THE ROLE OF IDEAS IN THE CIVIL RIGHTS SOUTH

SE

The Role of Ideas in the Civil Rights South

Essays by
Tony Badger
David L. Chappell
Elizabeth Jacoway
Richard H. King
Ralph E. Luker
Charles Marsh
Keith D. Miller
Linda Reed
Lauren F. Winner

Edited by
Ted Ownby

UNIVERSITY PRESS OF MISSISSIPPI
Jackson

www.upress.state.ms.us

Copyright © 2002 by University Press of Mississippi

10   09   08   07   06   05   04   03   02   4   3   2   1
∞
Library of Congress Cataloging-in-Publication Data

The role of ideas in the civil rights South / essays by Tony Badger ... [et al.] ;
edited by Ted Ownby.
    p.   cm. (Chancellor Porter L. Fortune Symposium in Southern
    History Series)
    Includes bibliographical references and index.
    ISBN 1-57806-467-8 (cloth : alk. paper)
    1. African Americans—Civil rights—Southern States—History—20th
century.   2. African Americans—Civil rights—Southern States—
Philosophy.   3. African Americans—Southern States—Intellectual life—
20th century.   4. Civil rights workers—Southern States—Intellectual
life—20th century.   5. Civil rights movements—Southern States—
History—20th century.   6. Southern States—Race relations.   7. Southern
States—Intellectual life—1865–   I. Badger, Anthony J.   II. Ownby, Ted.

E185.61 .R74   2002
323.1′196073075—dc21   2001046781

British Library Cataloging-in-Publication Data available

Contents

Acknowledgments

The papers in this volume began as part of the annual Porter L. Fortune, Jr. History Symposium at the University of Mississippi. Thanks go to my colleagues in the History Department, especially Robert Haws, chairman of the department, for working to make that event a success, and my colleagues at the Center for the Study of Southern Culture. Thanks as well to department secretaries Betty Harness and Michelle Palmertree, and to the Southern Studies graduate student, Molly McGehee, who helped coordinate travel and publicity for the symposium.

My greatest thanks are to the scholars who attended that symposium. Along with those who contributed essays, participants included Thomas Borstelman, Walter Jackson, Charles Payne, Daryl Scott, and Gerald Smith. Enhancing discussions were civil rights participants Lawrence Guyot and Ed King, and many students, scholars and visitors to campus.

Ralph Luker was not at the symposium, but his paper fits perfectly in this volume. My thanks to Charles Marsh for suggesting that the paper be included.

The Mississippi Humanities Council helped fund the symposium, as did an endowment honoring Porter L. Fortune, Jr., a former chancellor at the University of Mississippi.

Helping prepare this volume were Molly McGehee, Molly Campbell, and Vanessa Bliss in the Southern Studies program, Antoine Alexander in the History Department, Susan Ditto, and friends at the University Press of Mississippi.

Introduction

Our primary images of the American South in the 1950s and 1960s concern vivid struggles over power. Some of those struggles took place in the streets, some in the courts, some in legislatures, some in schools. Our images involve protest and counter-protest, demands to be heard and refusals to acknowledge those demands, marches and violence, heroism and stubborn resistance to change.

We tend to think more about people acting than people thinking. How can we understand how people connected thought and action? The essays in this collection examine ideas and the roles they played in the South in the civil rights era. Studying ideas should help add some nuances and complexities to stories we already know. It may also be a way to tell new stories and reconceptualize some old ones.

These essays investigate a wide range of thought in the civil rights era South. When people challenged authority, or defended it, what ideas did they uphold? What were their moral and intellectual standards? What language did they use, and what sources did they cite? What issues did they feel needed explaining, what issues did they take for granted, and what issues did they avoid?

The history of ideas asks us to study people trying to figure things out. Some people sought ideas that satisfied their own search for what Charles Marsh calls "ultimacy and the divine." Some sought ideas that would buttress their own place in power structures or would challenge society as it existed. Some people's confrontation with ideas was more about strategies; they wanted to know what worked. Others confronted ideas about morality and justice; they wanted to know what the world might be, at its best. The history of ideas is often best at studying people in the process of asking questions.

For some time now, historians of intellectual life have made efforts to go beyond the work of well known systematic thinkers with university training, literary ambitions, and publishers. Thus, this collection studies both people who hoped the published versions of their intellectual efforts would convince other people to follow them, and also those like Fannie Lou Hamer or Jim Johnson who never saw themselves as intellectuals. While several essays concentrate on the most studied southern intellectual in the 1950s and 1960s, Martin Luther King, Jr., others deal with activists, preachers, editors, and politicians whose ideas have received relatively little attention.

Intellectual history also brings into the picture some characters we do not often confront in southern history. Hegel and Karl Barth. Arthur Schlesinger, Jr. and Lionel Trilling. William F. Buckley and Daniel Patrick Moynihan. These are not southerners, obviously, but their place in this volume emphasizes that southern life, especially southern thinking, took place in national and international contexts.

What one also finds in this volume are serious efforts to make judgments about the power and validity of the ideas under discussion. Were they *good* ideas? Did they make sense? When people tried to apply them, did they work, and did anyone agree with them? Do we agree with them, and should we? Some of these essays challenge existing orthodoxies and may therefore draw criticism. I hope so. Thinking seriously about ideas in history should force us to reconsider things we felt comfortable that we understood.

The civil rights movement established most of the agenda for southern thinking in the 1950s and 1960s, so this volume begins with five analyses of ideas within the civil rights movement, especially those of Martin Luther King, Jr. The volume then moves on to people who responded to the civil rights movement, with equivocation, denial, or resistance. It includes a discussion of white southern moderates and the reasons they had little success, and it concludes with discussions of intellectual and political conservatism, and finally discusses the thinking of African Americans who did not join the civil rights movement.

David Chappell begins the volume with a discussion of the dramatic differences between "The Intellectual Roots of the Second Reconstruction" and the intellectual assumptions of most American liberals in the mid-twentieth century. Liberalism, he argues, stressed optimism about the potential of both individuals and groups to identify and overcome problems, to pursue justice and even perfection once they understood they had the chance. He identifies that strain of liberalism with the thought of Swedish writer Gunnar Myrdal, author of the widely read and quoted *An American Dilemma*. Running counter to that sense of optimism about overcoming problems were the ideas of theologian Reinhold Niebuhr, who always reminded readers about the imperfectability of mankind, the limits of human potential, and the need for and the costs of activism to further justice in the world. Chappell stresses that Martin Luther King, Jr. and other civil rights activists leaned more toward a Niebuhrian view of the world that stressed mankind's inherent sinfulness, the need for coercion that might cause pain and disorder, and a deep commitment that individual actions could bring some improvements, but never perfection.

Charles Marsh asks "what a theological analysis of the civil rights movement might look like" and reaches some conclusions that differ from Chappell's. Both believe that we must take theology seriously to understand the movement, and both view Martin Luther King, Jr. as outside the optimistic traditions of American liberalism. But for Marsh, the primary theologian who inspired King's activist ideas was not Reinhold Niebuhr but Swiss thinker Karl Barth, developer of the "theology of crisis" that demanded recognition of sin in society and dramatic action against it. Barth stressed not only the essential sinfulness of man but also the need to name it and condemn it. In Marsh's analysis, as King moved from emphasizing the Beloved Community to the Kingdom of God, he was moving toward a Barthian model of a prophet, judging the world by a rigid theological standard.

Ralph E. Luker examines Martin Luther King, Jr.'s use of the concept of the Beloved Community. Arguing that King came to the concept in the 1950s and seems to have moved away from it in the mid-1960s, Luker shows that King saw the Beloved Community not as a final destination, like the Kingdom of God, but as an inspiring example of what groups can do. The Beloved Community meant, more than anything else, the community of activists holding up goals of equality and desegregation; there was something ennobling in the experience of work and protest that King saw as Beloved. The idea became less central to King's thinking, Luker argues, when war and divisiveness left many activists frustrated.

Keith D. Miller's intricate analysis of Martin Luther King, Jr.'s "I Have a Dream" speech shows the strong connections between King's metaphors and the language common in the hymns and sermons of African American Protestants. Exploring King's use of the common metaphors of Light and Dark, Up and Down, Life as a Journey, and Heaven as Home, Miller shows how King used religious language for political ends by joining the political language to the religious. By connecting heaven and freedom through repetition and association, King created a speech that was

at once familiar to African American listeners and also a powerful statement of protest.

Linda Reed places the thinking of Fannie Lou Hamer in the context of
her own life and the particular story of the Democratic Party in the 1960s.
From her own experience, Hamer knew the close connections between
economic deprivation and a lack of access to the political system. Arguing
that a politics that would serve poor people needed to include poor people
as representatives, Hamer was a prophetic voice urging the Democratic
Party to embrace more people and more efforts to fight poverty. Finally,
Reed stresses that Hamer's religious convictions lay at the center of her
thinking and her activism.

Tony Badger analyzes the politics of the possible in his story of the failures of white southern moderates. The substantial number of quite ideal-
istic and innovative southern politicians who supported New Deal
policies in the 1930s and 1940s, he argues, stumbled and fell when they
faced they issue of racial segregation. They were fatalistic about the possibility that white voters might overlook issues of segregation, so they
stayed quiet, becoming "closet moderates." In the closet, they had no
chance of attracting the small but growing numbers of African American
voters. With most of the old white liberals either closeted or voted out of
office, they had little role in the actual process of desegregation.

Richard H. King's ambitious essay places Southern conservative thinkers such as M. E. Bradford and Richard Weaver in a trans-Atlantic context
of post-World War II conservatism. Bradford and Weaver, along with
numerous European conservatives, saw the liberal state as the enemy of
their understanding of an organic society. They feared that liberalism contributed to the breaking down of order and declining respect for merit.
Conservative thinkers tried—not always successfully—to steer clear of
specific issues that civil rights protesters raised. Some argued that school
desegregation was not really an issue of justice but of local control, and
most misread the movement as a fairly minor outgrowth of the welfare
state.

Elizabeth Jacoway traces the development of Arkansas political leader
Jim Johnson as a segregationist on the white-supremacist right of Orval
Faubus. Johnson led interposition efforts in the name of local government,
local schools and local culture, white supremacy, and anti-communism.
Jacoway critiques the ways liberals at the time and since have dismissed
Jim Johnson as irrelevant. Because so many people have failed to take

seriously the depth of his commitments, she argues, people like Johnson continue to see themselves as outsiders and losers rather than as part of an ongoing historical process.

Lauren F. Winner's paper explores the largely unknown subject of African Americans who opposed segregation. Questioning the assumption of many historians that virtually all African Americans supported the civil rights movement, Winner investigates three subjects. A small number of African American preachers supported the segregationist status quo both out of traditional interpretations of the Old Testament and out of fears for their privileged position in the community. Secondly, Zora Neale Hurston and others doubted the *Brown* decision for its emphasis on spatial relations. Finally, businesspeople who feared the decline of an African American market and teachers and maids who worried that desegregation might mean the loss of their jobs did not share all of the ideas of most civil rights leaders.

THE ROLE OF IDEAS IN THE CIVIL RIGHTS SOUTH

Niebuhrisms and Myrdaleries

The Intellectual Roots of the Civil Rights Movement Reconsidered

DAVID L. CHAPPELL

I am going to discuss two things:

(1) American liberalism's principal weakness, as described by the most sensitive and articulate liberals of the mid-20th century: that it could not by its nature inspire the solidarity and sacrifice needed to win its own goals.

(2) The extra-liberal, even anti-liberal, quality of the ideas that made the civil rights movement *move* out of the black churches, into the streets, and into the laws, constitution, social structure, and culture of the country (and much of the rest of the world)—achieving something like liberalism's goals by other means and other inspiration.

I am arguing that there is a radical distinction and discontinuity between what we call liberalism and the intellectual sources of what we call the civil rights movement. Looking back from the perspective of today, commentators assume an identity between liberalism and civil rights, assimilating the end of segregation and disfranchisement in the 1960s to a historic trend of progress away from tradition, superstition, prejudice, and other marks of backward, undereducated, unenlightened culture.[1] This habitual way of thinking gives too much credit to the progress of liberalism and too little credit to what I think of as eminently traditional prejudices and superstitions rooted in Judeo-Christian myth.[2]

This is not to deny liberals' role in the civil rights movement: post-WWII liberalism and the civil rights movement are not as watertight as I may sometimes seem to imply. They leaked all over each other, and drew in some instances from common sources. Northern liberals became the key political allies of the civil rights movement, and the great victories of that movement probably could not have happened were it not for the alliance. But I am concerned that we misunderstand the great cultural sea-change symbolized by Martin Luther King and the mass movement of the 1950s–1960s, by thinking of it too much as part of the unfolding history

3

of American or "western" liberalism. I think it is better to see it rather as another great historic clash between liberalism, which I am identifying here with Gunnar Myrdal, Arthur Schlesinger Jr., and others, and what I'm calling a prophetic tradition, running from David and Isaiah in the Old Testament, through Augustine and Luther, and best encapsulated in the twentieth century American intellectual history in the thought of Reinhold Niebuhr. Simply put, liberals see "progress" in society more or less automatically solving the social "problems" inherited from the "past."[3] Prophets by contrast see society in decline, getting worse, because of human pride, and they are driven to isolation and austere demands of repentance.[4]

At the outset I want to ward off confusion: after World War II, Niebuhr identified himself with liberals in the Cold War, and they eagerly claimed him. I lean heavily on Richard Fox's observation in his biography of Niebuhr that after World War II Niebuhr was so harried—almost panicky, as he lent his name to liberal causes and burned up his days in speaking engagements—that he lost touch with himself, and ceased to be much of a Niebuhrian.[5] And I'll make a related point Fox doesn't make, that the liberals who claimed to become Niebuhrian after World War II (like Schlesinger) only adopted the most superficial hints of the insights that made Niebuhr who he was, best expressed in his 1932 book *Moral Man and Immoral Society*.

Where Niebuhr stood out as a conservative was in his doctrine of sin and his generally pessimistic anthropology: he did not think man was perfectible, as liberals thought, but rather irretrievably tainted by original sin. He shared with liberals—indeed with the most avid social gospellers whose doctrines he claimed to repudiate—a strong belief in social action. His originality lay in his insistence that such action—however ethically necessary for a Christian—was necessarily tragic: to be viable, such action had to be political, that is, collective rather than individual, and being necessarily coercive, rather than voluntary, such action had to create new injustice even when it succeeded in alleviating old injustice. His ideas are closer than those of any American thinker to the prophetic ideas that animate and distinguish the civil rights movement from the general backwash of our history.

My story is intended to explain how the civil rights movement caught liberals off-guard in the 1950s.[6] The alliance they nonetheless formed with the movement was an alliance of convenience, more a matter of coincidence than of deep ideological or cultural affinity. Against this background, I hope, the poignant unraveling of that alliance, in the post-1960s era, will not seem so surprising and baffling as it ordinarily does.

Civil rights was one of the crowning achievements of the period when liberals dominated American politics, from 1929 to 1969. Yet there were no gains in civil rights in the first part of this period, the New Deal era of the 1930s,[7] when liberals' power was greater and more secure than ever before or since. Civil rights was a distinctly postwar achievement, and its achievement must be understood in the context of a distinct postwar liberalism.

To judge them by their own words, liberals at the end of World War II were in deep trouble. They feared that Franklin Roosevelt's personality, rather than their own ideology, was what had attracted vast majorities to the New Deal, a fear reinforced by their great loss in popularity upon FDR's death. For this and other reasons, they trimmed their sails.[8] The Depression was one of the many great things the war killed, but in doing so it killed a lot of liberal hope. The absence of economic crisis made serious reform hard to sell, and FDR's successor, Harry Truman, was at once less committed to reform and a lousier salesman than FDR. The Depression did not return (as experts had expected). Liberals had to convince voters of the urgency of reform through the greatest boom in American history, which was rather like urging medicine upon a healthy and increasingly spoiled child. Liberals abandoned the large-scale planning by which they had tried to soften the structural inequities of capitalism during the 1930s, and emphasized instead greater individual rights and increased opportunity through economic growth.[9]

But liberals' lack of confidence, their fear that they were alienated from the public they so earnestly wanted to help, goes back further in their history than the postwar period.[10] John Dewey, for example, was possessed by a sense that something was missing from liberalism—something that religion *had* and something that liberals could appropriate if they changed their thinking about it. With a remarkable insensitivity to the commitments of faith, Dewey thought it was possible to graft some form of "religion" onto a secular, optimistic world view based on instrumental reason. Dewey hated superstitious belief in the supernatural but thought some positive aspects of "religion" could be reconstructed without supernatural faith.[11]

Other liberals expressed the same concern.[12] Malcolm Ross, for example, who was to become head of the Fair Employment Practices Committee in World War II, one of the first non-southern liberals to gain experience in racial issues, published his autobiography, *Death of a Yale Man*, in 1939. A story of disillusionment before its time, *Death* looked back on Ross's invigorating adventures as a young newspaperman in the 1920s, when he covered Billy Sunday's revivals in Louisville. Of that evangelist, Ross wrote, "there is a certain dignity about anyone entirely engrossed in his profession, and Billy was a knockout at the business of saving, pro tem, the souls of the emotional." Ross wrote nostalgically that he remained "pleased to have seen the last of those who could barnstorm America on a hell-and-damnation platform." But he caught himself, correcting this rapturous memory in the tones of Sinclair Lewis or H.L. Mencken. He was pleased above all "because America has outgrown the stage where storekeepers can subsidize a revivalist to attract crowds into town."

Ross's liberal cynicism about religion (as always, mostly justified) kept him from developing religious commitments of his own. But through his own irony Ross could yearn, "Lord of Hosts, if thy servant Billy Sunday had been a man with an honest tongue to tell people where they stand and to what cause they should deliver their hearts, what a healthy jolt those meetings might have given Louisville." Ross blamed the storekeepers for allowing only preachers who preached a strictly personal salvation beyond this world, to speak in town. He blamed his own newspaper for being in league with the storekeepers. "I wish now that I had had the inspiration to ask Billy Sunday . . . how he stood on the question of the coalfield battles being fought at the other end of Kentucky. That would really have made a story, and I should probably have been fired for filing it."[13]

Dewey's feeling that liberalism sorely lacked a congealing, inspiring faith, like Ross's specific regret, is a theme that runs through modern liberal thought. It is there in Mill, in Matthew Arnold. It might be called pulpit envy—a phrase Ann Douglas uses in another context in another century.[14] Other prominent New Deal intellectuals said similar things.[15] After the war this envy becomes more pronounced. Lionel Trilling expressed the feeling in his 1949 bestseller, *The Liberal Imagination*. The keynote of this book was melancholy, though it was premised on the complete triumph of liberalism in mid-20th century America. "Liberalism is not only the dominant but even the sole intellectual tradition," Trilling famously said. "For it is the plain fact that nowadays there are no conservative or reactionary ideas in general circulation." While this state of affairs would "seem to some liberals a fortunate thing," Trilling warned that conservatism's lack of ideas is precisely what made conservatism such a danger—a danger for which liberals were entirely unprepared.

The rise of Nazis, fascists, and "totalitarian" socialists in Russia shaped Trilling's thought, and that of the whole generation of "chastened" liberals after WWII. It was dangerous for liberals to dismiss movements that had no ideas, Trilling said: "the experience of Europe in the last quarter-century suggests. . . . it is just when a movement despairs of having ideas that it turns to force." And force would be disguised with "ideology," a kind of pseudo-intellectual program that could be all the more destructive for its lack of intellectual rigor. Ideology became a dirty word in these years, and liberals fell all over themselves to show they had outgrown it—a tendency that culminated in Daniel Bell's bestseller at the end of the 1950s, *The End of Ideology*. I haven't been able to document the point precisely, but I feel sure it must be that it was in this era that Americans picked up the habit of pronouncing the word with short "i"—as though its root were *idiot* rather than *idea*.

To Trilling, Bell, and others, politics in a mass age was inescapably cultural and spiritual. It was "no longer possible to think of politics except as the politics of culture," Trilling said. Political thinkers who hoped to influence political events could not ignore cultural and spiritual dynamics. And liberalism was at a great disadvantage here: Liberalism unfortunately viewed the world in a rationalistic way, a "prosaic" way; what it needed was the "poetic" insight, the fire, of reactionaries and Romantics. Trilling saw it as his task, "the job of criticism," to "recall liberalism to its first essential imagination of variousness and possibility"[16]: in short to leaven liberalism—thus extend and protect its triumph—with a quasi-spiritual discipline. Trilling's sad tone suggested that squaring this circle would be as difficult as it was desirable.

But it was a short step from wistful thinking to wishful thinking. In the same year that Trilling's essay appeared (1949), Arthur Schlesinger Jr. published *The Vital Center*, which became a manifesto of postwar liberalism. *The Vital Center* grew out of the same horror of totalitarianism, the same recoil from all efforts to make the world conform to utopian ideals, in which liberals felt complicit. But it was a more cheerful expression of the chastened liberal spirit than Trilling's. Schlesinger claimed that a new and improved liberalism already existed. Schlesinger's new liberalism had learned from the mistakes of earlier, utopian liberalism (he resisted the temptation to call his liberalism scientific). The advent of the Americans for Democratic Action, "a new liberal organization, excluding Communists and dedicated to democratic objectives. . . . marks. . . . the watershed at which American liberalism began to base itself once again on a solid conception of man and history."[17] Schlesinger provided a way for liberals to worry about their past limitations without calling their very liberalism into serious question, as Trilling had done. Schlesinger did not mention Trilling, but in effect answered him.

Schlesinger did mention Reinhold Niebuhr, who had given Trilling's theme a more extended treatment in his *Children of Light and Children of Darkness* (1944), and especially in his *Moral Man and Immoral Society* (1932). Schlesinger claimed to have learned his new brand of liberalism from Niebuhr, yet he could never quite make it to the edge of the abyss with Niebuhr.[18] Niebuhr had criticized the naïve hope that a new system of education, or a revival of religion, or any other human program could ever make social conflict unnecessary in the future. Relations between groups, Niebuhr said, must always be based on force. And the owners of Capital, in particular, "possess so much power that they win the debate no matter how unreasonable their arguments."[19] No disadvantaged group could hope to win justice through discussion, as liberals hoped; it could only wrest away some measure of justice by force or threat of force.

Schlesinger, on the other hand, said that although industry inevitably drives the individual "to the wall," there were still "common values" between businessmen and liberals. These common values could be the basis of a successful battle against "totalitarianism" (the incubus that lurked in Soviet expansion and in ideologies of perfection at home). Schlesinger said, "I am certain that history has equipped modern liberalism . . . to construct a society where men will be both free and happy."[20]

The most striking differences between Schlesinger and Niebuhr appear in what they say on race and related subjects. Niebuhr thought that race was a central injustice in American society, a tragedy. In 1932, Niebuhr had expressed hope (prophetically, it turned out) that the American Negro—*not* the working class—would be the group to struggle successfully against oppression in the U.S. He also expressed the hope (again prophetically) that the American Negro would do this by nonviolent force, a technique of struggle that Niebuhr, following Gandhi, understood as having more in common with war than with pacifism.[21]

But Schlesinger, writing 17 years later—after all the years of agitation and outrage over lynching and the poll tax, after the "rising wind" of black militancy in World War II—had little to say (and nothing original) about race. He did say something about nonviolence—only to dismiss it. The very year that Gandhi's movement succeeded in driving the British Empire out of India, Schlesinger claimed that Gandhi's notion of nonviolence was just a form of egotism. Gandhi's faith was something that "enthusiasts" follow with "serenity," but like anarchism and decentralization, nonviolent methods could not solve anything except the psychological "complexes" of "the individual who adopts them."

Schlesinger was deaf to what was happening in what became the largest democracy in the world, and deaf to the important distinction that Niebuhr, influenced by Gandhi from the 1920s on, made between nonviolent force, à la Gandhi, and "pacifism," which Niebuhr defined (and denounced) as Tolstoyan nonresistance—turning the other cheek self-sacrificially and individualistically, and leaving it at that. Niebuhr thought *that* was a form of egotism, but he invested great hope in nonviolent force.[22] As to racism more generally, Niebuhr believed in a power struggle, whereby the Negro would gain ground only through coercion. Schlesinger, by contrast, said "prejudice" would yield to education.[23]

Schlesinger's attitude pervaded the ADA and helps explain why organized post-World War II liberals never saw race as a pressing crisis: with few exceptions, they never ranked it very high among their priorities. They gave dutiful, not to say perfunctory, support to anti-lynching & FEPC bills, but never saw racial discrimination as fundamental or urgent: they never could adopt Niebuhr's view of the issue.[24]

On that increasingly important subject, liberals had to find another touchstone. The one they found, was of course Gunnar Myrdal's *An American Dilemma*. A more striking contrast to Niebuhr could not be found. It is one of the most optimistic books published in the 20th century—as well as one of the longest. Perhaps the greatest evidence of Myrdal's overweening faith in human generosity was his apparent assumption that anybody was going to read 1,117 pages.

It is odd that the book that provided postwar liberals' inspiration on what would become their most important historical achievement made none of Schlesinger's show of skepticism, of disillusionment, of recovery from naive optimism. Myrdal's report, whose collaborators included many of the most prominent social scientists in America, boiled down to a prophecy: Americans' "creed" of equality contradicted their practice of racial discrimination, and in the battle between the two, the practice sooner or later had to yield to the creed—undoubtedly sooner, because white Americans, even southerners, were becoming more enlightened and more honest about the practice all along.

Myrdal had a very different experience with totalitarianism from Trilling or Niebuhr. He acknowledged his book was optimistic, saying it had to be optimistic in order to counter disillusionment. Myrdal found the danger of totalitarianism not in the optimism of those who supported it but in the pessimism of those who submitted to it. Myrdal believed that disillusionment pervaded Europe in the 1920s and 1930s, particularly in his gloomy native Sweden, where it spawned a deadly passivity, even in the face of fascist insurgencies. Myrdal's own brand of liberalism, Swedish Social Democracy, was in his mind too pessimistic. Swedish liberalism was on a very different trajectory (or as Schlesinger might say, in a different phase of its cycle) from American liberalism. When Myrdal came to America, he interpreted mainstream American social science as being similarly pessimistic.[25] He saw American complacency, one might say, as a result of fatalism rather than optimism.[26]

More striking than Myrdal's general optimism was the way his views on institutions contrast directly with Niebuhr's (whom he does not seem to have read, though his reading of American social thought was otherwise staggeringly vast). Not only would white Americans act better towards Negroes in the future as individuals, Myrdal said, they would become even more moral through collective institutions than they would be as individuals. On the basis of his observation that schools, churches, and the government were becoming more sympathetic to black demands, while individual white persons were not so bold, Myrdal came to the general belief that institutions would lead Americans in resolving the conflict between their creed of equality and the reality of their lives. Since America, like all modern societies, was becoming more institutionalized, Myrdal's general optimism was related to this belief in institutions leading the way to morality.

The thesis conveyed in the title of Niebuhr's greatest work, *Moral Man and Immoral Society* (1932), was precisely the opposite. Niebuhr said that

where individuals could often be counted on to respect moral rules, institutions and other collectives were, by their nature, incapable of being gov-
erned by the rules that restrained individuals. Institutions might pay lip
service and gain prestige by claiming moral purpose, but whenever it
came to a choice between such a purpose and the interests of the institution, an institution had to defend its interests. An individual man, though
tainted by original sin and incapable of perfection, was at least capable of
moral choice, and even of sacrificing his own interests for a greater good;
history was full of examples. But to Niebuhr it was meaningless to say a
nation or a class or an institution ever chose to "sacrifice" itself for a moral
cause. An individual man could be moral; society was "immoral."[27] To recognize that was the difference between realism and liberalism.

Myrdal's report had a more powerful effect on liberal opinion after
World War II than anything Niebuhr had ever said, which may be another
way of saying Myrdal's report reflected the uncodified and often unstated
liberal impulses. President Truman's special committee on civil rights first
drafted its 1947 report, *To Secure These Rights*, as little more than a gloss
of Myrdal, speaking of an "American Creed" at odds with the practice of
discrimination, and of the necessary triumph of creed over practice.
NAACP president Roy Wilkins, looking back years later, said the Truman
Committee report became "a blueprint that we used for the next two decades." Hubert Humphrey, second only to Truman in pushing the Democrats to begin supporting civil rights in 1948, was also strongly influenced
by Myrdal, whom he read before entering politics, and whom he often
echoed in speeches.[28]

Myrdal's militant anti-pessimism is a great irony, because his compen-
sating optimism became as strong a reason for inaction as pessimism.
Myrdal's report was welcomed by the liberals: it was in sync with the
thinking of those who did very little on racism in the late 1940s and 1950s,
who retreated from their limited gestures of 1948. Liberals did not *do*
anything until the battle was joined in the streets of the South in the mid-
1950s—something they did not anticipate. As Walter Jackson observes,
"The last thing that white liberals were expecting in the 1950s was a mass
movement among African-Americans in the South."[29] Similarly, Richard
King argues that the experience of the civil rights movement "failed to fit
comfortably, if at all, within the confines of conventional liberal politics";
"the civil rights movement was a great surprise."[30]

This is not to say that liberals were insincere in their expressed desire to better the lot of the Negro—I am not concerned with sincerity here. Indeed I think historians' obsession with sincerity grows out a very Myrdalian habit of thinking of race as primarily a matter of opinion and attitude, susceptible to psychotherapy or education or sensitivity training. Liberals were sincere. Their sincere concern with the suffering of the Negro in no way conflicted with their equally sincere desire to get his vote. The point here is simply that liberals felt the need for other things, especially their own power, much more strongly than they felt the need for civil rights. That sense of priorities is not surprising, and it may have been a good thing for liberalism and a host of programs the liberals supported. The point is that liberals were not the ones, for whatever reason, who gave civil rights its power as an issue: they were not the ones who made it *move*.

The ideas of those who *did* make the issue move are of a wholly different order. What I want to emphasize is the civil rights activists' rejection of this world and its natural tendencies, their unwillingness to leave social processes alone to work themselves out, their lack of faith in the power of education and economic development, let alone institutions, to cure society of the evils that oppressed them—an attitude more akin to that of the Hebrew prophets and the Reinhold Niebuhr of 1932–1944 than that of Myrdal and mid-century American liberals.

Martin Luther King's relationship with theological liberalism has been misunderstood. He expressed a strong dislike for what he called the "fundamentalism" of his father and the church in which he grew up. In that sense, he was liberal. But in that sense, so was Reinhold Niebuhr, who is so often mislabeled (even by King) "neo-orthodox." What's important is King's Niebuhrian rejection of optimism about man: he is conservative on the same issues Niebuhr is, the issues that matter most for his public work.[31]

In King's first truly original work, a 1948 paper on Jeremiah, the "rebel prophet," King sounds out the keynotes of his later speeches and public writings. There was the prophetic belief that the nation is in moral decline, partly because its traditional creed was defective and needed to be reformed. "Jeremiah realized that the covenant made at Mount Sinai had failed to accomplish its purpose. . . . Instead of being a spiritual asset it was a snare and a delusion. Instead of leading men to their knees it filled them with foolish presumption." Jeremiah, not only by the standards of his contemporaries, but also "by the standards of the world. . . . was a failure." There was the indictment of institutions. Jeremiah "saw that the Temple had been relegated to a position of empty formalism which substituted a superficial reverence for the doing of Yahweh's will." The Temple "had become in Yahweh's eyes, a cave for robbers to shelter themselves in," and "functionaries of the Temple . . . drifted into the belief that the Temple was more important than the distinction of good and evil, the sacrifices more vital than sin." And there was the rebellion and renewal that prophetic truth motivated. In articulating the Second Covenant, Jeremiah was correcting the naïvete of the Deuteronomists. For all their accomplishments in organizing their religion, the Deuteronomists "failed to see that religion is not something which can be organized, rather it is a spontaneous outflow from men's contact with a divine spirit." Since the Temple was "a national institution, linked intimately with the fortunes of the race," to "attack" it was political and social rebellion—an anticipation of King's chosen namesake, Martin Luther. "It took the fortitude and mind of Jeremiah to expose these pressing faults." Jeremiah "seized upon a revolutionary truth"; he remains "a shining example of the truth that religions should never sanction the status quo."[32]

King's attraction to Jeremiah put him on the same path as Reinhold Niebuhr, who in his rejection of both liberalism and neo-orthodoxy came up with "prophetic religion" as the best name for the doctrines he emphasized.[33] King frequently referred to "prophetic Christianity" in later writings and speeches, and frequently cited Jeremiah, Amos, and Isaiah as examples of brave men who sacrificed their social position and standing when they preached to society of its corruption and insisted on total, rather than incremental, reformation.[34] As he grows closer to Niebuhr, more conscious of his affinity for Niebuhr's thought, King points to the important way the "neo-orthodox" theologians of his own day call us back to the message of the prophets.[35]

The point here is not that King got these emphases solely from Niebuhr—indeed the rather obvious point scholars lately stress that King learned most of his abiding commitments in the black Baptist church in which he grew up does not conflict with the argument here: whatever useful things he learned from that rich and diverse tradition, though he later condemned it as "fundamentalist," were compatible with what he later learned from Niebuhr. The point is not that Niebuhr invented the prophetic tradition, but rather that Niebuhr codified its teachings and expressed them for his contemporaries in vivid, arresting language that King understood and embraced. King's striving to reconcile his peculiar tradition with the best of the rest of American Protestantism and with the best of the American civic tradition is what made his thought converge with Niebuhr's. The important question of King's relationship to Niebuhr is not a question of roots—historians have an occupational susceptibility to the genetic fallacy—but rather a question of affinities. Recent scholarship implies, in effect, that everything King needed to know he learned in kindergarten—his spiritual kindergarten, "the" black church. But it was the mature King who communicated with a world beyond his church, who brought much of his church with him into the "mainstream," who reminded his church and the mainstream how much they had in common.

King's first full-fledged discussion of the doctrine of man, in an essay written in 1949–50, is also the first to bring in his personal experiences with racism. In this essay, King suggests that his own neo-orthodox tendencies may "root back to certain experiences that I had in the south with a vicious race problem." Some of these experiences "made it very difficult for me to believe in the essential goodness of man." This essay cites Niebuhr, whom King calls neo-orthodox, as a more realistic authority on sin and man.[36] In this essay, King develops his understanding of Niebuhr, attributing to Niebuhr the important insistence that "men sin through intellectual and spiritual pride." On the basis of that point, King rejects liberal optimism, concluding, like Niebuhr, that "the modern Christian must see man as a guilty sinner who must ask forgiveness and be converted."[37]

Niebuhr becomes more important in King's graduate school writings at Boston University in 1951–54. Whatever King's academic attraction to the Personalists,[38] Niebuhr is the thinker King takes most often into his *public* statements, beginning with an essay he read to the Dialectical Society, a group of young intellectuals over which King presided in Boston. This point needs emphasis. Too many scholarly works on King offer an uncritical inventory of the contents of his brain—there's a little Rauschenbush folded in with a little Niebuhr, a soupçon of neo-orthodoxy, a dash of Kant and Thoreau, all Hegelized together in and suspended in a vast broth of Personalism (later inventories add, all this was superfluous after the primordial influence of "the" black church)—as a substitute for an analysis of which ideas make him historically significant. The Personalists loom large in King scholarship, it seems, simply because King spent more time in Boston and cranked out more pages under their influence than anywhere else. But there is no analysis that shows a greater influence of the Personalists on King the public man, the leader of a mass movement—no analysis to show that Personalist ideas *matter* in the work he did as a civil rights leader, or that Personalist ideas differentiate him from thousands of preachers nobody has ever heard of.[39] My point is not that King read more Niebuhr or cited Niebuhr more than, say, the Personalist Edgar Sheffield Brightman, but that what makes King a world-historical figure is his Niebuhrian pessimism about man and human institutions and his Niebuhrian insistence that coercion is tragically necessary to achieve justice.

King told the Dialectical Society in 1954 that "Niebuhr differs from Barthianism," which rejects the human experience of contact with God in Biblical history. "For Niebuhr, the only adequate religious expression of the human situation is a combination of this-worldly and other-worldly hopes." Niebuhr's synthesis "contains a realistic pessimism which balances the initial Renaissance optimism." King then focused on the matter that had already drawn *him* away from liberalism: "Niebuhr's anthropology," King said, "is certainly the cornerstone of his thought." There can be no doubt that King agrees with Niebuhr's view of man: "Niebuhr's anthropology is the necessary corrective of a kind of liberalism that too easily capitulated to modern culture." According to modern culture, which tends to reduce religion to ethics, "Man who has come so far in wisdom and decency may be expected to go much further as his methods of attaining and applying knowledge are improved. Although such ethical religion is humane and its vision a lofty one, it has obvious shortcomings. This particular sort of optimism has been discredited by the brutal logic of events. Instead of assured progress in wisdom and decency, man faces the ever present possibility of swift relapse not merely to animalism but into such calculated cruelty as no other animal can practice. Niebuhr reminds us of this on every hand." Since the Dialectical Society was apparently all-black, the charge that Keith Miller and some black nationalist critics have made that King quoted "white" thinkers only when he hoped to manipulate white audiences, could not apply.[40]

All the themes from the Dialectical Society discussion of Niebuhr recur in King's later work. It is Niebuhr, not Brightman or any other contemporary theologian, whom King quotes in his "Letter from the Birmingham City Jail" (1963) and his explanation of his intellectual sources in his *Play-*

boy interview (1965) (two public statements that are relatively immune to the questions, often exaggerated in any case, of the influence of ghostwriters over King's thinking). Niebuhr—or to invoke a broader tradition behind Niebuhr—prophetic Christianity, is more of a key to what happens in King's *public* life than the mushy cloud that scholars call "the" black church, or "African-American tradition." It is no more useful to say King was shaped by the black church than to say that he breathed oxygen or was a Georgian. What set him *off* from the black church is what makes him significant. What set King off from the black church is the same thing that set him off from liberalism—what led him out of both of those Egypts.

All this pessimistic emphasis on man's sinfulness and the need for coercion in King's writings appears before the members of the Fellowship of Reconciliation got to King and began teaching him the doctrines of nonviolent resistance. Though most scholars now stress the role that Bayard Rustin, Glenn Smiley, Stanley Levison, Harris Wofford, and others had in writing many of King's major works, Rustin said he and Levison "were analyzing Martin and saying 'how did he view these kinds of problems, what would be the way for him to tackle them?' It was not we directing him so much as we working with him and giving expression to ideals we knew he had or would quickly accept. . . . I don't like to write something for somebody where I know he is acting like a puppet. I want to be a real ghost and write what the person wants to say. And that is what I always knew was true in the case of Martin. I would never write anything that wasn't what he wanted to say."[41] I am suggesting that Rustin understood King's mind better than recent scholars who imply King allowed his signature to appear under writings he did not agree with.

A similar prophetic emphasis comes through in the writings and speeches—and, I think, the actions—of other movement intellectuals such as Bayard Rustin (in his independent writings as well as his ghostwriting), James Lawson, Modjeska Simkins, Bob Moses, and John Lewis. Space does not permit a full exploration of these other voices, but a few examples will convey their prophetic flavor. In 1942, Rustin saw a crisis coming in race relations: "The average Negro has largely lost faith in middle-class whites. . . . He looks upon the middle-class idea of long-term educational and cultural changes with mistrust."[42] Writing in 1956, Rustin agreed with Myrdal's first premise that discrimination created psychic

tension in the white mind, but he came to the opposite of Myrdal's conclusion: white people, far from finding dehumanization of Negroes an
intolerable contradiction of their creed, simply "rationalized" it, "insisting
that the unfortunate Negro, being less than human, deserved and even
enjoyed second-class status." White people came to believe the Negro
was exempt from their belief in progress, and their cognitive dissonance
evaporated. "White men soon came to forget that the southern social culture and all its institutions had been organized to perpetuate this rational-
ization." The system was breaking down, not because white minds
changed, but because black minds changed. "We discovered that we had
never really smothered our self-respect and that we could not be at one
with ourselves without asserting it. From this point on, the South's terrible peace was rapidly undermined by the Negro's new and courageous
thinking and his ever-increasing readiness to organize and to act." The
Negro would act not in a gradualist way, but in a "revolutionary," coercive
way, forcing white people to change.[43]

In 1948, the black South Carolina activist Modjeska Simkins berated
her own people for their failure to resist the normal course of history: "too
many of us are all American souls . . . satisfied to move slowly along like
contented cows, swishing flies and chewing cud and following the beaten
path of the common herd."[44] Simkins often compared herself and fellow
activists to Job, saying in a later speech that, "Like ourselves," Job found
himself in a "great struggle against power." She also identified with the
early Christians in Ephesians 6:12: " 'For we wrestle not against flesh and
blood, but against principalities and powers, against the rulers of darkness
of this world, against spiritual wickedness in high places.' " They were
struggling against "obstinate opposition," and "Black Quislings," and
must "Realize that politicians cannot be changed."[45]

Nashville leader Jim Lawson responded to the post-World War II liberals' lack of a sense of purpose and direction, or at least to the malaise that
liberals' children felt. In a speech in April 1960, Lawson noted the sudden
political visibility of the younger generation, which had been written off
as " 'silent,' 'uncommitted,' or 'beatnik.' " Now, however, with the sit-ins
that began earlier that year, not just black students but "all the white
American students were simply waiting in suspension; waiting for that
cause, that ideal, that event, that 'actualizing of their faith' " that would
allow them to "speak powerfully to their nation and world." This was a
religious event: "God has brought this to pass."[46]

John Lewis, who became president of SNCC in 1963, spoke of the sacrifice and risk that activists were taking in challenging the system. He said SNCC was aiming for a "social revolution" that raised more "basic questions" than "the question of negro rights." He did not think that "the South and those in power are going to give up their interest without some form of struggle." He found "in the history of Judeo-Christian tradition . . . the idea that there can be no salvation without the shedding of blood." He believed non-violent methods would probably lead to such a shedding of blood.[47] Lewis repeated many of these points in his March on Washington speech at the Lincoln Memorial in 1963, even after toning down the original draft, which had included a statement that he wanted to re-enact Sherman's march and other statements that older leaders found too belligerent. At the Lincoln Memorial, Lewis said, "we are involved in a serious social revolution. . . . American politics is dominated by politicians who build their careers on immoral compromises and ally themselves with open forms of political, economic, and social exploitation."[48]

These and other activists who were (or tried to be) self-conscious and/or systematic about what they believed and did not believe, shared a prophetic pessimism about man and human institutions, about the general drift of social development. They did not necessarily get this from Niebuhr, or from King. It was in the air—the air got it from the Bible, from King and Rustin, and like-minded leaders, but there were other sources. Bob Moses found the best source for unifying and justifying his prophetic impulses in Albert Camus, and he helped to popularize that writer among the younger generation of activists (often unChristian or much more casual in their Christianity than the generation of King, Lawson, and Simkins). Camus's warnings about the necessity yet danger of moral action on behalf of the oppressed were almost identical with Niebuhr's warnings on the same subject—the danger that the victims, in Camus's memorable metaphor, will become the executioners as soon as you give them a chance.

This prophetic pessimism has more to do with the civil rights activists' embrace of nonviolence—non-violent *force*—than any faith in the efficacy of moral suasion, or confidence in appeals to the innate goodness of white people. They called themselves a non-violent army—and they meant to win, and they did. They did not bring heaven on earth—but they had no such liberal utopian expectation; they achieved a considerable victory, measured by real-world standards, a victory they knew from the start would never be complete. For that and other reasons, we still have a great deal to learn from them.

The Civil Rights Movement as Theological Drama

CHARLES MARSH

In this paper, I ask what a theological analysis of the civil rights movement might look like and how such an analysis might open up an interpretive framework within which scholars and activists could learn new lessons from the period. A good place to begin is with a basic question. I raise the question—which may at first appear slightly crude in its formulation—as a way of clarifying the two contrasting fields of discourse available to us. Did the church people in the movement believe what they said about God or did they use religion as an opiate of social reform?

More specific questions follow: Did Martin Luther King, Jr. believe that the universe came into being through the gracious decision of a divine Creator, that human dignity and the "sacredness of all human life," as he said, would be forever grounded in an ontological certainty; and that this divine Creator had revealed himself in Jesus Christ, reconciling the world to himself? "In Christ there is neither Jew nor Gentile. In Christ there is neither male nor female. In Christ there is neither Communist nor capitalist. In Christ, somehow there is neither bound nor free. We are all one in Christ Jesus."[1] Or did King seize upon Pauline language because he liked the way it subverted the claims of white supremacy? Further, did King believe that agape love had become incarnate in this same Jesus, such love that transforms the intent of human desire and community? Did he care about faith's integrity, its truthfulness and coherence? Or were his gestures to the church and Christian tradition always performed with a free-wheeling sense of irony? Did King really believe that the "Word of God" fell upon him when he preached and when he spoke—"like a fire shut up in my bones," that "when God gets upon me, I've got to say it?" Or did he indulge in a little "Pythian madness" as a clever means of revving up the troops?[2]

One could ask similar questions to King's fellow travelers. Did Andrew Young believe that "God had changed the world through the shedding of innocent blood," that the unshackling of humanity's bondage to sin in the

19

Easter event enabled the movement's own liberating energies?[3] Or did the black struggle's idea of freedom emerge from essentially human aspirations? Did Victoria Gray Adams really believe what she said about the movement being "the journey toward the establishment of the kingdom of God"? Or did she use eschatological language as an effective way of dramatizing the urgency of change? Was John Lewis's civil rights life a testament to radical discipleship? "I had to learn to turn myself over and follow," he said, "to be consistent and follow, and somehow believe that it's all going to be taken care of; it's all going to work out."[4] Or was he simply giving voice to his presumption that time was on his side?

The questions are important not only because they raise issues critical to the role of ideas in the civil rights movements and to the historiography of the movement, but even more for the fact that they force one's hand on theological matters great and small. Was Fred Shuttlesworth's life embraced "by the everlasting arms of Jesus," as he always believed, or was his sense of the divine "Yes" something like a psychic defense against feelings of worthlessness? Were Fannie Lou Hamer's prayers answered in the summer of 1964, as were those of her friends and family, when hundreds of student volunteers came South to work alongside local Americans in voter registration and civil rights organizing? Or was her piety a quaint though heartwarming expression of her desperation and desire? Similarly, when Mrs. Hamer emerged from a night of torture in a Winona, Mississippi, jailhouse and said, astonishingly—"It wouldn't solve any problem for me to hate whites just because they hate me. Oh, there's so much hate, only God has kept the Negro sane"—was she bearing witness to the complex Christian tradition of redemptive suffering and cruciform forgiveness, or just using the language of "costly grace" as a cover for her crushing humiliation?

These questions force our hand on theological matters. What I mean is that the questions require us to make up our minds about the way theological ideas "functioned" in the civil rights movement. For example, are we willing to say that the African American women and men who believed that God was working through his church and his children were mistaken, however well-intentioned or useful in social utility these delusions may have been?

Even more questions follow. How has it come to pass that a social movement so thoroughly saturated with theological conviction and religious passion has been, at the same time, so frequently deracinated by its interpreters from the living energies of its communities? What has led well-meaning and politically-committed scholars of history to redescribe "the beloved community"—an idea that King would in some measure come to use interchangeably with the "Kingdom of God"—as a liberal, multicultural coalition of citizens committed to various strategies of social transformation for the sake of some universal notion of the Good? Can we show appropriate respect for the women and men of the civil rights movement without reckoning with the substance of their beliefs?[5] Does it not matter greatly whether King believed what he said about God, and if so, must not the question also be asked whether his beliefs about God have credibility as theological claims? And if we agree that the people of faith who filled the movement ranks believed what they said about God, don't we have to reckon with the unsettling question of whether their beliefs are true or false, whether these beliefs are credible as theological claims, and whether a causal relation exists between those beliefs and the course of events that followed?

So to rephrase the questions: If Dr. King believed what he said about God—again that, "God is love, because Christ is love . . . that God is just because Jesus Christ is just. And . . . that God is a merciful God, full of grace and glory, because Jesus Christ is merciful"—then does not intellectual honesty, if not decency, require us to accept these beliefs as essential to his life in the movement, if not to the very existence of the movement itself?[6] For if King believed that (one more time) "standing up to the truth of God is the greatest thing in the world," the "end of life" no less, then it seems undeniable that these beliefs and passions were in every way related to his civil rights life, and that, as King wrote of the prophet Jeremiah in a 1948 essay at Crozer Theological Seminary, "it was this trust in the unerring righteousness of God that was the basis of his personal religion."[7] Apart from these beliefs, King would have acted quite differently.

In other words, there is no such thing as a civil rights religion, no monolithic spiritual energy available to all who joined the struggle, emerging outside of particular traditions of belief and practice, no free-floating piety, no cosmic interconnectedness of undelineated confessional origin. There were particular ways of thinking about God, Jesus Christ, and the Church that framed the basic purposes and goals of the movement, to be sure, purposes and goals shifting in emphasis and meaning at different historical moments and in different political and social contexts, and purposes and goals that were no doubt supplemented and often nurtured by other philosophical and religious traditions. But the spiritual energies of the movement were born of particular forms of theological expression.

In his first public address, at the Holt Street Baptist Church, a twenty-six year old Martin Luther King, Jr., cast the events of the burgeoning Montgomery bus boycott in a Biblical framework of meaning that proved decisive for the emerging movement. "We, the disinherited of this land," he said, "we who have been oppressed so long, are tired of going through the long night of captivity." The "strange new world within the Bible," to borrow the phrase of the theologian Karl Barth (whose influence on King we will examine later), gave the civil rights movement its inner sense as well as its ultimate point of reference. In this one sentence King, evocative of rich biblical images, relocates the common hopes for liberation in a particular narrative, each image alive with meaning for the sufferings and hopes of both Israel and African Americans. "From that night forward," wrote Richard Lischer in his groundbreaking book, *The Preacher King: Martin Luther King, Jr. and the Word that Moved America*, "King and the black church community forged an interpretative partnership in which they read the Bible, recited it, sang it, performed it, Amen-ed it, and otherwise celebrated the birth of Freedom by its sacred light."[8]

Although such organizations as the Student Nonviolent Coordinating Committee (SNCC) and the Conference on Racial Equality (CORE) have often been described as the secularizing wave of the movement, a particular theological self-understanding had been articulated in one of SNCC's founding documents. In the staff meeting of April 29, 1962, members of the organization had resolved their firm commitment to the creation of "a social order permeated by love and to the spirituality of nonviolence as it grows from the Judeo-Christian tradition."[9] To be sure, there were plenty of SNCC activists whose moral energies were driven by purely humanistic ideals. Still, the progressive, grass-roots organization was anchored firmly in the language, imagery and energies of the black church, committed to what John Lewis described as a "circle of trust, a band of sisters and brothers, the beloved community."[10] SNCC brought to the civil rights movement youthful energy and a bold and impatient vision of social change, more restless and edgy than King's perhaps, but still spiritually defined by the Biblical narrative and the story of the new Kingdom inaugurated by Jesus Christ. Love was "the central motif of nonviolence," the "force by which God binds man to himself and man to man", that goes to the "extremes" in radical acts of compassion and forgiveness—"even in the midst of hostility." "Peace dominates war; faith reconciles doubt," read the statement: "[the] redemptive community supersedes systems of gross social immorality."[11] In the 1962 document, staff members further resolved their firm commitment to the creation of "a social order permeated by love and to the spirituality of nonviolence as its grows from the Judeo-Christian tradition." Such love as this would forge a new social habitation, an "atmosphere in which reconciliation and justice becomes actual possibilities."

A theological analysis of the civil rights movement that brings to clarity the complex array of confessions, commitments and convictions is obviously far too ambitious a task for this essay, or any single study. Moreover, in addition to a theological analysis of the civil rights movement, there is another level of theological engagement—a more theologically constructive level—that seeks to clarify or explicate theological ideas by observing them in their concrete social settings. That is to say, the questions raised above also press the issue of how we interpret lived theological experience, the relation between religious appropriations of life and life's dense textures, as it relates to the claims and beliefs of the movement community. What do we see when we look at lived experience? We see perduring solidarity gathering around shared longings for ultimacy and the divine. We see a more evanescent solidarity gathering around contingently shared desires, needs and values. What I mean by contingently shared desires, needs and values has to do with goals that are satisfiable through campaigns of action: in the history of race, these would include abolition of slavery, anti-lynching laws, public accommodations laws, school desegregation, and affirmative action. What is not included is reconciliation. Reconciliation involves too many interconnecting, overlapping and perpetually contradictory processes to be considered satisfiable through campaigns of action: in the movement toward reconciliation, the processes and transactions of personal, spiritual, and cultural negotiation are renewed every morning, without fail, and always without consummation. That is to say, racial reconciliation requires affective, moral and spiritual resources that are not properly human.

Finally, if we grant that these above questions should be answered on the side of faith's integrity, we are compelled to further recognize that the interpretation of "religion and civil rights" is not a matter of tracing moral

sources of social action to various regions of civic piety or to representations of human goodness. Rather, what awaits us is the distinctively theological task of understanding the confessional details of the movement's
convictions, confessions and commitments as observed in its language and
actions, for the very specificity of these convictions, confessions and commitments has been largely overlooked by scholars, even among those
sympathetic to the black church and the Christian tradition. This level of
analysis, which may be called "lived" or "embodied" theology, would not
be primarily concerned with analyzing the specific theological sources of
particular social movements or of persons and people in historical narrative; rather, it would ask how certain theological themes or doctrines may
reach an intensity of meaning and application in the context of social existence. This might also be another way of saying that in order to explain
who "God the Lord is," we sometimes have to be willing to honestly tell
the stories of what people have actually experienced.[12] Interpreting the
movement as theological drama presents us with a plotline that far
exceeds the movement's significant political or economic achievements.

There is much exciting work ahead. I wish to advance this work in the
present essay by focusing on two dimensions of a theological analysis: the
theological commitments and convictions of Martin Luther King, Jr. and
the appropriation of the movement as historical context for theological
inquiry.

Martin Luther King, Jr. often described the civil rights movement's
mission as the pursuit of the beloved community. "A boycott is just a
means to an end," he said of the Montgomery bus boycott in his 1956
address, "The Birth of a New Age." "A boycott is merely a means to say,
'I don't like it.' It is merely a means to awaken a sense of shame within
the oppressor but the end is reconciliation. The end is the creation of a
beloved community . . . [and] the creation of a society where men will live
together as brothers . . . not retaliation but redemption. That is the end
we are trying to reach . . . The old order is dying and the new order is
being born."[13] In King's mind, the goal of political action informed by
agape love involves nothing less than the creation of a new social space.[14]

Of course, King and his fellow travelers in the Montgomery Improvement Association also wanted—and not only wanted, but intended and
demanded—more immediately visible goals as well. They wanted, for
example, fair seating arrangements on city buses as specified in the 1955

Holt Street Resolution and in his December 8, 1955, letter to the national office of the National City Buslines in Chicago:

1. Courteous treatment of bus drivers.
2. Seating of Negro passengers from rear to front of bus, and white passengers from front to rear on first-come-first-serve basis with no seats reserved for any race.
3. Employment of Negro bus operators in predominantly Negro residential sections.[15]

But the strategic goals and the complex negotiations, demonstrations and confrontations required to achieve them—in this time of transition "from the old order into the new"—were constituent parts of a larger theological vision, parts of what King called "the great camp meeting in the promised land of freedom."[16]

Most scholars agree that King's use of term "beloved community" borrows from a discourse fashionable in American philosophical and theological circles during throughout the early and middle twentieth century.[17] But King always kept a guarded distance between his own use of the term and its philosophical and cultural formulations. The American philosopher, Josiah Royce, who had taken the term from Hegel's philosophy of religion and revised it, talked about the historical realization of "a perfectly live unity of individual men joined in one divine chorus."[18] The dichotomy between divine and human would be fully overcome in the beloved community, so that the consciousness of God could be seen to be residing in the community. According to Hegel, this consciousness of God in community would be a fully realized apprehension of the present time in its essence—the "Kingdom of reconciliation," as he said in his 1831 lectures on the philosophy of religion.[19] Hegel considered it the ultimate task of philosophy to illuminate this reconciliation. "[Philosophy] presents the reconciliation of God with himself and us with nature, showing that nature, otherness, is implicitly divine, and that the raising of itself to reconciliation is on the one hand what finite spirit implicitly is, while on the other hand it arrives at this reconciliation, or brings it forth, in world history."[20] And since this reconciliation is an expression of the "peace of God," "[p]hilosophy is to this extent theology," Hegel said. All social oppositions, as in the spirit's march toward a final reconciliation, reach its most abundant expression in concrete community. "In the Kingdom you, and your enemy, and yonder stranger, are one," wrote Royce in *The*

Christian Doctrine of Life, "For the Kingdom is the community of God's beloved."[21]

Not only Hegel's self-positing spirit but the whole tradition of nineteenth century historical optimism echoes throughout Royce's formulations. Kant's ethical rationality, for example, shapes Royce's own moral admonitions, albeit with a robustly American spin. Kant's imperative— "Act in conformity with that maxim and that maxim only which you can at the same time will to be a universal maxim"—is recast in language suitable for social reform in America—"So act as to help, however you can, and whenever you can, towards making mankind one loving brotherhood, whose love is not a mere affection for morally detached individuals, but a love of the unity of its own life upon its own divine level, and a love of individuals in so far as they can be raised to communion with this spiritual community itself."[22] The result captures the essence of liberal Protestant ethical religion, the location of the divine-human relation in some modulation of human experience, in this case in a certain moral affection for universal community. Framed against its philosophical antecedents, the term beloved community shimmers with liberal hopes of human progress and perfectibility.

In more systematic theological form, as in Royce's book, *The Real World and the Christian Ideas*, the catalog of Christian doctrine is reconceptualized according to the basic axiom, "making mankind one loving brotherhood."[23] Christology—the doctrine of Jesus Christ—becomes something called "the practical acknowledgement of the Spirit of the Universal and Beloved Community." Beloved community is the inevitable conclusion of the evolutionary and synthetic energies of the Cross and Resurrection. "Love this faith," Royce says, "use this faith, teach this faith, preach this faith, in whatever words, through whatever symbols, by means of whatever forms of creeds, in accordance with whatever practices best you find to enable you with a sincere intent and a whole heart to symbolize and to realize the presence of the Spirit in the Community. All else about your religion is the accident of your special race or nation or form of worship or training or accidental personal opinion, or devout private mystical experience,—illuminating but capricious."[24] All we need to know of God is discovered in ethical religion, the Kantian imperative slightly adjusted for church-goers in capitalist economies.

Historian Casey Nelson Blake, in his study of the period from 1915–1930, *Beloved Community: The Cultural Criticism of Randolph Bourne*,

Van Wyck Brooks, Waldo Frank and Lewis Mumford, described the early twentieth century concern with beloved community as an intellectual attempt to rebuild "communities that engaged the self in the language and civic association of a democratic culture" in an era of corporate expansion and economic marginalization.[25] Philosophers and cultural critics such as Bourne, Brooks, Frank and Mumford spoke of "beloved community" as a regenerated American society in which all people could take part in the creation of social goals.[26] The present shape of things—however fragmented or frustrating—could then be judged from the perspective of an emerging new sociality, which itself would take the form of a common culture of lived experience—"the only possible source for genuine self-realization," as Blake said.[27] The beloved community would constitute an "American spiritual and cultural renaissance, grounded in a full understanding of human experience," and likewise prepare the way for a thrillingly new democratic politics.[28] Indeed, a politics in which the individual reaches his full potential as part of a collective venture toward complete social harmony—this is beloved community.

King's vision of "the camp meeting" trades on this philosophical discourse, while it also nicely illustrates the synthetic ingenuity of his spirituality, his ability to bring into a unified perspective the two dimensions of the movement reality: everyday people gathered in beloved fellowship surrounded by great expanses of divine freedom. But unlike Hegel's famous synthesis and Royce's American adaptation, King preserves the difference between God and community, as one sees in his sermons and speeches. How could he not? The Jim Crow South—like the history of the African American diaspora—hardly yielded a theodicy. Still, in King's theology, a unity does exist between God and the world, but this unity is sustained asymmetrically from the side of God's majesty—the great camp meeting in the promised land of freedom has been prepared by God. And for this reason, even the most forlorn southern towns and backwater hamlets could "become the theater of operations for God's righteousness," says Lischer.[29] You might say, too, that the great camp meeting gives imaginative life and power to King's non-dualistic conception of God, his repair of the Christian tradition's Gnostic dislocations, the segregation of spirit and flesh, God and world, the life hereafter and the here-and-now. Herein, King stands in the good company of theologians like Dietrich Bonhoeffer, the German pastor and resistance activist who waged war against the idols of race and blood in a different historical context, and who offered similar testimony to an integrated conception of God and world. Christian faith and practice "puts us into many different dimensions of life at the same time," Bonhoeffer had written in *Ethics*, but without segregating the individual from the world, or the world from God.[30] "There are not two realities, but only one reality," Bonhoeffer wrote, "and that is the reality of God, which has become manifest in Christ in the reality of the world. Sharing in Christ we stand at once in both the reality of God and the reality of the world. . . . A Christianity which withdraws from the world falls victim to the unnatural and the irrational, to presumption and self-will."[31] The "forces of darkness," to use King's vocabulary, "the iron feet of oppression," "the dark chambers of pessimism," "the tranquilizing drug of gradualism," "the dark and desolate valleys of despair," "the sagging walls of bus segregation"—have been defeated once and for all. The divine power that has spoken the decisive "Yes" on the Cross and has defeated these "forces of darkness" is the same power that fuels the spirit of the "fifty thousand Negroes in Montgomery."[32]

As I said above, King's use of beloved community was always permeated with the raw material of his own formative experiences in the southern black church. As Richard Lischer says, "The 'Beloved Community' he would later discover in the writings of the philosophical idealists preexisted in the earthly community at the crossroads of Sweet Auburn."[33] King could never use the philosophical discourse without revision; for this discourse finally gave rise to a defense of democratic capitalism and its diverse modes of authority and operations. This is a point Eugene McCarraher makes in his recent book, *Christian Critics: Religion and the Impasse in Modern American Social Thought*. "[P]rogressive religiosity—a mutation of liberal Protestant religion—ratified the cultural power of the professional and managerial elite," McCarraher writes. "Under this Protestant aegis of religion, the 'intellectual gospel' baptized by liberal theology slowly degraded the authority of the Protestant intelligentsia and promoted a secular mode of legitimacy for the professional-managerial class."[34] Such naive legitimization could not have been more unfamiliar to the sensibilities and daily experiences of African Americans in the Jim Crow South—hence King's ambivalence about the philosophical formulations. In King's hands, an increasingly banal liberal abstraction was invested with theological vitality and prophetic urgency, so that the prospects of social change came to look less like a bland and bourgeois cozying-up of the divine and the human and more like God's crashing into the

human—a sudden and new theological reality appearing quite paradoxi-
cally on the streets of Montgomery and Birmingham and Jackson. The
theological defines the social, it would seem, at least if we take King's
1956 address, "The Montgomery Story," as any indication: King calls the
civil rights movement a "spiritual movement." "We have the strange feeling down in Montgomery," he said, "that in our struggle we have cosmic
companionship. We feel that the universe is on the side of right and righteousness. That is what keeps us going."[35]

While "cosmic companion" and the morally-attuned universe hardly
amount to meaningful identifications of the God of Israel and Jesus Christ
and may seem to lack the specificity I mentioned in the first section of the
essay, King proceeded in two other 1956 speeches to situate these general
cosmological notions in a Christian framework. In "The Montgomery
Story" (July 27), he does this with a slight deferral on the specificity, "Oh,
I would admit that, yes, it comes down to us from the long tradition of our
Christian faith."[36] The cosmic companion of the Montgomery struggle is
the divine "something," and this something may go by the name of Jesus,
at least on Alabama soil, or remain an unnamed mystery—"there is something in the universe that justifies Carlyle in saying, 'No lies can live forever."[37] Yet, even in this formulation, the Cross of Jesus remains central
to the movement's vision, as well as to Christianity's integrity. "Good Friday may occupy the palace and Christ the cross. But one day that same
Christ will rise up and split history into A.D. and B.C. so that even the
life of Caesar must be dated by his name." The story of the death and
resurrection of Jesus injects the Montgomery movement with inner meaning and power. "That is why we can walk and never get weary because
we know that there is a great camp meeting in the promised land of freedom and equality."

Still, when King gave the same speech at the American Baptist Assembly and American Home Mission Agencies Conference, in July of 1956,
the slight hesitation, "Oh, I would admit," is gone. The "something" is
identified without qualification as the "great epic" of Good Friday and
Easter.[38] He says, "There is something that stands at the center of our
faith. There is a great epic. There is a great *event* that stands at the center
of our faith which *reveals* to us that God is on the side of truth and love
and justice."[39] I do not mean to say that the difference in emphasis
between the speeches of June 27 and the July 23, 1956, indicates any

theological change of mind on King's part, not in this short span of time in any case. My purpose is rather to show that King understands the fading of the "old order" and the emergence of a "new age" as a pervasively theological, if not ecclesiological, *event*. "God is working in history to bring about this new age," he says. Therefore, the stumbling block to America's partaking in the great epic of resurrection and reconciliation is not racial division as such, but division in the Church. "[The] church is the Body of Christ. So when the church is true to its nature it knows neither division nor disunity. I am disturbed about what you are doing to the Body of Christ."[40] The new age will be a time when "men will live together as brothers; a world in which men will beat their swords into ploughshares and their spears into pruning-hooks."[41] But the new age is not an inevitability, built into the evolutionary code of human history. The brotherhood and sisterhood of humankind, if it is realized historically at all, will radiate out from the fellowship of the camp meeting; this is the "broad universalism" discerned at "the center of the gospel."[42]

In the July 23, 1956 speech, King cites the lines by James Russell Lowell, as he had in "The Montgomery Story," though now with direct reference to the movement and its strategies:

> Truth forever on the scaffold
> Wrong forever on the throne,
> Yet that scaffold sways a future,
> And behind the dim unknown stands God
> Within the shadow keeping watch above his own.

He describes the "great epic" of the Cross as "the event" that *interprets* the non-violent direct action—"this is what the method of nonviolent resistance says to the individual engaged in the struggle."[43] And he describes the Cross as the event that *enables* resistance—"this is why the nonviolent resister can suffer and not retaliate." The "great epic" *activates* the mission of the church—its meta-narrative, as academic theologians might say, its comprehensive retelling of the human story. No longer is the church solely in the business of saving individual souls from damnation (as in white southern Christendom), but it represents (one might even say embodies) the great event by making free space for the worldly enactment of reconciliation with God and others. If "[s]egregation is a blatant denial of the unity which we all have in Jesus Christ," King says, then reconciliation demonstrates to the world that "it is still true that in Christ there is neither Jew nor Gentile (Negro nor white) and that out of one blood God made all men to dwell upon the face of the earth."[44]

Where then does the non-violent teaching of Mahatma Gandhi fit into King's christological account? As I see it, King describes Gandhi's astonishing sacrifices as gifts to the Montgomery movement, parables of justice, if you will, that stand beside and compliment the Christian tradition's inner resources. "Christ furnished the spirit and motivation," King wrote in "Experiment in Love," "while Gandhi furnished the method."[45] Gandhi's witness supplied the "Christian doctrine of love" with a strategy of social protest, just as Negro spirituals had at times nourished the soul of the Indian peace movement.[46] In his "Six Talks in Outline," written for his 1949 Crozer Theological Seminary Course, "Christian Theology for Today," King, in his earliest written reference, mentions Gandhi in his sketches on pneumatalogy entitled, "How God Works Through His Spirit." Gandhi is counted among David Livingstone and Albert Schweitzer (*and* Jesus Christ) as individuals who "reveal the working of the Spirit of God."[47] "As the circle is narrowed from the world to the Church and from the Church to the individual, the work of the Holy Spirit becomes more specific and intense," the young Baptist minister writes.[48] Later, in his 1958 essay, "An Experiment in Love," King made clear that although it was the Sermon on the Mount that initially inspired the Montgomery protests, the witness of the "little brown saint of India" and his "doctrine of passive resistance" helped inspire the work of local black churches as the movement unfolded.[49]

To speak of Gandhi's sacrifices as "parables of justice," as I have, invokes the unlikely ally of Karl Barth, the Swiss theologian and father of the so-called theology of crisis, who *apropos* of this description, in the late volumes of his *Church Dogmatics*, talked about certain "parables of the Kingdom," words and actions not directly associated with the Christian proclamation but which in their particular coming-into-being become genuine forms of Christian expression. These parables have to do with "true words which are not spoken in the Bible of the Church" but which have to be heard as true in relation to the Word of God—true because they bear witness to the reach and majesty of the Incarnation—"in the lowest depths He has triumphed, in the supreme heights He rules at the right hand of the Father."[50] Parables of the Kingdom are possible because God rules supreme in the "depths" and in the "heights," and the majesty of God's reign overflows the church onto regions of existence otherwise unbaptized. The "sphere of His dominion and Word is in any case greater than that of their prophecy and apostolate, and greater than that of the *kerygma*, dogma, cultus, mission and whole life of the community which gathers and edifies itself and speaks and acts in their school."[51] Barth's formulation breaks with liberal Protestant notions of the essential divinity of the human by insisting that humanity derives its dignity precisely from the one divinity, the God of Israel and Jesus Christ, who invites sinful humanity into its saving love through grace. Barth says, "If we recognize and confess Him as the One who was and is and will be, then we recognize and confess that not we alone, nor the community which, following the prophets and apostles, believes in Him and loves Him and hopes in Him, but *de iure* all men and all creation derive from His cross, from the reconciliation accomplished in Him, and are ordained to be the theater of His glory and therefore the recipients and bearers of His Word."[52] Gandhi's words register this kind of power in King's theology (as perhaps they do in Barth's as well), for the words of the little brown man from India "lead the community more truly and profoundly than ever before to Scripture."[53]

Therefore, the beloved community is the new social space wherein the "triumph and beat of the drums of Easter" invade the highways and byways of the Jim Crow South. This new social space is not shaped by a "religion of loyalty" (Royce) or by "the good life of personality lived in the Beloved Community" (Bourne) or even by the "social egalitarianism" of Jesus Christ (Rauschenbusch);[54] the beloved community is shaped by the "*great event* on Calvary," as King exclaimed again in his sermon at Dexter Avenue, "Paul's Letter to American Christians."[55] Although it is a regrettable, but undeniable, fact that this great event has been performed by white American Christendom as a "meaningless drama," still the love that God has poured out on the Montgomery movement—a costly but embracing love—is now revealing itself through the movement like a summons of grace. Changing his metaphors, King also calls the great event "a telescope through which we look out into the long vista of eternity and see the love of God breaking forth into time."[56]

We must take some caution in comparing King and Barth, because Barth's dialectical theology was sometimes vilified and caricatured by King's mentors, and sometimes written off as the austere piety of a fideist. In his Boston University studies, King too indulged at times in the fashionable stereotyping of Barth—i.e., Barth's God as the wholly other, wholly transcending time and history, distant and aloof—and one would not really expect anything less. King was a graduate student working with a faculty suspicious of the new European theology. (King's assessment is plausible, though unoriginal, in the context of Barth's dialectical writings of the years 1919–1931, but by 1955, Barth had moved to a position that resolved the kinds of conflicts stemming from his earlier description of revelation as pure act.[57] In 1948, Barth spoke of his "supratemporal" characterization of God as a kind of theological exaggeration; "although I was confident to treat the far-sidedness of the coming kingdom of God with absolute seriousness, I had no such confidence in relation to its coming as such."[58] And in 1960, he would write in his book, *The Humanity of God*, that he had overstated his criticisms of nineteenth century experiential theology and that it was now time to accord to "that earlier theology, and the entire development culminating it" a "greater historical justice than appeared to us possible and feasible in the violence of the first break-off and clash."[59] And yet the intent of Barth's defiant "Nein" to Protestant liberalism is exceedingly important in helping Martin Luther King clarify the drift, if not the intent as well, of his theology.

No doubt, King's academic vocabulary bears the imprimatur of mid-twentieth century Protestant American thought. Boston University especially retained many of the original convictions of the Protestant liberal tradition in its approach to theological studies. The Boston Personalist School considered itself to be a "species of Personal Idealism" that valued the human person as the "ontological ultimate" and personality as "the fundamental explanatory principle."[60] In this manner, a doctrine such as the Incarnation was understood not as the miraculous event of the Word made flesh but a symbol bearing lessons about a person of consummate will and devotion; that "only a person of holy love could do what God has done in Christ. As the Boston religious philosopher, John Lavely, explained, "When Jesus says, 'He who has seen me has seen the Father,' it is doubtful that he is asserting that he is ontologically identical with God. He is rather saying something like: I cannot tell you anything more about God than by being my (best) self. That is, there is no other analogy for God than a person at his or her best and the best analogy is the best person."[61] This kind of blurring of the difference between the divine and human—and at the same time unraveling of the trinitarian nature of God—represents the very tradition against which Barth makes his famous protest, and against which is directed his idea of the event-character of revelation, revelation as the self-disclosure of the trinitarian God in time. Hence, the question of Barth's influence—or at least the Barthian resonances, of King's thought—is appropriate. Like many young theological minds, King was taken by Barth's shattering critique of liberalism. King had already begun to discern theologically the naiveté of liberalism's hopes, which, of course, had been personally evidenced in his childhood in the Jim Crow South, even in the childhood of a protected middle-class boy. Just as the philosophical formulation of the beloved community seemed offensively optimistic, the notion of essential human goodness did not fit the facts of black experience. "Liberalism is ignorant—even innocent—of matters African-American children understand before their seventh birthday," as Lischer explains.[62] And so, in his essay, "Contemporary Continental Theology," King praises Barth's radical project and "the almost complete collapse of liberal Protestantism" left in its wake, and this point—however guarded—is made all the more striking for the fact that King was writing the essay in Harold DeWolf's seminar in Systematic Theology.* Karl Barth and the "theologians of crisis", said King, were

---

*Harold DeWolf was part of the formidable Personalist School, though not as well known as Edgar Brightman (who died during King's first year in Boston), nor as deeply invested in personalist jargon. Still, DeWolf was influential in King's theological formation. DeWolf's theological sympathies lay unequivocally on the side of the great German liberals, Ritschl, von Harnack, and Schleiermacher, as seen in his definition of religion as "devotion to supreme ideals". [Richard Lischer, *The Preacher King*, p. 58] Although Dewolf tempered his criticisms of Barth with charity—one does not encounter the kind of hostility running through the criticisms of American Reformed and evangelical theologians such as J. Gresham Machen and Carl F. H. Henry—DeWolf made it clear that he parted company with any theology that diminished the importance of natural knowledge of God in the divine-human relation. Barth's theology, DeWolf claimed, issued in a confusing social ethic—"arbitrary", "unpredictable" and "historically irresponsible"— precisely because it belittled the natural. Having no stake in human experience as a theologically significant category leaves Barth with "no principles by which to guide decisions in regard to social problems, and what we do has no direct and significant connection with the reign of God which, in any event, God will bring to full manifestation in his own good time." [L. Harold DeWolf, *The Case for Theology in Liberal Perspective* (Philadelphia: The Westminster Press, 1959), p. 168.] Barth's radical testimony to the provenience of grace over all worldly reality finally diminished the integrity of the world, Dewolf charged, and encouraged sectarian withdrawal and political quietism along the way. DeWolf would have no share in this. "A healthy, vigorous faith, firm in its conviction of truth and aggressive in its God-given mission to the world, accepts without fear the hazards of maximum involvement in the world's travail, thought, and toil." [L. Harold DeWolf, *The Case for Theology in Liberal Perspective*, p. 189.] On a related matter, Barth's praise of democratic socialism fell on deaf-ears among cold-war American Protestants. Martin Luther King, Jr. was no exception. Anthony Dunbar's book, *Against the Grain: Southern Radicals and Prophets, 1929–1959*, introduces us to an earlier generation of radical theologians in America who made a direct connection between Barth's theme "calling us back to the depths of the Christian faith," warning us "that we too easily capitulated to modern culture."[63]

To put the essay in clearer perspective, King's survey of the European theological scene in his "Continental Christian Theology" was less influenced by DeWolf's views than those of Harvard theologian, Walter Marshall Horton, particularly his 1938 book, *Contemporary Continental Theology: An Interpretation for Anglo-Saxons*. As a result, King's survey leans toward a more slightly sympathetic treatment than would be found on the east side of the Charles River. Horton was one of the few North American proponents of Barthian theology, and in 1928 he had published his brilliant translation of Barth's *Das Wort Gottes und die Theologie*. At the time a Congregational minister in Brookline, Massachusetts, Horton had run across *The Word of God and the Word of Man* (as the book would be titled in English) while browsing through the "New Books" shelf in the Harvard-Andover Library at Harvard Divinity School. Horton later recalled the decisive encounter: "[There] was undeniable exhilaration in rehearing and relearning that God is God, that he *will* will what he will *will*, that he is not caught in the trammels of the world he himself has created, and that man can produce him neither as the conclusion of a syllogism, the Q.E.D. of an experiment, nor the crown of a civilization." After falling under the spell of the book's "passionate and penetrating faith," and completely losing track of the passage of time, Horton resolved that never again would it be possible for his generation to "listen with equanimity to the teaching that an optimistic humanism is all that man needs to be himself."[64]

King's encounter of Barth, though certainly not as dramatic as Horton's,

---

of God breaking into time and history and the form of the socialist movement. Dunbar laments the civil rights movement's unwillingness to consider racial inequality in the larger historical context of the southern radicals' campaigns against unfair labor practices and social inequities endemic to market economies. Dunbar writes, "Martin Luther King, Jr. made the point in an address he gave to the final large gathering of the Fellowship of Southern Churchmen just as he was beginning to rise to national prominence. 'I never intend to adjust myself,' he said, 'to the tragic inequalities of an economic system which takes necessities from the many to give luxuries to the few.' Yet rarely did King, or any other leader of the emerging black movement, call capitalism his enemy. Their struggle altered the fundamental characteristic of southern society, the second-class citizenship of blacks, but it set aside for consideration by future generations many of the historic demands of southern dissenters: 'land for the landless,' 'full and decent employment,' a halt to the invasion of carpetbag industry, the holding in common of 'all natural resources and all scientific processes,' and the 'liberation of all workers from enslavement to the machine.'" [*Against the Grain: Southern Radicals and Prophets, 1929–1959* (Charlottesville: University Press of America, 1981), p. 258.]

was decisive still, and has been understated by scholars. In *The Papers of Martin Luther King, Jr.*, Volumes II and III, the writings of King's student years, there are as many references to Barth as to Reinhold Niebuhr. King likes what he hears—Barth's penchant for overturning established categories of thinking and his serious reckoning with human fallenness and divine transcendence. "We in the Anglo-Saxon world," King wrote, "securely relying upon our vast natural resources, our highly developed science and technology, and our fairly stable social institutions, have been thinking and talking far too glibly about the Kingdom of God as of something that we might hope to 'bring in' by our own human efforts. Half unconsciously, we have been confusing the ancient hope of the coming of God's Kingdom with the modern doctrine of progress. Have not we depended to much on man and too little on God?"[65] King confesses that "maybe man is more of a sinner than liberals are willing to admit." Man should also admit that "many of the ills of the world are due to plain sin."[66] While it may be true that "the sinfullness [sic] of man is often overemphasized by some continental theologians"—not only Barth but Emil Brunner and Friedrich Gogarten as well—King dissents from the liberals here and insists that the word sin must "come back into our vocabulary." "The tendency on the part of some liberal theologians to see sin as a mere 'lay of nature' which will be progressively eliminated as man climbs the evolutionary ladder seems to me quite perilous." For "only the one who sits on the peak of his intellectual ivory tower looking unrealistically with his rosey colored glasses on the scene of life can fail to see this fact."

Over the course of King's lifetime, the deep wounds wrought by the "sinfullness of man" in American society intensified the idea of the beloved community theologically; in time it came to express with an even greater sense of crisis the eschatological in-breaking of God in history. (There is no evidence King continued reading Barth after seminary.) In fact, according to Lischer, after 1966, King altogether dropped the term "beloved community" from his speeches and sermons, preferring to stick solely with the "Kingdom of God," the Biblical term for the eschatological reign of God that was tearing its way onto the soil of ordinary towns. Lischer explains: "As King's social idealism was succeeded by more realistic appraisals of human evil, references to the Beloved Community gradually disappeared from his sermons, their place taken by the theological symbol 'the Kingdom of God'. On the basis of King's published writings and utterances, scholars have debated the question of the kingdom's this-worldly as opposed to other-worldly character, but they have not commented on the radical conversion implicit in the shift from the humanism of the 'Community' to the theology of the 'Kingdom'. The former carries overtones of utopian idealism; the latter acknowledges God's claim upon all human achievements."[67]

I might add to Lischer's helpful insight by suggesting that King's beloved community was always different in tone and intention than its liberal formulations—for the theological reasons already stated. But be that as it may, Lischer is correct to say that the rhetorical shift in emphasis from beloved community to Kingdom of God echoes the shift from "identification to rage" that King made in the final years of his life. "Confrontation was the theological flip-side of identification," Lischer says. Identification with mainstream values—the hints of civil religion and Americanism in King's middle years—gives way to searing judgment. Racism was as American as apple pie, as human as pride. This became King's final message. No doubt, confrontation had never been absent from King's repertoire of proclamation and provocation; but after the riots and uprisings, after the movement had swept through the South without its revival call answered, and as the shadows of Vietnam began to cover the American soulscape, King dropped the inclusive "we" in talking about the movement's aims. He dropped the "we" of national redemption and social transformation—"to redeem the soul of America" read SCLC's motto— the "we" of the beloved community. The soul of America was unredeemable, King concluded, for a nation "born in genocide," can never be redeemed apart from the cleansing fires of the righteous God. "Life is a continual story of shattered dreams," King told his Ebenezer congregation in March of 1968. A few weeks later, on the eve of his assassination, he lamented to the Memphis crowd gathered in support of the sanitation workers' strike, "The world is all messed up. The nation is sick. Trouble is in the land. Confusion all around."[68] The righteousness of God would not transmogrify the human frame from the inside out like some inexorable and innate force—like some moral arch of the universe. The righteousness of God divides and sunders, wreaks havoc on the smug and the pious. In these final speeches, Barthian crisis has surfaced in a particularly visceral form. The hour is late. The reconciling gesture remains unreciprocated. Judgment falls on the land.

CONCLUSION

Such ideas offer a wealth of material for further consideration, and much exciting work lies ahead. Still, I hope in this essay to have made clear that the interpretation of "religion and civil rights" is not a matter of writing religious genealogies of moral actions, civic piety or representations of human goodness, or of attending to the non-material influences of social activism. The interpretation of religion and civil rights involves the task of understanding the specific details of theological convictions in their inner-logic and their dynamic particularity. In future discussions, it will not be enough to say that King, Hamer, Lewis, Young, Shuttlesworth and all their fellow travelers in the Spirit were civil rights activists influenced by religion, and that religion motivated acts of courage and compassion. Theologians, working together with historians and other scholars, will have to reckon with the meaningful fact that religious persons believe particular things about God and these beliefs create a new world from which all life is interpreted.

Kingdom of God and Beloved Community in the Thought of Martin Luther King, Jr.

RALPH E. LUKER

Martin Luther King, Jr., is more closely associated with language about the "beloved community" than any other preacher or public intellectual in the twentieth century. Indeed, two scholars argue that it was "the organizing principle" of his public ministry, the "capstone" of his thought. "The centrality of the 'Beloved Community' in King's intellectual concerns," they argue, "is demonstrated by the fact that it can be traced from his earliest addresses and articles to his latest writings and public speeches."[1] Some themes or ideas can be traced from King's earliest through his last addresses and articles. His ultimate hope for the establishment of the Kingdom of God, his belief that all life is interrelated and his conviction that humanity's moral development had failed to keep pace with its technological achievement weave from his earliest sermons through the whole of his work.[2] By contrast, "beloved community" was an adopted language, one which he did not use until near the end of the Montgomery bus boycott and one which he increasingly abandoned in the last years of his life.[3]

COMMUNITY AS PRIMAL EXPERIENCE

King's "An Autobiography of Religious Development," written in 1950, speaks most clearly about his early sense of community. He recalled a "congenial" and "intimate" family life which extended from the two story frame home on Atlanta's Auburn Avenue through the quadplex apartments and "shotgun" duplex cottages of neighbors who belonged to his father's Ebenezer Baptist Church just up the street. "The church has always been a second home for me," young King wrote.

It is quite easy for me to think of a God of love mainly because I grew up in a family where love was central and where lovely relationships

39

were present. It is quite easy for me to think of the universe as basically friendly mainly because of my uplifting hereditary and environmental circumstances. It is quite easy for me to lean more toward optimism than pessimism about human nature mainly because of my childhood experiences.

Thus, King's early sense of community centered in a loving home and extended to a second home at church, both of them encompassed by a "deeply religious," "unsophisticated," "wholesome community," relatively free of crime.[4]

Atlanta was both profoundly his home and, yet, a city in which he was only marginally at home, for King's early community was one largely circumscribed by race. The racially mixed neighborhood of businesses and residences along Auburn Avenue had witnessed the horrors of Atlanta's race riot of 1906. White folk clearly were the aggressors in the riot, but in the city's first experience of "white flight," Auburn Avenue became predominantly black within the next four years. By passing residential segregation ordinances, Atlanta's white power structure sought to re-enforce the tendency to define neighborhoods by race. Thus, when King was born in 1929, "Sweet Auburn" was almost exclusively black.[5] A white-owned grocery store across Auburn Avenue from King's childhood home was the rare exception. His preschool playmates included the son of its owner, but when they entered school, the white child's parents insisted that the two boys could play together no longer. "I was greatly shocked," King recalled, "and from that moment on I was determined to hate every white person." His parents' enjoinders nonetheless to love them were unsatisfying. "How could I love a race of people [who] hated me and who had been responsible for breaking me up with one of my best childhood friends?" he wondered.[6] For another ten or twelve years, King's experience with white folk was commonly marked by their requirement of his exclusion or subordination.[7] For the rest of his life, racial prejudice and discrimination gave specificity to the theological meanings of "sin."

Young Martin Luther King, Jr., was spared the searing fundamentalist/modernist controversy among Northern white Protestants early in the twentieth century.[8] He may never have known about the public intellectuals' debates about "community" in the 1920s.[9] Thus, his answers to profound questions about community would have been quite traditional. In 1948, had you asked him to name the present reality of the community of redemption, he would undoubtedly have said: church; and had you asked the name of its future hope, he would undoubtedly have said: Kingdom of God. While he may have encountered talk about the "beloved community" in studies at Morehouse College, Crozer Theological Seminary and Boston University, there is little significant evidence of it.[10]

COMMUNITY AND ACADEMIC THEOLOGY

As a student at Crozer, Martin Luther King, Jr., studied the works of liberal white Northern theologians, William Newton Clarke and William Adams Brown, on the Kingdom of God. From Clarke, he learned to contrast pre-millenial and post-millenial expectations, concluding that "however varied the interpretations are, it is probably commonly agreed by all Christians that God's final purpose is the building of a regenerated human society which will include all mankind in a common fellowship of well-ordered living."[11] Several scholars, including two who knew him well, argue that for Martin Luther King, Jr., "beloved community" was synonymous with the Kingdom of God.[12] The passage which they cite as confirming their case, however, is from two subsequent papers based on William Adams Brown's book, *Beliefs That Matter*. The passage does not mention "beloved community" and its combination of legitimate quotation, paraphrasing and plagiarism is so complex that one knows what Brown thought, but the papers are dubious sources for what Martin Luther King thought.[13] In any case, he never again cited William Newton Clarke or William Adams Brown as significant influences on his thinking about Kingdom or community.

The two theologians who did influence King's thinking about community throughout his adult life were Walter Rauschenbusch and Reinhold Niebuhr. Preferring to use the traditional theological categories, neither of them wrote about "beloved community." In 1950, King's mentor at Morehouse College, President Benjamin E. Mays, published a popular anthology of Rauschenbusch's thought and shortly thereafter King encountered Rauschenbusch in seminars at Crozer. In later years, he wrote that the social gospel's pre-eminent theologian made "an indelible imprint on my thinking." His insistence that the gospel deals with the social and economic conditions of communities as well as their spiritual well-being would be fundamental to King's theology throughout his life. By the early 1950s, however, Rauschenbusch was being read in the light of a widespread neo-orthodox critique of theological liberalism and King repeated much of it in his intellectual autobiography, "Pilgrimage to Nonviolence." Rauschenbusch had "fallen victim to the nineteenth-century 'cult of inevitable progress' which led him to a superficial optimism concerning man's nature" and had come "perilously close to identifying the Kingdom of God with a peculiar social and economic system—a tendency which should never befall the Church," King wrote.[14] Subsequent readings of Rauschenbusch suggest that he was largely innocent of those charges, commonly made by a generation which read Reinhold Niebuhr.[15]

In seminary, King became convinced that Reinhold Niebuhr's arguments about the pervasive implications of sin in human communities must be accommodated.[16] His engagement with Niebuhr deepened in graduate school at Boston University between 1952 and 1954. Near the end of his first year, King prepared an oral report and a seminar paper for his mentor, L. Harold DeWolf, on Reinhold Niebuhr's social ethics. Here, he grappled with Niebuhr's insights about the impotence of moral suasion on inherently egoistic communities and the limits that fixes on what can be expected within history. King borrowed his criticism of Niebuhr, his failure to admit the capacity of agape to motivate perfectionist communities to acts of self-transcending love, from DeWolf's faculty colleague, Walter G. Muelder. Nonetheless, the exercise familiarized him with Niebuhr's primary insights. Two years later, he prepared a paper, "The Theology of Reinhold Niebuhr," for the Dialectical Society, a discussion group of African American graduate students in the Boston area. Still, King relied on Muelder for questioning whether Niebuhr's theology was adequately biblical, but his paper was a more mature explication of Niebuhr's thought. He was undoubtedly aware of, but made no reference to, Niebuhr's prophetic recommendation of nonviolent resistance to structures of racism in America.[17]

When King first reviewed his own "Pilgrimage to Nonviolence" in 1958, he acknowledged the influence of Rauschenbusch on his thinking, but devoted much more attention to Niebuhr. "I became so enamored of his social ethics," King wrote, "that I almost fell into the trap of accepting uncritically everything he wrote." By 1958, Niebuhr's rejection of pacifism, his insistence that there was "no intrinsic moral difference between violent and nonviolent resistance," and his insight into the "complex relation between morality and power" in groups and nations would offer a substantial intellectual challenge to King's own experience beyond academic speculation.[18]

MOVEMENT AS COMMUNITY

The context in which King began to talk about "beloved community" suggests that, for King, it never was simply equivalent to the Kingdom of God. From the beginning of the Montgomery bus boycott, he often spoke of the immorality of violence and the necessity of love and establishing the Kingdom of God on earth.[19] In the struggle, King was elated to find that divisions of religious denomination and social class were eroded and miracles of self transformation occurred as ordinary people translated accumulated resentments from sullen acquiescence into determined courage.[20] King referred to "beloved community," however, only after a federal district court ruled favorably in the Montgomery Improvement Association's suit to desegregate the city's busses. He did so in two major addresses. The first was to his Alpha Phi Alpha fraternity brothers on 11 August 1956, while the boycott continued and the city appealed the lower court's decision to the United States Supreme Court.

> As we move in this transition from the old age into the new we will have to rise up in protest. We will have to boycott at times, but let us always remember that boycotts are not ends within themselves. A boycott is just a means to an end. A boycott is merely a means to say, 'I don't like it.' It is merely a means to awaken a sense of shame within the oppressor but the end is reconciliation. The end is the creation of a beloved community. The end is the creation of a society where men will live together as brothers. An end is not retaliation but redemption. That is the end we are trying to reach. That we would bring these creative forces together we would be able to live in this new age which is destined to come. The old order is dying and the new order is being born.[21]

King referred to it again in an address to the Montgomery Improvement Association on 3 December 1956, three weeks after the Supreme Court's confirmation of the lower court's favorable ruling.

> This love might well be the salvation of our civilization. . . . Not through violence; not through hate; no, not even through boycotts; but through

love. It is true that as we struggle for freedom in America we will have
to boycott at times. But we must remember as we boycott that a boycott
is not an end within itself; it is merely a means to awaken a sense of
shame within the oppressor and challenge his false sense of superiority.
But the end is reconciliation; the end is redemption; the end is the creation of the beloved community. It is this type of spirit and this type of
love that can transform opposers into friends. It is this type of understanding good will that will transform the deep gloom of the old age
into the exuberant gladness of the new age. It is this love which will
bring about miracles in the hearts of men.[22]

"Beloved community," then, is where "miracles" occur "in the hearts
of men." King's use of the parable of the Prodigal Son in an address to
the Montgomery Improvement Association on 14 November 1956 is more
specific. One day earlier, the United States Supreme Court affirmed the
lower federal court's decision that segregation on busses was unconstitutional. The next evening, before two packed mass meetings, King urged
black Montgomery to return to the busses, when the time came, with dignity, forbearance and love. They had long since occupied the moral high
ground and were now assured by the Supreme Court that they were there
by right. In call and response, King said white segregationists, "like
the . . . prodigal son . . . have strayed away to some far country of sin and
evil."

> I must still believe that there is something within them that can cause
> them one day to come to themselves (*That's right, Yes*) and rise up walk
> back up the dusty road to the father's house. (*Yes*) And we stand there
> with outstretched arms. That's the meaning of the Christian faith. . . . I
> believe that the Ku Klux Klan can be transformed into a clan for God's
> kingdom. (*Yes*) I believe that the White Citizens Council can be trans-
> formed into a Right Citizens Council. (Yes) I believe that. That's the
> essence of the Gospel.[23]

Beyond church, yet short of the Kingdom, "beloved community" was
where such unlikely but real transformations would occur.

For King, "beloved community" was adopted and defined in the cruci-
ble of an intense struggle for social change when it was already experienced by those who shared the struggle and then only after the hope of a
successful result was confirmed by legal authority. Rhetorically, it bridged

the yawning gap between the present reality of "church," burdened by the scandal of denominational and racial division,[24] and the distant hope for the "Kingdom of God." For another decade, King appealed to the establishment of the "beloved community" in sermons and speeches, in his most widely read books and articles.

COMMUNITY AND THE BROADENING STRUGGLE

Shortly after the successful conclusion of the Montgomery bus boycott, Martin Luther King and other southern clergymen organized the Southern Christian Leadership Conference as a coordinating civil rights agency among their communities. He continued to celebrate the expectation of the Kingdom of God.[25] As a spokesman for SCLC, however, he made establishing the "beloved community" its theme. A month after its founding, he wrote that

> nonviolent resistance does not seek to defeat or humiliate the opponent, but to win his friendship and understanding. The nonviolent resister must often express his protest through noncooperation or boycotts, but he realizes that noncooperation and boycotts are not ends themselves; they are merely a means to awaken a sense of moral shame in the opponent. The end is redemption and reconciliation. The aftermath of nonviolence is the creation of the beloved community, while the aftermath of violence is tragic bitterness.[26]

For years, King repeated these arguments in shifting coalitions of words.[27]

Within the next two years, for example, King visited newly independent third world nations, Ghana in March 1957 and India in February 1959, to identify the African American freedom struggle with their own. In both cases, he returned to the United States with illustrations of the benign aftermath of nonviolent social change. At a state dinner in Accra, Ghana, King recalled, President Mordecai Johnson of Howard University drew his attention to the fact that the new Prime Minister, Kwame Nkrumah, was dancing with the Duchess of Kent.

> I said, 'Isn't this something? Here it is the once-serf, the once-slave, now dancing with the lord on an equal plane.' And that is done because there is no bitterness. These two nations will be able to live together and work together because the breaking aloose was through nonvio-

lence and not through violence. The aftermath of nonviolence is the creation of the beloved community. The aftermath of nonviolence is redemption. The aftermath of nonviolence is reconciliation. The aftermath of violence are emptiness and bitterness.[28]

Similarly, when he returned from India in 1959, King reflected on the friendship of Prime Minister Nehru and Lady Mountbatten. "They were lasting friends only because Gandhi followed the way of love and nonviolence," King said. "The aftermath of nonviolence is the creation of the beloved community, so that when the battle is over, a new relationship comes into being between the oppressed and the oppressor."[29]

At the same time, however, King knew that "beloved community" was not achieved by making an easy adjustment to the reigning social order. Rather, it required a "maladjustment" or "nonconformity" to its injustices.[30] Beloved community occurred as a consequence of struggle to establish justice in the land. Indeed, if talk of "beloved community" threatened to become mere sentimentality, King quickly invoked the far ranging requirements of the Kingdom of God as the standard. Questioned by a white leader in Montgomery about his disturbing the status quo, King replied that disturbing the status quo was what Jesus meant when he said: "I have come not to bring peace, but a sword." Jesus drew his sword to cut a dramatic line of distinction between the status quo and the Kingdom of God.[31] For King, the Kingdom of God's far ranging requirements extended not merely to social relationships but also to economic relationships. Earlier than most scholars have acknowledged, King was asserting the economic requirements of the Kingdom. "The Kingdom of God is neither the thesis of individual enterprise nor the antithesis of collective enterprise, but a synthesis which reconciles the truths of both," he argued.[32]

In order to avoid sentimental or other misreadings of his argument, King offered the most important of many efforts to explain agape as love which would not surrender the quest for community. It occurred in his an autobiographical account of the Montgomery bus boycott, *Stride Toward Freedom.* "Agape is not a weak, passive love," he wrote.

> It is love in action. *Agape* is love seeking to preserve and create community. It is insistence on community even when one seeks to break it. Agape is a willingness to go to any length to restore community. It is a

willingness to forgive, not seven times, but seventy times seven to restore community.

For King, community was central to the message of the gospel.

The cross is the external expression of the length to which God will go in order to restore broken community. The resurrection is a symbol of God's triumph over all the forces that seek to block community. The Holy Spirit is the continuing community creating reality that moves through history.

The consequential implications for the self were massive.

He who works against community is working against the whole of creation. Therefore, if I respond to hate with a reciprocal hate I do nothing but intensify the cleavage in broken community. I can only close the gap in broken community by meeting hate with love. If I meet hate with hate, I become depersonalized, because creation is so designed that my personality can only be fulfilled in the context of community.

Recognizing the brokenness of human communities, King offered a balm that restores and heals. "Love, *agape*, is the only cement that can hold this broken community together," he wrote. "When I am commanded to love, I am commanded to restore community, to resist injustice, and to meet the needs of my brothers."[33] Far from mere sentiment, it required a massive, militant discipline. "The movement for equality and justice can only be a success if it has both a mass and militant character," he wrote; "the barriers to be overcome require both. Nonviolence is an imperative in order to bring about ultimate community."[34]

Shortly after the publication of *Stride Toward Freedom* in 1958, King was nearly assassinated in New York, when a deranged woman plunged a seven-inch letter opener into his chest. Its blade came to rest just short of his aorta. Had it been penetrated, he would have died of massive internal bleeding almost immediately. It was as near to death as he would come for another decade. Two weeks later, while still recovering from his wound and pneumonia in New York, King wrote to friends in the Montgomery Improvement Association. He spoke of neither community nor Kingdom. "Our final destination is the city of freedom," King wrote, "and we must not stop until we have entered the sublime and lofty Metropolis."[35] A decade later, he would return to that metaphor.

As the walls of segregation began to crumble under the pressure of executive orders, legal decisions and direct action, white communities commonly offered token compliance. Thus, King found it necessary to distinguish among segregation, desegregation and integration. "The word *segregation* represents a system that is prohibitive," he told a Nashville, Tennessee, church conference in 1962;

> it deprives the Negro of equal access to schools, parks, restaurants, libraries and the like. *Desegregation* is eliminative and negative, for it simply removes these legal and social prohibitions. Integration is creative, and is therefore more profound and far-reaching than desegregation. Integration is the positive acceptance of desegregation and the welcomed participation of Negroes into the total range of human activities. Integration is genuine intergroup, interpersonal doing. Desegregation then, rightly, is only a short-range goal. Integration is the ultimate goal of our national community.

What was at stake, King said, was the hope for civil community itself. "At the heart of all that civilization has meant and developed," he argued,

> is 'community'—the mutually cooperative and voluntary venture of man to assume a semblance of responsibility for his brother. What began as the closest answer to a desperate need for survival from the beast of prey and the danger of the jungle was the basis of present day cities and nations. Man could not have survived without the impulse which makes him the societal creature he is.[36]

Assuming the responsibility of moving the nation, King held out hope for a racially integrated society as the beloved community. "With every ounce of our energy we must continue to rid this nation of the incubus of segregation," he said. "But we shall not in the process relinquish our privilege and our obligation to love. While abhorring segregation, we shall love the segregationist. This is the only way to create the beloved community."[37]

Even as Martin Luther King celebrated the beloved community, however, he continued to refer to the Kingdom of God. It need not necessarily have been so, even among black Baptist preachers. Sam Williams, the pastor of Atlanta's Friendship Baptist Church and an SCLC official, had been King's philosophy professor at Morehouse College and co-taught a philosophy seminar there with King in the fall of 1960. Williams was an iconoclast, nurtured in an old fashioned rational theological liberalism at the University of Chicago. Talk about the Kingdom of God was irrelevant in the modern world, he argued. In a modern democracy, King was only a good last name.[38]

Yet, Martin Luther King did appeal to the hope of the Kingdom of God. "All progress is precarious, and the solution of one problem brings us face to face with another problem," he acknowledged in one of his most widely admired sermons. "The Kingdom of God as a universal reality is not yet. Because sin exists on every level of man's existence, the death of one tyranny is followed by the emergence of another tyranny."

> But just as we must avoid a superficial optimism, we must also avoid a crippling pessimism. Even though all progress is precarious, with limits real social progress may be made. Although man's moral pilgrimage may never reach a destination point on earth, his never-ceasing strivings may bring him ever closer to the city of righteousness. And though the Kingdom of God may remain not yet as a universal reality in history, in the present it may exist in such isolated forms as in judgment, in personal devotion, and in some group life. 'The kingdom of God is in the midst of you.'[39]

On the eve of his confrontation with segregation's citadel in Birmingham, Alabama, King "granted that we face a world crisis which leaves us standing so often amid the surging murmur of life's restless sea. But every crisis has both its dangers and its opportunities. It can spell either salvation or doom. In a dark, confused world the Kingdom of God may yet reign in the hearts of men."[40] It was a distant hope. Five years later, King's friend, Vincent Harding, would tell him that hope for "beloved community" was no brighter and no less sure.

Readers of Martin Luther King's "Letter from the Birmingham Jail" may be struck by its author's preoccupation with "church." It was, after all, a letter by one southern clergyman addressed directly to other southern clergymen and intended for circulation among church people across the land. King conceived of it as another of his modern versions of a Pauline letter to the ancient churches.[41] Here, the language of "beloved community" and, even, Kingdom of God disappears as King talks about the obligations and failures of "church people in the struggle."[42] If reference to the Kingdom of God appears nowhere in King's "Letter," its author asserts the judgment of a God who is not democratically elected, as if he had never heard Sam Williams on a roll. It was the church, not the Kingdom of God, whose relevance was at issue. ". . . the judgment of God is upon the church as never before," King wrote. "If the church of today does not recapture the sacrificial spirit of the early church, it will lose its authentic ring, forfeit the loyalty of millions, and be dismissed as an irrelevant social club with no meaning for the twentieth century."[43]

The other noteworthy element in King's "Letter" is its reassertion of Reinhold Niebuhr's thirty year old argument about the inexorable egocentricity of groups. "Lamentably, it is an historical fact that privileged groups seldom give up their privileges voluntarily," he noted. "Individuals may see the moral light and voluntarily give up their unjust posture; but, as Reinhold Niebuhr has reminded us, groups tend to be more immoral than individuals."[44] King, the personalist, was never a thoroughgoing Niebuhrian, however. A few months later, at the peak of his influence as a prophet of American civil religion, King seemed to identify the "beloved community" with the "American Dream." If the old man on Morningside Heights had not already begun to mellow, even a theological neophyte could have heard the thunder roll.[45]

After the assassination of John F. Kennedy in November 1963, Lyndon Johnson's ghost writers began reaching widely—from Martin Luther King to Walter Lippmann—for language of hope. ". . . we hope that the world will not narrow into a neighborhood before it has broadened into a brotherhood," Johnson said at the lighting of the nation's Christmas tree on 22 December 1963.[46] When the old New Dealer's slogan of "a better deal" failed to catch on, he emphasized Richard Goodwin's suggestion, "the great society," in a speech on 23 April 1964. "We have been called upon—are you listening?" he said. "—to build a great society of the highest order, a society not just for today or tomorrow, but for three or four generations to come. . . . We are going to build a great society, and we have just begun to fight." A month later, Johnson told an audience at the University of Michigan: ". . . in your time we have the opportunity to move not only toward the rich society and the powerful society, but upward to the Great Society."[47] With that slogan, he proposed and won passage of a flood of legislation designed to end poverty and promote civil rights. In another year, the President would even be singing the Movement's song, "We Shall Overcome."

Many veterans of the civil rights movement, however, date the unraveling of King's dream of a "beloved community" to the summer of 1964, when Lyndon Johnson's strong arm tactics at the Democratic national convention rejected the credentials of the Mississippi Freedom Democratic Party. In the hour of trial and in the face of power, the beloved community met the Great Society and found it looked like a raw deal. White liberal allies had failed a crucial test.[48] Neither a politician nor a social engineer, King was a preacher and he continued to preach his gospel. On 25 March 1965, at the climax of the Selma to Montgomery March, he repeated earlier themes.[49] Later, King recalled a scene at Montgomery's airport after the march. There,

> several thousand demonstrators waited more than five hours, crowding together on the seats, the floors and the stairways of the terminal building. As I stood with them and saw white and Negro, nuns and priests, ministers and rabbis, labor organizers, lawyers, doctors, housemaids and shopworkers brimming with vitality and enjoying a rare comradeship, I knew I was seeing a microcosm of the mankind of the future in this moment of luminous and genuine brotherhood.[50]

It may have been his last sighting of beloved community. He may have last expressed his hope for it in October 1966 to readers of *Ebony*. "I must continue by faith or it is too great a burden to bear and violence, even in self-defense, creates more problems than it solves," he wrote. "Only a refusal to hate or kill can put an end to the chain of violence in the world and lead us toward a community where men can live together without fear. Our goal is to create a beloved community and this will require a qualitative change in our souls as well as a quantitative change in our lives."[51]

THE DISINTEGRATING COMMUNITY

After 1965, according to Richard Lischer, King seemed to abandon references to the "beloved community" as the language of liberal humanist illusions for the biblical language about "the Kingdom of God." He was increasingly conscious of his own "inner civil war," Vincent Harding suggests, disturbed by the fragmenting of the movement and distressed by entrenched, violent resistance to the massive social reformation he believed necessary. In his last three years, King took refuge in the "loving community" which he had known from childhood and, in his "Ebenezer sermons," both acknowledged the persistence of sin and reaffirmed the biblical vision of the "Kingdom of God."[52]

Martin Luther King's sense of the crisis was broadcast in the title of his book, *Where Do We Go From Here? Chaos or Community?*. In it, he sought a way to community between the white liberals' disappointing Great Society programs on the one hand and the inflammatory rhetoric of black power spokesmen on the other. "The daily life of the Negro is still lived in the basement of the Great Society," King said, as he offered an extended critique of its programs.[53] The inclination of black power spokesmen to violent language was also disturbing. "Violence is the antithesis of creativity and wholeness," he reminded them. "It destroys community and makes brotherhood impossible." Rejecting both inadequate public programs and alienating ideologies, King called for a renewed devotion to militant, nonviolent social change. The "structures of evil do not crumble by passive waiting."[54] King's use of the parable of the Prodigal Son in the book is a fair measure of how his thinking had changed in a decade. Once it had been the Ku Klux Klan and the White Citizens Council, now it was America itself which had "strayed to the far country of racism" and needed miraculously to return to a welcoming home.[55]

Responding to the publication of *Where Do We Go From Here?*, King's friend and sometime ghostwriter, Vincent Harding, published a critique of its reaffirmation of biracial coalitions. "Perhaps there is still a Beloved Community ahead," he wrote.

> But if it is, it must be seen as the Kingdom whose realization does not depend upon whether whites (or anyone else around) really want it or not. If it comes, it may come only for those who seek it for its own sake and for the sake of its Lord, recognizing that even if He is black, the final glory is not the glory of blackness, but a setting straight of all the broken men and communities of the earth.[56]

If Harding seemed to collapse King's distinction between Beloved Community and Kingdom of God, it was because by late 1967 both seemed to be equally remote.

Nonetheless, in his 1967 "Christmas Sermon on Peace," first given at Ebenezer Baptist Church in Atlanta and then for the Canadian Broadcasting Corporation, King repeated his position in a passage from a much earlier sermon. ". . . if we are to have peace on earth, our loyalties must become ecumenical rather than sectional," said King.

Our loyalties must transcend our race, our tribe, our class, and our nation; and this means we must develop a world perspective. No individual can live alone; no nation can live alone, and as long as we try, the more we are going to have war in this world. Now the judgment of God is upon us, and we must either learn to live together as brothers or we are all going to perish together as fools.[57]

In his last years, the war in Viet Nam seemed to frustrate all that King had hoped for in the future. On the one hand, it undermined the hope for a Great Society at home. "All these human-relations problems are complex and related, and it's very difficult to assign priorities—especially as long as the Vietnam war continues. The Great Society has become a victim of the war," he wrote. "I think there was a sincere desire in this country four or five years ago to move toward a genuinely great society, and I have little doubt that there would have been a gradual increase in federal expenditures in this direction, rather than the gradual decline that has occurred, if the war in Vietnam had been avoided."[58] In order to renew hope for a Great Society, he spoke of plans to recruit three thousand of the poorest citizens from across the land for training in nonviolent direct action and then marching on Washington with this "nonviolent army, this 'freedom church' " to demand executive and legislative action on employment and income.[59]

On the other hand, the war in Viet Nam was the antithesis of all sense of community abroad. "One day somebody should remind us that, even though there may be political and ideological differences between us," King argued; "the Vietnamese are our brothers, the Russians are our brothers, the Chinese are our brothers; and one day we've got to sit down together at the table of brotherhood." The preacher King stretched a mystical Pauline sense of community to embrace even those who would resist embrace. "But in Christ there is neither Jew nor Gentile. In Christ there is neither male nor female. In Christ there is neither Communist nor capitalist. In Christ, somehow, there is neither bound nor free. We are all one in Christ Jesus. And when we truly believe in the sacredness of human personality, we won't exploit people, we won't trample over people with the iron feet of oppression, we won't kill anybody."[60]

If King replaced "beloved community" after 1965 with references to a more familiar biblical language about the Kingdom of God, he spoke with increased urgency about the community of hope in the last months of his life. He had occasionally referred to a "new Jerusalem" in earlier years.[61] In his last weeks, however, that language reappeared with near apocalyptic urgency. On 31 March 1968, his sermon at the National Cathedral in Washington, D.C., concluded with an appeal to it. "Thank God for John, who centuries ago out on a lonely, obscure island called Patmos caught vision of a new Jerusalem descending out of heaven from God, who heard a voice saying, 'Behold, I make all things new—former things are passed away.' "[62] Four days later in Memphis, as though in answer to his own appeal, King said:

> It's alright to talk about "streets flowing with milk and honey," but God has commanded us to be concerned about the slums down here, and his children who can't eat three square meals a day. It's alright to talk about the new Jerusalem, but one day, God's preacher must talk about the New York, the new Atlanta, the new Philadelphia, the new Los Angeles, the new Memphis, Tennessee. This is what we have to do.[63]

Martin Luther King's experience of and appeals to community have much to teach us. The ecstatic wonder of Montgomery's African Americans at the unanimous response to the call for a boycott of the city's busses and its solidarity throughout long months of struggle suggests that community is a gift, one not readily contrived out of the ordinariness of class divisions, personal ambitions and tribal jealousies. Alas, even the prepared heart is no guarantee that community will be achieved. When it occurs, wondrous things can happen, as the victory in the bus boycott makes clear. In subsequent years, King expected the beloved community to expand beyond the community of struggle to encompass those who had opposed the movement. He did not live to see the prodigal sons of racism transformed into repentant children of righteousness. Indeed, he did live to see the movement itself rent by ambitions, divisions and jealousies. King himself abandoned all talk of beloved community in the years immediately prior to his death. Yet, his death and the painful anguish of that era were a sober summons to repentance. George Wallace sought repentance. So, may we.

Beacon Light and Penumbra

African American Gospel Lyrics and Martin Luther King, Jr.'s "I Have a Dream"

KEITH D. MILLER

Before James Farmer founded the Congress of Racial Equality and led the Freedom Rides, he earned a master's degree in religion at Howard University. There he studied with Benjamin Mays and Howard Thurman, who later served as two of Martin Luther King, Jr.'s most important mentors. Like Mays and Thurman, Farmer's father was an ordained minister. The senior Farmer had completed a Ph.D. in religion at Boston University, where, years later, King also graduated with a Ph.D. in religion.

Yet, when James Farmer graduated from Howard, despite his rich religious background and training, he declined to be ordained as a minister. When I asked Farmer why he refused ordination, he explained that he did not think that the African American church would ever contribute significantly to the struggle for racial equality. He admitted that his analysis proved incorrect.[1]

How did certain African American churches—which Farmer and others considered extremely otherworldly and apolitical—become a potent political force during the 1950s and 1960s? Scholars have not seriously addressed this question.

Here's a preamble to another question. King's "I Have a Dream" is easily the most popular speech included in anthologies used in freshman and sophomore English courses in colleges and universities. In fact, King's famous oration is often the *only* example of public address included in such collections. Imagine. In their college English courses, many students encounter no speeches by Malcolm X or John Kennedy or Barbara Jordan. They read no orations by George Washington or Thomas Jefferson or Abraham Lincoln or Sojourner Truth or Franklin Roosevelt or Clarence Darrow or Cesar Chavez. None by Elizabeth Cady Stanton or Helen Keller or Margaret Sanger or Mary McLeod Bethune or Chief Joseph. None by any other American. And not only that. They also read no addresses by Winston Churchill or Queen Elizabeth I or Cicero or Pericles or any other European, ancient or modern. And no speeches from Africa, China, India, or South America. Instead, many anthologies represent the entire panorama of oratory through a single speech—"I Have a Dream."

While English professors grade students' writing, they invariably correct students' clichés, prodding them to coin original expressions instead of mindlessly repeating shopworn phrases.

But—here comes the question—if "I Have a Dream" can exemplify the total, historical cavalcade of speeches, why does "I Have a Dream" feature so many clichés? And feature them it does. During the twentieth century, anyone who attended almost any Sunday worship service in any African American Baptist church almost certainly heard about "trials and tribulations." No set of words is more routine among black Protestants. Why does King insert "trials and tribulations" into "I Have a Dream"? Why does he also employ such utterly familiar expressions as "beacon light of hope," "joyous daybreak," "dark and desolate valley," "sunlit path," and "valley of despair" to mention a few? Why would any gifted orator sprinkle such triteness into his most acclaimed speech? And by what magic would the clichés appear not to harm King's eloquence, but somehow to enhance it? While students often raise such questions about "I Have a Dream," no one has tried to answer them in print.

In this essay I explain how, in "I Have a Dream," King transmutes traditional African American Protestant language for political ends. I do so by making two new claims. First, a single system of metaphors underlies a large number of African American spiritual and gospel lyrics. Second, this system of metaphors structures much of "I Have a Dream" and largely accounts for King's majestic clichés. Understanding these previously unexamined metaphors is crucial to understanding "I Have a Dream."

I build my argument in four steps. First, adapting the metaphor theory of George Lakoff and his co-authors, I identify the network of metaphors in African American spiritual and gospel lyrics. Second, I examine the value and function of the metaphors for churchgoers. Third, I analyze King's use of the metaphors prior to "I Have a Dream." Fourth, I explore the value and function of the tropes in "I Have a Dream."

George Lakoff and Mark Johnson explain that systems of metaphors structure everyday speech, often reinforcing each other. Such metaphors include LIGHT/DARK and UP/DOWN, LIGHT signifying good and DARK indicating evil, UP representing good and DOWN designating evil.[2]

Metaphors of LIGHT/DARK and UP/DOWN also appear frequently in the Bible and in Christian discourse, including, for example, John Milton's *Paradise Lost*, Frederick Douglass's speeches, and many Christian hymns. In these texts, LIGHT and UP spell holiness, revelation, joy, freedom, Jesus, or God; DARK and DOWN indicate suffering, sin, oppression, slavery, or evil.

Lakoff and Mark Turner note another common metaphor: LIFE IS A JOURNEY.[3] This trope underlies much of the Bible and world literature, including the Book of Exodus, Homer's *Odyssey*, Chaucer's *Canterbury Tales*, Dickens's *Great Expectations*, and African American slave narratives. Christians modify LIFE IS A JOURNEY to LIFE IS A JOURNEY MADE EASIER BY GOD AND JESUS. Reflecting on their hardscrabble lives, African Americans adjust this standard Christian figure to LIFE IS AN EXTRAORDINARILY DIFFICULT JOURNEY MADE EASIER BY GOD AND JESUS.

Lakoff and Turner claim that LIFE IS A JOURNEY precedes another metaphor: DEATH IS GOING TO A FINAL DESTINATION.[4] Christians alter this trope to FOR THE FAITHFUL, DEATH IS ARRIVAL AND FULFILLMENT IN HEAVEN. Black lyricists embrace this metaphor and add another: HEAVEN IS HOME.

Lyricists, especially Baptists, have extended workaday and Biblical metaphors into a system that expresses orthodox Christianity and African American experience. This system embodies what Lakoff and Turner call "poetic thought" that "uses the mechanisms" of common tropes but "extends" them, "elaborates them, and combines them in ways that go beyond the ordinary."[5] By extending metaphors of LIGHT/DARK and UP/DOWN, African American religious lyricists together weave a system of "poetic thought."

This system features the following metaphors:

    I. LIGHT/DARK
       Examples of LIGHT:
       DAWN, DAYBREAK, NOON, DAY, BEAMS, STAR, SUN,
         SUNSHINE, RAYS, BRIGHTNESS
       Examples of DARK:
       GLOOM, NIGHT, OR MIDNIGHT
       Elaboration:
       STORM

II. UP/DOWN
   Examples of UP:
   HIGH, HIGHER, STAND, RISE, CLIMB, LIFT, STAR, SUN,
   SUNSHINE
   Examples of DOWN:
   LOW, LOWER, FALL, STUMBLE, SLIP, SINK
   Elaboration:
   HILLS, MOUNTAINS, VALLEYS, HEAVEN (above the sky)

III. LIFE IS AN EXTRAORDINARILY DIFFICULT JOURNEY
    MADE EASIER BY GOD OR JESUS
    Elaboration:
    DAUNTING OBSTACLES:
    STORMS, MOUNTAINS, TRIALS, TRIBULATIONS
    JESUS HELPS BELIEVERS OVERCOME DAUNTING
    OBSTACLES
    BELIEVERS CARRY A HEAVY LOAD OR BURDEN
    JESUS RELIEVES THE LOAD OR BURDEN

IV. FOR THE FAITHFUL, DEATH IS ARRIVAL AND
    FULFILLMENT IN HEAVEN
    Elaboration:
    HEAVEN IS HOME[6]

According to these metaphors, everyone undertakes a spiritual JOUR-
NEY: sinners move LOW, STUMBLING or FALLING; faithful Christians withstand STORMS, TRIALS, and TRIBULATIONS before
advancing UP and into the LIGHT, LIFTED and saved by Jesus.

These tropes customarily interlock. In these lyrics, SUN and STARS
are HIGH, close to heaven and holy. For that reason, SUN and STARS
merge metaphors of LIGHT/DARK with those of UP/DOWN. Because
storms are literally dark, STORM embodies and elaborates LIGHT/
DARK, thereby fusing LIFE IS A DIFFICULT JOURNEY with LIGHT/
DARK. MOUNTAINS impose obstacles on the JOURNEY. But, because
MOUNTAINS are close to the SUN and heaven, they also serve as sites
of holiness, revelation, and joy. MOUNTAINS thus fuse metaphors of UP/
DOWN with those of LIGHT/DARK.

These metaphors enliven spirituals sung by slaves. For example, one
spiritual urges believers to "steal away home" to heaven. In the most popular of all spirituals, the narrator longs for a "chariot" to "swing low" and
"carry" her "home" to heaven. "Steal Away" and "Swing Low, Sweet

Chariot" blend LIFE IS A JOURNEY, DEATH IS FULFILLMENT IN HEAVEN, and HEAVEN IS HOME; "Swing Low, Sweet Chariot" merges those three metaphors with UP/DOWN. In another well-known spiritual, the narrator plaintively laments, "Been in the storm so long." But, she adds, "If ever I get on the mountaintop . . . I'll shout and shout and never stop." Because mountains are closer to heaven, ascending the MOUNTAIN means triumphing over the STORM and attaining holiness.

In a gospel lyric by Lucie Campbell, a dominant musical presence at the National Baptist Convention, the narrator experiences "trials" and is "burdened" until "heavenly sunshine" penetrates the "shadows" and "rain" when she hears Jesus say, " 'Do not falter' " and " 'Follow me.' " In this lyric, Campbell brilliantly combines LIFE IS A DIFFICULT JOUR-NEY, FILLED WITH TRIALS, BUT MADE EASIER BY JESUS; UP/DOWN (sunshine, falter); LIGHT/DARK (sunshine, shadows); STORM (rain); and CARRY A BURDEN ("burdened").[7]

In the best loved of all gospel songs, "Precious Lord," Thomas Dorsey's narrator petitions Jesus to "Take my hand. . . . Let me stand. . . ./Lead me on through the night, through the storm, to the light."[8] The narrator then asks Jesus to help him reach "home" or heaven. These lines imaginatively and seamlessly fuse LIFE IS A DIFFICULT JOURNEY MADE EAS-IER BY JESUS (lead me on), UP/DOWN (stand), LIGHT/DARK (light, night), STORM, and HEAVEN IS HOME.

In William Herbert Brewster's "I'm Climbing Higher and Higher," the narrator is "sinking in sin" and suffers "great tribulation" until "a ladder" descends "from heaven" and she begins "climbing" in search of "higher ground." She plans to "pass the sun moon and stars" and planets. These lyrics intertwine and elaborate LIFE IS A DIFFICULT JOURNEY, FILLED WITH TRIBULATION, BUT MADE EASIER BY JESUS; LIGHT/DARK and UP/DOWN. Brewster's lines also associate "sun" with "heaven."[9]

Some gospel lyrics only include one or two of these metaphors. But, for veteran churchgoers accustomed to this system of interlocking figures, a single metaphor entails the entire system.

These mutually reinforcing tropes appear in many, many prayers, hymns, and sermons in African American Protestant services, especially among Baptists. Indeed, the metaphor system is so pervasive and so for-midable that it seems virtually inseparable from the Black Baptist experi-ence itself. Because the tropes overlap and intertwine, someone who wanted to challenge any one of them would need to challenge all of them. One could hardly do so without seeming to advocate atheism—an extremely unpopular position in the highly churched African American community.

The metaphor system affords four enormous advantages. First, the tropes are extremely clear and accessible. Second, they provide hope. Amid the inconceivable barbarism of slavery and the mental (and sometimes physical) torture of segregation, the metaphors affirm that a loving God governs a highly ordered, reliable cosmos and cares for the oppressed. Third, the ubiquity of the metaphors contributes to African American solidarity with those living throughout the nation and with many generations of the dead and unborn. All are included—a vast African American society. Fourth, the tropes proclaim that, far from being isolated, lost, or worthless, each individual life embodies ultimate meaning.

Martin Luther King, Jr.'s father, a folk preacher, and his mother, who played the organ each Sunday, ensured that King, Jr. would attend church every week of his childhood and adolescence. There he was soaked in spiritual and gospel music and lyrics, including those by Campbell, Dorsey, and Brewster—titans of gospel music whose lines were often sung in Baptist churches and at the annual National Baptist Convention, which the King family attended.

King, Jr. sometimes harnesses the metaphors to articulate basic Protestant theology about the struggle of the individual who, by relying on God, can resist sin and experience salvation. For example, in one sermon, King incorporates lyrics from the gospel song "Never Alone," merging his voice with that of the narrator. He declares that he observed the "lightning flash" and the "thunder roll," that he experienced "sinbreakers dashing" that aimed "to conquer" his "soul." Then, he states, Jesus urged him to resist the STORM—a typical image in gospel lyrics. In this passage King refers only to his individual religious experience, not to African Americans' political struggle.[10]

Like Campbell, Dorsey, Brewster, and other spiritual and gospel lyricists, King interlaces the metaphors. For example, by explaining that God enables people to "rise from the midnight of desperation to the daybreak of joy," he fuses metaphors of UP/DOWN, LIGHT/DARK and LIFE IS A DIFFICULT JOURNEY.[11] He also criticizes humanism as an attempt to "live without a sky," rhapsodizes about "beautiful stars" that "bedeck the heavens like swinging lanterns of eternity," and implores listeners to reject humanism and "reach up and discover God." Again, this passage blends UP/DOWN and LIGHT/DARK. Here, like Brewster, King identifies "sky" and "stars" with "God" and "eternity."[12] In these statements King orchestrates the metaphors to proclaim God's ability to redeem individual humans, who are prone to excessive pride and sin. Implicit in King's declaration is the promise of heaven to all who live faithfully. These passages also fail to mention black political struggle.

Generally, however, King secularizes the metaphors. But never completely. In order to understand this process, consider the gospel song, "Woke Up This Morning with My Mind Stayed on Jesus." When civil rights leaders sang the lyrics and tune of this song, they retained the tune and only changed one word: "Woke Up This Morning with My Mind Stayed on Freedom." In this alteration, when singers substitute the word "Freedom" for "Jesus," people who know the song can still "hear" the word "Jesus" even though they no longer literally hear it. Though absent, "Jesus" remains present. I call this effect a penumbra. Although "Freedom" eclipses "Jesus," the sacredness of "Jesus" continues to surround "Freedom," which gains a penumbra of holiness when it substitutes for "Jesus," which—for most African Americans—is indisputably an ultimate term.

When King secularizes the spiritual and gospel metaphors, he creates a similar effect. He notes that Jews

> have been forced to walk through the dark night of oppression. . . . But this did not keep them from rising up with creative genius to plunge against cloud-filled nights of affliction new and blazing stars of inspiration.[13]

To his list of Jewish achievers, he adds exemplary African Americans: ". . . Booker T. Washington rose to the stature of one of America's greatest leaders; he list a torch and darkness fled." King applauds gifted singers Roland Hayes and Marian Anderson, who also "rose." He relates that Mary McCloud Bethune, Ralph Bunche, Joe Louis, Jesse Owens, and Jackie Robinson each "grabbed" a "star."[14] Like a gospel lyricist, King here blends LIFE IS A JOURNEY, UP/DOWN, and LIGHT/DARK, elaborating the metaphors through lyricists' typical references to NIGHT and STARS.

While these metaphors normally articulate standard Christian theology, King uses them here to evoke not God, but the earthly accomplishments of notable Jews and Blacks. But he does not altogether secularize the metaphors. Because they are used so pervasively in a sacred context and because King is a highly regarded minister, a penumbra of sanctity clings to each trope.

As a civil rights orator, King wields the entire system of metaphors. During the first rally of the Montgomery Bus Boycott, he bemoans African Americans' "long night of captivity" and longs for a "daybreak of freedom"—a double metaphor that resurfaces in "I Have a Dream."[15] Like gospel lyricists, he consistently reprises such phrases as "dark days," "dark skies," "ray of hope," "daybreak," and "new dawn." He often urges listeners to "rise" or "stand up" for their rights.

Why does King choreograph these figures? Doing so affirms the unity of the sacred and secular. He constantly rails at any version of Christianity that focuses on heavenly bliss while ignoring earthly injustice. By choosing the same network of religious metaphors to represent Christian redemption and earthly achievements, he pictures goodness on earth and goodness in heaven as essentially identical.

This rhetorical practice is not unusual among African Americans. Spirituals, for example, express the simultaneous desire to escape from slavery and to reach heaven. Also, black women's groups have sometimes used the motto "Lifting as We Climb" to explain their simultaneous dedication to altruism and personal achievement. Their slogan combines UP/DOWN with LIFE IS AN EXTRAORDINARILY DIFFICULT JOURNEY. In Langston Hughes's renowned poem, "Mother to Son," a mother informs her child about her travails. No one offers her a "crystal stair"; instead, she struggles arduously up rough wooden steps, pierced by splinters. Both the women's phrase and Hughes's verse are secular; for many African Americans, however, their metaphors resonate with those of spiritual and gospel lyrics.

In "I Have a Dream" King seizes and politicizes this entire ensemble of metaphors, including its clichés. Note the following tropes in "I Have a Dream":

UP:
 high plane of dignity
 rise from the dark and desolate valley
 majestic heights of meeting physical force with soul force
 From every mountainside, let freedom ring.
 Let freedom ring from

the prodigious hilltops of New Hampshire
the mighty mountains of New York
the heightening Alleghenies of Pennsylvania
the snow-capped Rockies of Colorado
the curvaceous slopes of California
Stone Mountain of Georgia
Lookout Mountain of Tennessee
every hill and molehill in Mississippi

DOWN:
Let justice roll down like waters.
dark and desolate valley of segregation
quicksand of injustice
valley of despair
down in Alabama

LIGHT:
great beacon light of hope
joyous daybreak
sunlit path of racial justice
bright day of justice

DARK:
long night of captivity
dark and desolate valley of segregation

LIFE IS AN EXTRAORDINARILY DIFFICULT JOURNEY:
rise from the dark and desolate valley of segregation
trials and tribulations
wallow in the valley of despair
Our bodies, heavy with the fatigue of travel, cannot gain lodging in the
    motels of the highways and the hotels of the cities.
battered by the storms of persecution and staggered by the winds of
    police brutality
mountain of despair

In "I Have a Dream" King pleads for America to "rise from the dark
and desolate valley of segregation to the sunlit path of racial justice." In
this sentence he fuses LIFE IS A DIFFICULT JOURNEY, UP/DOWN
(rise), and LIGHT/DARK.

"I Have a Dream" secularizes gospel lyricists' LIFE IS A DIFFICULT JOURNEY and STORM by describing the experiences of civil rights agitators who are "battered by the storms of persecution and staggered by the winds of police brutality." King secularizes LIFE IS A DIFFICULT JOURNEY and CARRY A BURDEN by explaining that African Americans' "bodies heavy with the fatigue of travel, cannot gain lodging in the motels of the highways and the hotels of the cities." Because demonstrators' JOURNEY is EXTRAORDINARILY DIFFICULT and replete with "excessive trials and tribulations," he urges them not to "wallow in the valley of despair," which resembles the low places evoked in gospel lyrics and the "valley of the shadow of death" walked by the narrator of the Twenty-third Psalm. He also politicizes the metaphor of MOUNTAIN as obstacle by proclaiming the ability of protestors with "faith" to "hew out of the mountain of despair a stone of hope."[16]

King's quotation from the Book of Amos—"Let justice roll down like waters . . ."—is an UP/DOWN metaphor but also an image of transformation in which God dispatches justice in heaven down to earth. This citation uses the Bible to argue that the sacred and the secular are inseparable.

Throughout "I Have a Dream" King's status as a minister, his overt Biblical citations, and his use of the anaphoras and the delivery of the folk pulpit—starting calm and rocking almost imperceptibly to a momentous climax—help contribute a godly penumbra to each secularized metaphor. For African American Protestants, religious meaning suffuses all of these metaphors. No matter how secularized the figures might seem, the penumbra of the holy persists.

The entire pattern of metaphors prepares listeners for King's conclusion, the litany of "Let Freedom Ring," which King borrows and adapts from Rev. Archibald Carey.[17] King introduces the litany by quoting lyrics from "America" that compare "freedom" to a bell that can "ring" "from every mountainside." Then, following Carey, King extends the lyrics of "America" by enumerating mountains from which, he hopes, freedom, will eventually ring:

Let freedom ring from the prodigious hilltops of New Hampshire!
Let freedom ring from the mighty mountains of New York!
Let freedom ring from the heightening Alleghenies from Pennsylvania!
Let freedom ring from the snow-capped Rockies of Colorado!
Let freedom ring from the curvaceous slopes of California!

But not only that.
Let freedom ring from Stone Mountain of Georgia!
Let freedom ring from Lookout Mountain of Tennessee!
Let freedom ring from every hill and molehill in Mississippi!

By the time he finishes, "every mountainside" is included as a site for freedom to "ring."

Earlier in the speech, King climaxes his famous "I Have a Dream" litany by incorporating a prophecy from Isaiah:

I have a dream that one day every valley shall be exalted, the hills and mountains shall be laid low, the rough places shall be made plain, the crooked places shall be made straight, the glory of the Lord will be revealed and all flesh shall see it together.

In this passage, King yearns for the day when God will transform the pain of racism, smoothing and straightening all obstacles—valleys, mountains, rough places, and crooked places—that interfere with racial justice.

In his conclusion, King essentially repeats the prophecy. "The valley of despair" will become "the mountain of despair," and activists working with God will ensure that mountains ring with freedom. Freedom will even peal "from Stone Mountain of Georgia"—an infamous meeting place for the Ku Klux Klan—and "from every hill and molehill in Mississippi," a flat state dominated by white supremacy.

King's conclusion also secularizes the metaphors of spiritual and gospel lyrics, metaphors that are especially prominent in "I'm Climbing Up the Rough Side of the Mountain" by Thomas Dorsey, "When I Get Home" by Lucie Campbell, and "Heaven Bells" by Kenneth Morris, another well-known gospel composer.

In "I'm Climbing Up the Rough Side of the Mountain," Dorsey's narrator scales a decidedly "rough" MOUNTAIN that poses huge difficulties but is also HIGH and blessed. The narrator struggles to tackle the MOUNTAIN because conquering it means reaching heaven. King's metaphors parallel those of Dorsey's lyric. Shortly before King reaches the "Let freedom ring" litany, he mentions a giant obstacle—"the mountain of despair." But when, soon afterward, King articulates his "Let freedom ring" anaphoras, "every mountainside" rings with freedom. Thus, at the end of "I Have a Dream," as in Dorsey's lyric, cloud-piercing MOUN-TAINS supply the most awesome challenge, but also the greatest imaginable possibility—heaven for Dorsey's narrator, freedom for those listening to King.

In "When I Get Home," Campbell's narrator celebrates the long-anticipated day when she will "get home" to heaven. When that happens, "the bells will be ringing" and "the saints will be singing." Likewise, in Morris's lyric, the narrator hears "heaven bells" and knows that she soon will die and enter the next life. Campbell and Morris thus associate ringing bells with the ultimate experience—life in heaven.

King's ministerial status, Biblical citations, anaphoras, delivery, and network of religious metaphors add a penumbra to his concluding imagery. For many of King's African American listeners who sang Campbell's and Morris's lyrics, bells ring in heaven. Thus, King's "freedom" that "rings" from mountains carries the penumbra of the holy because King overtly associates "freedom" with mountains and implicitly, but strongly, associates "freedom" with "heaven."

In spiritual and gospel lyrics LIFE IS AN EXTRAORDINARILY DIFFCULT JOURNEY MADE EASIER BY GOD OR JESUS.

The arduous JOURNEY often involves TRIALS and TRIBULATIONS.

The arduous JOURNEY often involves CARRYING A BURDEN.

The arduous JOURNEY often demands that one endure and surmount STORMS.

If successful on the JOURNEY, one moves from DOWN to UP and from DARKNESS to LIGHT.

When one overcomes all difficulties, the JOURNEY leads to heaven, which is UP and filled with LIGHT.

MOUNTAINS interfere with the spiritual progress of the JOURNEY.

But, because MOUNTAINS are HIGH, they can enable one to reach the ultimate destination of the JOURNEY—heaven.

BELLS can RING to celebrate one's arrival in heaven where people sometimes sing.

In "I Have a Dream" LIFE IS AN EXTRAORDINARILY DIFFICULT JOURNEY MADE EASIER BY GOD.

For African Americans, the JOURNEY still begins in slavery. ("One hundred years [after Lincoln's Emancipation Proclamation] the Negro still is not free; one hundred years later, the Negro is still sadly crippled by the manacles of segregation").

The arduous JOURNEY involves TRIALS AND TRIBULATIONS ("some of you have come here out of excessive trials and tribulations").

The arduous JOURNEY involves CARRYING A BURDEN ("our bodies, heavy with the fatigue of travel cannot gain lodging in the motels of the highways and the hotels of the cities").

The arduous JOURNEY demands that one endure and surmount STORMS ("Some of you . . . [have been] battered by the storms of persecution and staggered by the winds of police brutality").

If successful on the JOURNEY, one moves from DOWN to UP and from DARKNESS to LIGHT ("rise from the dark and desolate valley of segregation to the sunlit path of racial justice").

When one overcomes all difficulties, the JOURNEY leads to freedom, which is UP on a MOUNTAIN ("Let freedom ring from every mountainside").

Freedom and justice are filled with LIGHT ([The Emancipation Proclamation] "came as a great beacon light of hope," "the bright day of justice").

MOUNTAINS interfere with the spiritual progress of the JOURNEY ("mountains will be laid low [by God]," "mountain of despair").

But, because MOUNTAINS are HIGH, they can enable one to achieve the ultimate reward of the JOURNEY—freedom ("Let freedom ring from every mountainside").

FREEDOM IS A BELL that will RING on MOUNTAINS when African Americans achieve racial equality.

Fittingly, in the final sentences of "I Have a Dream," when "freedom rings," all Americans—"black men and white men, Jews and Gentiles, Catholics and Protestants"—will "join hands and sing in the words of the old Negro spiritual, 'Free at last, free at last. Thank God Almighty, we're free at last.' " After a long journey negotiating the valleys and mountains of injustice, King predicts, African Americans—and all Americans—will finally experience freedom. And they will sing—something people often do in heaven.

In composing "I Have a Dream," King marries the structure and content of the African American political jeremiad to an ensemble of metaphors from spiritual and gospel lyrics, metaphors that he partly but not entirely secularizes.[18] Knowing little or nothing about this jeremiad tradition and these metaphorical lyrics, many people wrongly assume that "I Have a Dream" is a highly original speech.

But, for King and other African American Protestants, this jeremiad and these metaphors were decidedly familiar. Fusing the two rhetorical systems enabled King to generate the wonder and majesty of "I Have a Dream" and thereby both to sanctify and to politicize the African American struggle.[19]

Fannie Lou Hamer

New Ideas for the Civil Rights Movement and American Democracy

LINDA REED

At the time of Fannie Lou Townsend's birth into the world, America had been involved in World War I for a little over a year. A war that was fought to make the world safe for democracy did not mean the same for Fannie Lou Townsend, her family and all other African Americans in the United States. As sharecroppers, the Townsends lived under desperate circumstances in Mississippi. Like other black people, they would remain second-class citizens, but their baby daughter would become a freedom fighter to include all Americans in democracy.[1]

Born Fannie Lou Townsend to James Lee Townsend, a Baptist preacher, and Ella Townsend on October 6, 1917 in rural Montgomery County, Mississippi, this youngest child of twenty shared a birth year with John F. Kennedy, and the two would coincidentally gain national notoriety in the 1960s. Ella and Jim moved to Sunflower County when Fannie Lou was two years old, and the child received her six to eight years of education there. School years for sharecroppers averaged only about four months, and Fannie Lou said she missed many of those, even, because she had very poor clothing. At the age of six, Fannie Lou began working in the cotton fields and worked many long years chopping and picking cotton until the plantation owner, W. D. Marlow, learned that she could read and write.[2]

In 1944 Fannie Lou Townsend became the time and record keeper for Marlow and in 1945 married Perry Hamer, a tractor driver on the Marlow Plantation. Fannie Lou married for the first time, but she numbered as the third wife for Perry Hamer. She affectionately grew to call him "Pap." For the next eighteen years of her adult life, Fannie Lou Hamer worked as sharecropper and timekeeper on the plantation four miles east of Ruleville, Mississippi, the place where she and Perry made their home. As time and record keeper, Hamer had a good knowledge of math, and she held the respect of the landowner and the other families who worked with the landowner as sharecroppers.

Fannie Lou Hamer's life changed August 31, 1962 when she suffered economic reprisal after an unsuccessful attempt to vote in the county seat of Indianola. The usual intimidation amounted to persons' names appearing in the local newspaper, but Fannie Lou Hamer said all her trouble with the landowner came immediately. Marlow, the plantation owner, appeared at the Hamers' home the very day to ask that she not attempt to register to vote. Familiar with physical violence that often followed economic reprisals and having received threats, Fannie Lou Hamer left her family to stay with friends. But the move did not stay the violence, and Hamer and her friends miraculously escaped rounds of gunshots fired into the friends' home when a person or persons yet unknown discovered her presence there.

Despite the denial of the right to vote and the subsequent violence and economic intimidation, Fannie Lou Hamer became an active member of the recently formed Student Nonviolent Coordinating Committee (SNCC) in Ruleville. Economic reprisals, long a way to obstruct concerted efforts by blacks who demanded equality, did not deter Hamer. She took the literacy test several times, and in 1963 at the age of 45, she became a field secretary for SNCC and a registered voter, an action that had led to death for a few determined persons.

It became clear in the 1960s that Fannie Lou Hamer, with the assistance of SNCC and other organizations, had new ideas for the civil rights movement and American democracy. From 1963 onward, Hamer worked in Mississippi with voter registration drives and with programs designed to assist economically deprived black families who faced problems with which she said she felt especially familiar. The youngest of twenty siblings whose parents seldom were able to provide adequate food and clothing, Fannie Lou Hamer saw a link between the lack of access to the political process and the poor economic status of blacks. She was instrumental in starting Delta Ministry, an extensive community development program in 1963.

On April 24, 1964 Hamer took part in the founding of the Mississippi Freedom Democratic Party, becoming vice chairperson and a member of its delegation to the Democratic National Convention in Atlantic City, New Jersey, which challenged the seating of the regular all-white Mississippi delegation. In this capacity she made a televised address to the convention's Credentials Committee.

Influential SNCC leaders Ella Baker (the MFDP founder who had given the keynote address at its founding) and Robert Moses enabled the MFDP to retain Joseph Rauh, a powerful attorney in Democratic Party machinations. Rauh was the vice-president of Americans for Democratic Action and general counsel for the United Automobile Workers. He understood the significance of showing the Democratic Credentials Committee how blacks in Mississippi had been denied access to the vote. He hoped the testimonies of Reverend Edwin King, Fannie Lou Hamer, and Rita Schwerner (wife of slain white civil rights worker, Michael Schwerner, killed in June 1964 in Mississippi in voter registration efforts) would convince the Committee that MFDP deserved seating at the 1964 Democratic National Convention.

In her testimony Hamer identified herself, told where she was from, stressing that Sunflower County was the home also of Senator James O. Eastland. She described her attempt to register to vote in August 1962 and the harassment that followed. Next she spoke about the brutal beating she, Annelle Ponder, and Ivesta Simpson (two middle-aged black women and one young black girl) had suffered as they and others returned from a voter registration workshop in South Carolina in June 1963. She finished:

> I was in jail when Medgar Evers was murdered. All of this is on account we want to register, to become first-class citizens, and if the freedom Democratic Party is not seated now, I question America, is this America, the land of the free and the home of the brave where we have to sleep with our telephones off of the hooks because our lives be threatened daily because we want to live as decent human beings, in America?[3]

President Lyndon B. Johnson upstaged Fannie Lou Hamer by calling a hasty press conference of his own, recognizing that he could not afford to upset southern politicians. For instance, Mississippi Governor Paul B. Johnson and other leading politicians (including former Governor Ross Barnett) spoke publicly about supporting Senator Barry Goldwater's presidential bid in 1964. The conservative Goldwater represented what they wanted to maintain in Mississippi, and it was addresses like those of Paul Johnson and Barnett that led the Credentials Committee to require that

Democratic National Convention delegates take a pledge to be loyal to the Democratic Party.

The 1964 challenge failed despite compromises offered through Hubert Humphrey and Walter Mondale. On the first compromise, MFDP delegates could participate in party proceedings without any vote; MFDP totally rejected this offer. The second face-saving effort would have allowed two nonvoting MFDP members (African American Aaron Henry, president of Mississippi NAACP chapters, and European American Ed King, chaplain at historically black Tougaloo College) selected by Humphrey to have at-large seats; the remaining MFDP delegates would be "guests." This too was rejected. The MFDP's actions resulted in an unprecedented pledge from the National Democratic Party *not* to seat delegate groups that excluded blacks at the next convention in 1968.

Fannie Lou Hamer had been the one who insisted on not compromising when national black leaders such as Martin Luther King, Jr. and Roy Wilkins, had wanted to accept the Humphrey/Mondale compromise. Hamer emphatically said, "we did not come all this way from Mississippi to Atlantic City sharing bologna sandwiches and hot soda water to take less than what we deserve." Having less (nothing) to lose than her middle-class black male counterparts in the struggle, Fannie Lou Hamer insisted on demanding that the Democratic Party implement changes that could be seen in the near future. Although it had not gotten its delegates seated at the national convention of the Democratic Party, the MFDP came out of 1964 confident that history had been made and that it had indeed demonstrated for the nation that Mississippi blacks could lead toward a more inclusive democracy.

Also in 1964 Hamer unsuccessfully attempted to run for Congress. Since the regular Democratic Party disallowed her name on the ballot, the MFDP conceived the "Freedom Ballot," which included all the candidates' names, black and white. Fannie Lou Hamer defeated her white opponent, Congressman Jamie Whitten (33,099 to 41). Hamer, both in Atlantic City and with the Freedom Ballot race, wanted to show poor people, especially poor people of Mississippi, that poor people could become agents of change for themselves.

In 1965 Hamer, Victoria Gray of Hattiesburg, and Annie Devine of Canton, appealed to the U.S. Congress, arguing that it was wrong to seat Mississippi's representatives who were all white, when the state's population was fifty percent black people—fifty percent poor black people. The three women observed as the House voted against the challenge 228 to 143. They came away moved by the fact that at least 143 congress members agreed with them. They also made history; no other Americans had ever questioned American democracy on representation in Congress, with the argument that poor people ought to represent poor people. No one else took up her idea that poor people needed to be represented by other poor individuals, but Fannie Lou Hamer had new ideas for how American democracy ought to be practiced.

Hamer remained active in civic affairs in Mississippi for the remainder of her life, becoming a delegate to the National Democratic Convention in 1968 in Chicago. Thus, she had seen in four years the importance of her uncompromising stance only four years earlier.

We hear Fannie Lou Hamer in an interview in 1965 say: "I was determined to see that things were changed." Later in the same sitting, she paraphrased John F. Kennedy, "And I am determined to give my part not for what the Movement can do for me, but what I can do for the Movement to bring about a change." On being tired, Fannie Lou Hamer put it best when she said:

> I do remember, one time, a man came to me after the students began to work in Mississippi and he said the white people were getting tired and they were getting tense and anything might happen. Well, I asked him 'how long he thinks we had been getting tired'? I have been tired for 46 years and my parents was tired before me and their parents were tired; and I have always wanted to do something that would help some of the things I would see going on among Negroes that I didn't like and I don't like now.[4]

Hamer consistently stated that she had *always* wanted to work to transform the South because she saw her parents work so hard to raise 20 children. She spoke often of the hardships of her mother and her enslaved grandmother. She also talked about her father. Once her father bought two mules after much sacrifice, and simply because this meant he might experience semi-independence from the landowner, his mules were poisoned. Hamer never could come to grips with this kind of hatred. It bolstered her with courage and initiative when the time came. Too, it made her angry and helped her envision an American democracy that would include poor people.

Fannie Lou Hamer's life is best framed in its religious and political context. She knew religion long before she became politically active in the formal sense, but of course, for many blacks religion and day-to-day survival often meant political manipulation of an oppressive racial system. Political activity in actual party politics came for Fannie Lou Hamer and others like her in the 1960s when they challenged the Democratic Party to live up to its pledge of democracy for all Americans. Religion and politics are significant components of African American culture as it has evolved in the United States. The civil rights movement is a perfect example of this when one considers the major role of the black church as the struggle reached new levels.[5]

Most people familiar with the civil rights movement of the 1960s know of Fannie Lou Hamer, sharecropper, determined voter registrant, field worker for SNCC, a founder (along with Annie Devine, Victoria Gray, Aaron Hen.y, Ella Baker, and others) of the Mississippi Freedom Democratic Party, orator, and all-around political activist. In addition to these contributions, Fannie Lou Hamer abided by strong religious teachings and often expressed that religious zeal through a sacred hymn before each of her speeches. She opened many gatherings with "This Little Light of Mine," one of her favorite songs.

Even Fannie Lou Hamer's religious zeal helped her to see things differently. At least on one occasion she also used her singing to give notice that a program needed to close. John Dittmer, professor of history at Depauw University and former faculty member at Tougaloo College, relates that one of his most vivid recollections of Hamer occurred at a Tougaloo Commencement ceremony when the school awarded her her first honorary doctorate. Dittmer recalled,

> It was hot in the chapel, and Aaron Henry had gone on far too long in his commencement speech. It was a very formal commencement, and after Mrs. Hamer got her degree[,] she whispered something in our president's ear. He appeared rather startled, then nodded his head. Mrs. Hamer signaled to the back of the room, and a small group of Ruleville people came forward to join Mrs. Hamer in a stirring rendition of "Go Tell It on the Mountain."

In Dittmer's assessment, Fannie Lou Hamer "symbolized the best of what was the Movement."[6]

Hamer followed the examples set by other leading women freedom warriors of her time, Rosa Parks (Alabama), Septima Clark (South Carolina), Daisy Bates (Arkansas), and Ella Baker (New York City), like them becoming an active participant in the civil rights struggle at the local level.

Fannie Lou Hamer's founding in 1969 of the Freedom Farms Corporation (FFC), a non-profit venture designed to help needy families raise food and livestock, showed her concern for the economic plight of blacks in Mississippi. FFC also provided social services, minority business opportunity, scholarships, and grants for education. When the National Council of Negro Women started the Fannie Lou Hamer Day Care Center in 1970, Hamer became the chairperson of its board. As late as 1976, even as she struggled to survive against cancer, Hamer served as a member of the State Executive Committee of the United Democratic Party of Mississippi.[7]

Initiative, courage, and selflessness best describe Fannie Lou Hamer's life. Her motivation to make a difference in the freedom struggle is best summarized by her repeated remark "I'm sick and tired of being sick and tired." The motto resembled the same sentiment expressed by Martin Luther King, Jr., when he began saying in the 1950s that black people had waited long enough for racial justice. Indeed, the 1950s gave rise to fundamental changes in American society that caused people to address the problem of racial segregation and discrimination.[8]

Keeping in mind that Hamer's frankness, determination, courage, and leadership abilities made her a memorable warrior in the 1960s civil rights struggle, her actions (especially her work with the Mississippi Freedom Democratic Party) are also well understood when placed within the historical context of the Democratic Party. MFDP'S challenge to the Democratic Party in August 1964 takes on greater meaning when viewed in light of the history of the Democratic Party, especially its place among white southerners. The 1964 MFDP's bid for political power threatened Lyndon B. Johnson's presidential nomination and ultimately changed Mississippi's political scene. When the MFDP refused to accept the compromise offered in 1964, it demanded an end to all-white delegations. This demand threatened the political success of local white politicians, putting Mississippi on notice that there would no longer be politics as usual. Between 1964 and 1976, essentially, the MFDP closed the last major avenues to white conservative Mississippi Democrats who were continuing what amounted to an all-white primary. As the MFDP persistently reported discriminatory practices from Mississippi to the national

Democratic Party, segregationists eventually began to break rank with the Democratic Party and started to build a Republican force, a development that had not occurred since Reconstruction. Indeed, only one instance prior to 1976, Democrat Alfred E. Smith's 1928 presidential bid, provided the Republican Party with inroads into the Solid South. Ironically, the 1960s and 1970s Mississippi Republicans hardly resembled the radicals of the century before; the new supporters of the Republican Party searched for a conservative home base.

The Democratic Party has had an extended history of conservatism and white supremacy far longer than it has of liberalism and social justice struggles. In the 1850s the party supported, with few exceptions, racial slavery. When southern states seceded and initiated the Civil War, the Democratic Party stood on the side of the southern cause. For the next century the Democratic Party remained the choice party of whites in the Solid South, people who held steadfastly to the status quo on conservatism and white supremacy. To maintain its conservative hold the party paid particular attention to the disenfranchisement of black people and used the violence and intimidation associated with the Ku Klux Klan, the grandfather clause, poll taxes, literacy tests, and various other discriminatory practices. Of the Deep South states, few were more determined to maintain white political power than Mississippi.

Conservatives were left intact even after *Smith v. Allwright* in 1944 and Harry S. Truman's 1948 attempt with the civil rights plank. After those episodes, most leading white segregationist politicians could still count on the usual ways to disenfranchise citizens, especially poll taxes, literacy tests or the discretion of voter registrars, intimidation, and violence. Voter registration drives and other efforts had begun to curb these practices. For instance, the 1938–1948 interracial Southern Conference for Human Welfare's National Committee for the Abolishment of the Poll Tax struggled unsuccessfully to stamp out the poll tax. The Southern Conference Educational Fund, SCHW's legacy, and SNCC in the 1960s worked forcefully for voter registration.[9]

The greatest success at curbing the power of white conservative southern Democrats came in 1948 with the push by President Harry S. Truman and young Minneapolis Mayor Hubert Humphrey to incorporate civil rights into the Democratic Party platform and transform the conservative party. In 1948 Truman surpassed the Franklin Delano Roosevelt administrations' reluctant gestures toward liberalism and racial equality. In protest against the liberalism of Truman and Humphrey, the entire Mississippi and half of the Alabama delegation, along with a few delegates from other southern states, marched out of the National Democratic Convention while the band played "Dixie." The youthful George C. Wallace stayed. The Dixiecrats or States' Rights Party with delegates from Mississippi, Alabama, South Carolina, and Louisiana nominated South Carolina Governor Strom Thurmond for president. Mississippi Governor Fielding L. Wright, whose idea it had been to stage the party revolt, became Thurmond's running mate. The conservatives had little interest in making states more vital as units of government. In the words of a Birmingham newspaper commentator, "When the Democratic party ceases to be the party of white supremacy, the deepest basis of Democratic loyalty has been destroyed."[10] The Dixiecrats lost miserably as Truman defeated the Republican Thomas E. Dewey.

During Truman's full-term administration, he integrated the armed services with Executive Order 9981, and after the Republican interlude of the 1950s, Kennedy and Johnson more actively supported legislation in support of civil rights and political rights for blacks. Kennedy's assassination in November 1963 left a forceful Lyndon B. Johnson to rally the necessary support for the bill. On July 2, after a fifty-seven day filibuster, Congress passed and Johnson signed the Civil Rights Act of 1964 which, among other things, prohibited employment discrimination based on race and sex and established an Equal Employment Opportunity Commission to implement it. Aaron Henry, chairman of the Mississippi Loyal Democrats, in the late 1960s, remarked, "Mississippi [was] the only state in the nation . . . that [had] an OEO [EEOC] program in every county." The Voting Rights Act met success in 1965, re-enfranchising the majority of southern blacks.[11]

Most Americans understood the importance of political rights. Fannie Lou Hamer and the MFDP had made their position on the subject clear in 1964. Lyndon Johnson even joined Fannie Lou Hamer and the MFDP in recognizing the link between political access and economic development. Johnson, in assessing his presidency in 1969, chose the Voting Rights Act as his greatest accomplishment, saying

I believe if [people have] the right to vote that they can take care of their own problems pretty well. As you see, when they are electing southern sheriffs, southern mayors, and southern judges, the Negroes have been emancipated a good deal. It is going to correct an injustice of decades and centuries. I think it is going to make it possible for this Government to endure, not half slave and half free, but united.

A member of the MFDP said it another way, "Voter registration is black power. Power is invested in the ballot and that's why the white man worked like hell to keep you away from it." By 1969, after seeing the difficulty of creating a majority rule, Fannie Lou Hamer proposed that "minority groups . . . have representation according to the percentage they represent in their communities. This should be guaranteed by law . . . [even] if this takes a constitutional amendment."[12] Hamer continued to push for new ideas in politics. Many people labeled her as too far left; she responded, "I admit I'm from the far left, to be exact, I am 400 years from being far left, I don't think it could be any further."[13] Thus, Fannie Lou Hamer embraced her connection to America through her identity of being African American. She understood that history to be a long one filled with economic pitfalls, among others, for black Americans.

Certainly, seeking representation in government was not a new or novel idea. However, to request that poor people represent poor people and that states send representatives according to the demography of the local setting were new and novel ideas. Indeed, Fannie Lou Hamer did see American democracy a little differently than most civil rights activists or any American, for that matter.

The numbers support the claim to empowerment. Between 1965 and 1968 black elected officials in southern states increased from 72 to 388. In 1969 that number jumped to 1,160 elected officials and increased to 5,038 by July 1981. Blacks, however, held only 1.03 percent of all elected offices in the nation in 1981. The painfully slow political progress had been steady and centered primarily in the southern states, where 53 percent of the black population of the country lived. Furthermore, by 1981 Mississippi led in the net increases.[14]

The steady growth in black elected officials meant a decrease for the white population. In Mississippi conservative white Democrats rallied to interfere with the political process and the success of blacks running for office. The most common tactics later used included the dual registration system in Mississippi, under which voters had to register in one location for state and national elections and in another for local elections; at-large elections as opposed to elections by districts; election-time purging of voter rolls to force voter re-registration; institutional obstacles, such as inadequate information concerning voter registration and procedures, inconvenient places and times of registration, and keeping the number of black registrars small or nonexistent.[15]

The message from the Democratic National Committee insured equal opportunity for participation in all party affairs "for all Democrats of all States regardless of race, color, creed or national origin." The National Committee also considered the matter of "paramount concern to the future . . . of the Democratic Party." In Mississippi Democratic Party leaders worried that the continued struggle for the protection of black voting rights would push conservative whites out of the Democratic fold.[16] Although it did not happen immediately, by 1976 Mississippi Republican strength placed in office Trent Lott and Thad Cochran, the second and third Republican Congressmen since Reconstruction.[17]

When the 1964 Atlantic City compromise failed, at least the national Democratic Party promised that in 1968 the delegation to the National Democratic Convention would be inclusive of all constituents without regard to race. Given the history of the conservative, white supremacy Democratic Party, segregationists had little room to maneuver within the confines of the state Democratic apparatus. For the next several years they tried all sorts of schemes to prevent all voters' full participation in the state party. The national Democratic Party held to its position that all voters had to be represented. Having lost support from the national Democratic Party, and with the MFDP's watchful eyes forever reporting continued discriminatory practices in Mississippi, white supremacists turned to the Republican Party, which had taken on some of the conservatism formerly associated with the Democrats. In the end the Democratic Party, with its long history of racism and conservatism, became a party of liberal forces, willing to represent everyone. The Republican Party, which for a long time represented liberalism for black people because of Abraham Lincoln's Emancipation Proclamation, acted as a haven for conservatism.

Fannie Lou Hamer received wide recognition for her part in bringing about such major political transition and raising significant questions that addressed basic human needs. In 1963 the Fifth Avenue Baptist Church in Nashville, Tennessee, presented her one of the first awards that she received; it was appropriately for "Voter Registration and Hamer's Fight for Freedom for Mankind." Among the numerous other awards the

National Association of Business and Professional Women Club, Inc. presented Hamer its National Sojourner Truth Meritorious Service Award as a tribute to Hamer's strong defense of human dignity and fearless promotion of civil rights. Delta Sigma Theta Sorority, Inc. awarded her life membership. Many colleges and universities honored her with honorary degrees, including her neighboring institution Tougaloo College in 1969.

Fannie Lou Hamer gave numerous speeches across the country into the 1970s. She grew weary by this time because she suffered with cancer, but she continued to accept invitations to speak about things most dear to her, basic human rights for all Americans. Indeed, she remained tired of being sick and tired until her life ended. She died of cancer on March 14, 1977 at Mound Bayou Community Hospital.

Fannie Lou Hamer is remembered as a political heroine.[18] She is probably remembered as such because she personally had overcome so much. She became a noted figure despite the fact that she had only about eight years of formal education. She even became a noted speaker. But Fannie Lou Hamer believed that she could compete equally with any high school graduate of the 1970s; she was an intelligent being. As a speaker, Fannie Lou Hamer was charismatic. She expressed her thoughts in a unique way, and she had a rich, deep husky voice. Many Mississippians who heard her speak have told me that she was spell binding.[19] Fannie Lou Hamer relied on what she knew best, and some of this was part of her African American culture: religion, politics, and self-help. Certainly self-help work was not new to the black community in the 1960s. Even Hamer's efforts with FFC in the 1960s (and the work of other Mississippi women in similar entities) were not new. We only have to remember the desperate situation for farmers in nineteenth-century America, when farmers turned to cooperatives as a way of surviving and helping themselves. In what historians have called the Populist movement, African Americans too played a significant role, as the movement held tremendous hope for improving their situation. In my estimation, some of Fannie Lou Hamer's questions that rested firmly in matters of economics place her squarely in the camp with Martin Luther King, Jr., who had come to focus on economics as a major issue for the civil rights struggle by 1966.

A few SNCC members objected to the political landscape offered by the regular Mississippi Democrats and national Democratic Party leaders of the 1960s. Stokeley Carmichael (the late Kwame Ture) preferred the third party route, but had SNCC leaders and the MFDP taken that route, the argument here would probably be that more could have been gained from working within the Democratic Party to have it live up to its promise of American democracy. Fannie Lou Hamer asked fundamental questions and convinced the MFDP that greater leverage would come without compromise. Fannie Lou Hamer's legacy, in part, is evident in the greater African American political representation in the Democratic Party. Additionally, she saw the lack of political access and its connection to the poor economic situation of blacks in the Mississippi Delta. Thus, like Martin Luther King, Jr., Fannie Lou Hamer must be remembered also for her work of connecting politics to matters related to economics.

"Closet Moderates"

Why White Liberals Failed, 1940–1970

TONY BADGER

I

Kerr Scott was the most liberal governor of North Carolina of the twentieth century. He was elected in 1948 in an upset victory over the State Treasurer, Charles Johnson. The blunt uncompromising Scott campaigned for his "branchhead boys"—isolated rural voters who lived not at the heads of the rivers but at the ends of the tributaries—and against "lawyer-business" rule. Johnson was supported by most members of the General Assembly, and by most state officials and county commissioners. Scott put together a coalition of lower-income, especially rural, whites and blacks to defeat him. For the first time for years, noted one observer, you did not know who was going to be governor. Johnson had been so confident of winning that allegedly he had ordered a new Cadillac with special hubcaps. Edwin Gill, protégée of Max Gardner, and later state treasurer himself, was so surprised, it was said, that he tried to jump out of his second-floor office window.[1]

In office, Scott rewarded his liberal coalition. He built 12,000 miles of farm-to-market roads, paving the dirt roads of rural North Carolina, and lifting the state out of the mud. He stimulated a dramatic increase in the provision of rural electrification and telephones. He improved teachers' salaries and pensions and increased spending on school construction. He raised welfare benefits and widened unemployment compensation coverage. For African Americans, he defused a proposed march on Raleigh by consulting black leaders, fought for increased appropriations for black institutions, monitored black efforts to register to vote, especially in eastern North Carolina, and appointed blacks to state government positions. Above all, he appointed Harold Trigg, president of St. Augustine's College, as the first African American to serve on the State Board of Education.[2]

For organized labor, Scott attempted to repeal the state's anti-closed shop law and to raise the minimum wage. Unlike his predecessors and successors, he intervened in strikes on behalf of the strikers, not the employers; he did not call out the National Guard to break strikes. When textile workers struck Hart Mills in Tarboro and spent most of 1949 on strike, Scott condemned the owners. He complained that the company "doesn't believe in unions," that they were inflexible, and set on busting the union.[3]

When Scott had campaigned for Commissioner of Agriculture he had criticized the lack of representation for the interests of thousands of farm-women: it was a repeated theme. He appointed the first woman, Jane McKimmon, to the state board of Agriculture. As governor, he attempted to secure more representation for women in state appointments and appointed North Carolina's first female superior court judge, Suzie Sharp, later chief justice of the state Supreme Court. Scott also appointed women campaign managers, notably in critical counties like Forsyth.[4]

Scott sought the economic modernization of the state but it was a New Deal-style modernization strategy, aimed not at attracting low-wage industry through cheap labor and tax incentives, but at creating economic growth through the creation of mass purchasing power, sustaining and increasing the income of black and white lower-income voters. There was a liberal cutting edge to Scott's policies: he confronted the state's bankers over state financial deposits and revenue; the oil companies over an increased gasoline tax; the utility companies over rural electrification and water resources; and employers over union rights, strikes, and the minimum wage. He recognized the essential ingredient of federal aid if the state was to solve its long-term economic problems: he supported federal aid to education, federal development of water resources, federal aid for hospital construction and low-cost housing, and some form of national health insurance. He was a southern politician firmly in sympathy with the economic policies of a liberal Democratic national administration, a sympathy emphasized when he appointed the former press secretary to FDR and Truman, Jonathan Daniels, as Democratic National Committeeman. He confirmed that liberalism by appointing the state's most advanced New Dealer, UNC President Frank Graham to the United States Senate. Scott was one of the last North Carolina politicians to be proud of the adjective liberal. As he praised Frank Graham to one audience, "You haven't got a better liberal in America than the Senator you've got."[5]

And there were North Carolinians who responded with zeal to this liberal politics. On September 16, 1949 one admirer wrote to Scott that he was "as far as I am concerned, . . . the first North Carolinian in my lifetime who has had the vision and the ability to become President of the United States." The admirer encouraged Scott "to set his cap for that accomplishment. This is the political era of the 'Little Man'. You have a way of getting along with that Little Man make the most of it." That enthusiastic admirer of North Carolina's most liberal governor was a young Jesse Helms.[6]

Almost twenty years later, Kerr Scott's son, Robert, set his sights on the governor's mansion. In 1967 in a speech in Dunn he blasted "the civil disobedience movement and its demonstrators," "hippies," "Black Power advocates," "coddlers of criminals," "the United States Supreme Court and the federal establishment," "peaceniks," and "free-wheeling academics," and blamed them for disorder in America. In 1968 Scott won a narrow election victory over Republican Jim Gardner by taking a tough "law and order stance" and distancing himself from the Johnson administration and the Hubert Humphrey campaign. As governor, he used the National Guard and state troopers to quell disturbances in Oxford and Wilmington and to end student occupations in Greensboro and Chapel Hill.[7]

In 1969–70 I was a graduate student supporting my research by teaching the History of Western Civilization to textile majors at North Carolina State University. On February 23, 1970 I wrote to my parents,

> On the Saturday I went to see 'Un Homme et une Femme' at the Union. A beautiful and sensitive film which had been inexplicably banned by the owner of the local TV network. This man, a Nixon supporter with Wallaceite tendencies who rather cleverly exploits anti-intellectual prejudices, would no doubt have apoplexy if he watched BBC 2 for an evening.

That television owner, Jesse Helms, announced that month that he had become a Republican. It was, wrote Thad Stem to Jonathan Daniels, no great surprise, "the next big surprise will be Raquel Welch's announcement that she has big tits. Maybe Harry Golden will confirm the fact that he is Jewish." In 1972 Helms defeated Democrat Nick Galifanakis for the Senate, implying that Galifinakis was neither American nor Christian, and like the Democratic candidate George McGovern, was soft on drugs. Helms won by winning over the Wallace Democrats from rural Eastern North Carolina. That same year Kerr Scott's campaign manager from 1954 and former governor, Terry Sanford, was overwhelmingly defeated in his effort to stop George Wallace from winning the state's presidential primary.[8]

The purpose of this essay is to ask how the South got from liberal hope to a conservative reality, how the liberal "politics of the Little Man" championed by Jesse Helms in 1949 became the reactionary "politics of the Little Man" espoused by Jesse Helms in 1972.

II

Kerr Scott was not an isolated figure for change when he was elected in 1948. He was part of a liberal window of opportunity that opened up for the South in the 1940s from the economic and social changes unleashed by the New Deal and World War II. John Egerton in *Speak Now Against the Day* concluded

> One of the things I have come to see in retrospect is how favorable the conditions were for substantive social change in the four or five years right after World War II. It appears to have been the last and best time—perhaps the only time—when the South might have moved boldly and decisively to heal itself, to fix its own social wagon voluntarily. But it didn't act, and the moment passed, and all that has happened in the tumultuous days since . . . has followed from the inability to seize the time and do the right thing, not simply because it was right, but because it was also in our own best interest.[9]

A wealth of recent scholarship has spoken to this liberal possibility. Egerton, himself, focussed his attention on academics, writers and journalists who had engaged in so much regional self-criticism in the 1930s and, drawing on the work of Patricia Sullivan, on the New Deal radicals and black activists who made up the Southern Conference for Human Welfare. Sullivan had shown how black voter registration campaigns at the local level had linked to NAACP membership drives, teacher equalization suits and protests against brutality. After 1944 those drives were underwritten by the CIOPAC as labor attempted to secure the election of liberal candidates in the 1946 elections. Adam Fairclough confirms Sullivan's picture in Louisiana. The revival of the NAACP did not involve merely a litigative, middle-class strategy but was crucially linked to voter registration, community organization against police brutality and local labor radicalism. Nelson Lichtenstein and Bob Korstad drew similar attention to the crucial interaction of militant, left-led interracial unions, their involvement in local politics and black voter registration, notably in Winston-Salem. Tim Minchin has demonstrated that textile workers attempted to capitalize on their wartime pay rises and newly signed contracts. The drive to unionize textiles persisted for some years after the time historians have dismissed Operation Dixie as a failure. The union mounted a general strike in 1951.[10]

Jennifer Brooks has demonstrated that returning white veterans, anxious to see a new modernized South, combined in GI revolts to overthrow long-standing, local political machines. Nor did southern women simply return to "domestic pursuits" after the war. Pam Tyler and Leslie Gale Parr have shown how New Orleans women strove to clean up their city and promote interracial cooperation in the late 1940s.[11]

What were the political implications of this ferment of reform? To John Egerton politicians were "conspicuously absent from the ranks of the critics and reformers," "progressive or moderate or even mildly conservative congressmen were as scarce as hen's teeth." But I have argued that there was a new generation of New Deal southern politicians. Just as in the North "issue-oriented" politicians in the Democratic Party replaced "patronage-oriented" politicians, so in the South, younger politicians ideologically committed to New Deal economic policies came to replace patronage-hungry congressmen who had only supported FDR in the economic emergency of the 1930s. John Sparkman identified himself as a "TVA liberal" and other congressman drew the lesson Sparkman learned from the TVA that the federal government could regenerate an entire region. Like Sparkman in 1946 they made the progress from the House to the Senate: Lister Hill and Claude Pepper in 1937 and 1938, William Fulbright in 1944, Estes Kefauver and Lyndon Johnson in 1948, Albert Gore, Sr. in 1952. In 1944 labor in Gadsen helped Albert Rains defeat anti-union, anti-communist representative Joe Starnes, and in 1946 textile workers in Rome, Georgia, helped Henderson Lanham defeat Malcolm Tarver. Albert Thomas and Lindley Beckworth in Texas, Brooks Hays and James Trimble in Arkansas, Robert Jones in Alabama, Charles Deane in North Carolina, even Frank Smith elected from the heart of the Mississippi Delta in 1950, helped constitute a liberal bloc which formed part of what Ira Katznelson and his colleagues have identified as a party-based liberal coalition of non-southern and southern Democrats on welfare state, fiscal and regulatory issues. Katznelson concluded that they "supported much of the party's social democratic agenda with a level of enthusiasm appropriate to a poor region with a heritage of opposition to big business and a history of support for regulation and redistribution."[12]

In the state houses governors were elected by a biracial alliance of lower-income whites and the small, but steadily increasing black electorate. Big Jim Folsom in Alabama in 1946, Sid McMath in Arkansas, Kerr Scott in North Carolina and Earl Long in Louisiana in 1948 exploited a common man appeal, took advantage of their states' relative prosperity since 1940, and offered a New Deal-style economic program that promised their lower-income supporters the welfare and public services long-denied them by the conservative elites. In response to the voter-registration campaigns that had quadrupled the percentage of voting age blacks registered to vote, they adopted a stand of racial moderation, protecting the black right to vote, improving services to the black community, seeking increased appropriations for black institutions and appointing blacks to state government jobs. They attempted to protect organized labor and worked closely with politically active women.[13]

At the local level, men like Jim Wright in Fort Worth, Jack Brooks in Beaumont, Frank Smith in Sidon, Terry Sanford in Fayetteville, Dante Fascell in Miami, and Joe Langan in Mobile came back from the War, went to graduate school, took control of the Young Democrats in their city and state, and got elected to their state legislatures, joining other veterans determined, in Smith's words, to "have a part in making a better day." Smith would go to Congress in 1950, Wright, Brooks and Fascell in 1954.[14]

III

These liberal and racially moderate politicians were not the force of the future in the South, despite the hopes of successive presidents and the Supreme Court. The latter's civil rights strategies were predicated until 1963 on the willingness of responsible southern leaders to lead their communities into voluntary acceptance of racial change. Instead, southern voters increasingly supported conservative candidates who most vociferously protested their loyalty to segregation and their determination to resist racial change. When racial change was eventually imposed on the South in the 1960s, the adjustment to that change was engineered not by the old liberals and racial moderates but by transmogrified segregationists, business leaders, and, after 1970, a new generation of business progressive New South politicians. The scene of liberal successes was also the scene of the most violent and vigorous segregationist resistance. It was under Jim Folsom that a mob would prevent Autherine Lucy entering the University of Alabama. It was his liberal protégé George Wallace who would stand at the schoolhouse door and defy the federal government. It was Sid McMath's liberal protégé, Orval Faubus, who would use the National Guard to prevent the desegregation of Central High School. Two years after Kerr Scott's election to the Senate in 1954, which one observer contended meant that race "will never again raise its ugly head" in North Carolina politics, Scott had signed the Southern Manifesto and endorsed the Pearsall Plan, North Carolina's version of Massive Resistance. It was racially moderate mayor, DeLesseps Morrison, who allowed mobs to roam the streets of New Orleans to enforce a boycott of desegregated schools in 1960.[15]

What had gone wrong?

One argument clearly is that the liberal window of opportunity never existed, that racial and economic liberals were neither sizeable nor liberal enough seriously to threaten conservative hegemony and the established racial and economic status quo.

First, organized labor failed in its bid to undermine the South as a bastion of the open shop. Textile unions, according to Tim Minchin, never solved the free rider question: if employers of non-union plants matched the wages of those plants which were under contract, why should non-union workers risk strike action to secure a contract which would not bring them any economic benefits but would threaten their ability to keep up the mortgage and credit payments that they now made as home-owning consumers. Were white workers interested in interracial cooperation? Time and again, the answer seemed no. As Bryant Simon argued in South Carolina, in response to black activism, even as early as 1938, mill hands had "emerged as a reactionary political force."[16]

Second, returning veterans were as likely to believe that their wartime sacrifice had been in order to maintain white supremacy as to establish a new racial order. As Jim Cobb and Jennifer Brooks have pointed out, returning veterans were the perpetrators of post-war racial violence, founders of the Citizens Council and core members of a re-invigorated Klan. Herman Talmadge, Strom Thurmond, and George Smathers were prominent among candidates who parlayed successful war records into post-war political success as defenders of the racial status quo. As Thad

Stem noted about Klan members in eastern North Carolina in the 1960s, they were not just "malcontents, freaks and oddballs," they were also financially successful men who were "as hot for the Klan as they were hell on Hitler, all the way from Libya to the Rhine."[17]

Third, "the political era of the 'Little Man' " was not necessarily conducive to liberal politics, either in racial or economic affairs. The common man, good ol' boy style of politics of a Jim Folsom was equally a style used by reactionary politicians like Eugene Talmadge. Populist suspicion of elites and special financial interests could equally be tapped as anti-statist sentiments that fuelled resentment of government spending and taxation and hatred of African Americans. Folsom, himself, noted the discrepancy:

> Gene Talmadge . . . got elected in 1946. I got elected cookin' turnip greens and he got elected on the race issue. That was his personal preservation, and I never did use it. The same time right in adjoining states —the same background—ethnic background . . . He got elected just raisin' hell about the race question. Negro, Negro, Negro, Negro, and I never mentioned the thing. And I shook hands with the Negro.

Conversely, economic liberalism did not automatically go with racial moderation, as the records of politicians like New Deal supporters and race-baiters Theodore Bilbo and John Rankin indicated, or as the resolute refusal of union-backing Olin Johnston to betray any public hint of racial moderation testified. Equally the ranks of racial moderates included economic conservatives. An analysis, for example, of those who did not sign the Southern Manifesto reveals conservative Texas congressmen, loyal to Sam Rayburn, a right-wing Republican and future Goldwater loyalist, and a union-busting, Liberty League, textile millionaire from North Carolina.[18]

Finally, women may have been influential in the churches, interracial groups and in the later campaigns to keep public schools open, but much of this activity for a long time scarcely entered the public space. White women were arguably more prominent in support groups for the Dixiecrats and in vocal segregationist groups like the Mothers' League for Central High in Little Rock and the Women for Constitutional Government in Mississippi. Gladys Tillett might proclaim that "Women Will Win This Election" for Frank Graham in 1950, but she was wrong.[19]

The second argument is that the liberal window of opportunity had always been closed by the race issue. The forces of popular white racism made it politically suicidal after World War II for any politician to deviate from staunch defense of white supremacy. To survive and preserve his influence, the aspiring liberal politician had to suppress any sentiments for racial moderation. Carl Elliott, courageous north Alabama liberal congressman, for whom Franklin Roosevelt was, and remained, a political god, recalled the inexorable process:

> There was no room left in the middle for anyone . . . you had to do what you could to somehow connect with the people, to find some way of appeasing them without sacrificing your principles . . . When that [Southern] Manifesto came along, neither these [Deep South] colleagues nor my constituents back in Alabama cared about moderation. You were either with them or against them. And if you were against them, you were gone. Voted out. Politically excommunicated . . . I knew there was no way I could survive and I hadn't yet achieved what I came to Congress to do.

Politicians like Elliott and the rest of the Alabama House delegation followed the lead of their liberal senators Hill and Sparkman and ran for cover. They became in Hodding Carter's words "closet moderates." It was a pattern repeated all over the South. Historians differ over the date when the race issue apparently closed the liberal window. Patricia Sullivan puts it as early as 1946 and the defeat of CIOPAC candidates in those elections and the subsequent travails of the Southern Conference and the failure of the efforts of Henry Wallace and the Progressive Party in 1948. For Morton Sosna, 1950 was the time when liberalism on race was fatal to political careers in the region, as the defeats of Claude Pepper and Frank Graham indicated. For Michael Klarman, the decisive moment comes with the violent backlash after Brown, which in turn stimulated black protest. Southern moderates were irrelevant in the ensuing battle between the southern conservatives and the federal government. "By propelling southern politics towards racial fanaticism, Brown set the stage for the violent suppression of civil rights demonstrations in the early 1960s, which in turn aroused previously indifferent northern whites to demand federal legislative intervention to inter Jim Crow."[20]

Anti-communism has been seen as part and parcel of the conservative resistance to racial change and liberal failure. For Patricia Sullivan the new national liberalism largely abandoned a bold civil rights strategy and the anti-communist issue, remorselessly exploited by southern conservatives, fatally divided the Popular Front coalition in the South. For Korstad and Lichtenstein, anti-communism was used to break up the alliance of left-led unions and black workers. In Louisiana, Adam Fairclough wrote

> The impact of McCarthyism was so profound that one could argue that a fundamental discontinuity separated the period 1940–54 from the following decade. Well before 1950 the Cold War had produced an ideological chilling effect that made criticism of the social order, so commonplace during the Roosevelt era, unfashionable, unpatriotic, and politically dangerous.

The dynamics of the potent mix of pervasive white racism and anti-communism were read differently by Numan Bartley. For Bartley, unlike Sullivan, national liberals were not too cautious on civil rights but too radical. Bartley blames the failure of post-war southern liberalism squarely on national cold war liberals. American liberalism, Bartley argues, abandoned its vision of economic reform and redistribution aimed at the biracial lower-income coalition in the South, and instead embraced the politics of anti-racism and desegregation. It substituted a moralistic concern for symbolic opportunity and the elimination of de jure segregation for the substance of a drive to tackle the problem of back and white disadvantage. Liberalism "became increasingly fixated on race relations," it lost "most of its substance and direction" and left white workers with "little aside from contempt and the right to compete for scarce jobs with black workers."[21]

According to Bartley, the civil rights movement chose the wrong target—de jure segregation, especially in education, where white fears for their children were so profound. The movement should have concentrated on voting rights and economic gains. Similarly Michael Klarman sees the litigative strategy on education, seeking redress from outside the region, undercutting southern moderates' efforts at gradual, internal change in the areas of interest that engaged southern blacks before 1954. Korstad and Lichtenstein also lament this direction away from issues of economic equality and working-class empowerment which Martin Luther King would vainly try to resurrect after 1965. This line of argument has clear contemporary resonance. Jim Sleeper in 1998 contrasted Vice-President Albert Gore's "racial moralism" unfavorably with "the honorable but more grounded approach of his father." Gore Sr. "favored government intervention in economic relations rather than in racial ones."

His was a "more authentically 'progressive' emphasis on economic redistribution."[22]

IV

All these analyses have a great deal of truth in them. But I want to argue for a different dynamic of the issues of race, class and anti-communism, one in which liberal possibilities persisted past 1954 only to be undermined in part by the liberals' own fatalism, which made it impossible through the particular biracial politics of the 1950s to deliver what African Americans wanted, driving African Americans to eschew politics for direct action protest. This protest marginalized southern liberals. On the one hand, it was transmogrified segregationists and business leaders who mediated the acceptance by southern communities of federally mandated racial change. On the other, black assertiveness, together with economic and cultural dislocation for lower-income and middle-income whites, provoked conservative southern Republican success.

It is obviously prudent not to overstate the political strength of postwar southern liberals. The structural obstacles which V. O. Key identified as perpetuating conservative hegemony and inhibiting the interests of the "have-nots" were, even with the slowly increasing black electorate, still formidable. In a state like Mississippi, the short-lived collaboration of a maverick newspaper editor, a university chaplain and a detached Nobel laureate in a spoof parody of Citizen Council magazines can scarcely be portrayed as a major threat to established interests. Nevertheless, I do believe that the existence of a southern New Deal style post-war political liberalism has been underestimated. Recently, I believe this reflects the persuasive case made brilliantly by Alan Brinkley in *The End of Reform*. Brinkley, who does not mention any southern liberals, argues that the New Deal legacy was for the next generation a national liberalism, aimed at consumers, not producers, committed to economic growth, not redistribution, and championing a limited, not interventionist, state in economic affairs. National liberalism had become, in Arthur Schlesinger's well-known formulation, qualitative, rather than quantitative. But this view of national liberalism in itself underestimates the extent that this "consensus" was contested and problematic in the 1950s. It also virtually ignores the South, where the time-lagged impact of the New Deal ensured that a redistributionist liberalism surfaced and struggled through the 1940s and

1950s. Most southern states saw a vigorous competition between liberals and conservatives over the appropriate modernization strategy for the region. The conservatives triumphed more often than not, and ultimately won, but that should not obscure the persistent conflict through these years.[23]

When William Colmer could seriously warn fellow Mississippi congressman, Frank Smith, to steer clear of hawk Henry "Scoop" Jackson of Washington on the grounds that Scoop Jackson was a communist, one clearly should not underestimate the power of anti-communism in the South. Indeed, Maury Maverick, Jr. recalled that in the South liberals were in favor of filibusters as the only weapon to stop anti-communist excesses. He recalled that in Texas,

> There was a bill for awhile to give anyone the death penalty who belonged to the Communist Party. I remember that I had a hand in reducing that to life imprisonment. That was a great liberal move at the time. (laughter) Well, hell, it sounds silly today, but you know, God Almighty, I was at least trying to keep the Reds from being put in the electric chair and now, I feel like a damn fool even talking about it.

There is no doubt that anti-communism, exploited by conservative elites, destroyed southern radicals in the 1940s—the Southern Conference, left-led unions, the Civil Rights Congress's work in Louisiana. Red scare politics played a major factor in the defeat of Claude Pepper and Frank Graham in 1950, though both incumbents were unusually vulnerable to guilt-by-association cold war fears. But anti-communism had been a staple of some southern conservatives, particularly some southern industrialists, since the early New Deal. Anti-communism was part of the staple of some southern politicians, the small change of the rhetoric of politicians like Herman Talmadge. It was not a major theme in the 1940s. Opponents of racial change in Georgia at that time did not need anti-communism to justify violent racial repression. It was later, as Michael Heale's study of little HUACs indicates, that southern anti-communism really flourished and stifled dissent. Massive resistance and black activism fuelled anti-communism, rather than anti-communism fuelling massive resistance. Many of the southern liberal politicians who espoused biracial politics in the 1940s and early 1950s were routinely red-baited, but equally routinely survived. Later, black activism, then, student anti-war protests in the 1960s fed anti-communism in southern states, as William Billingsley's new study of the Speaker Ban law in North Carolina, passed in 1963, demonstrates and the career of Jesse Helms exemplifies.²⁴ Race was the issue that overwhelmed southern liberals. But how did the mix of personal ideology and constituency pressure play out?

The standard reminiscence of southern politicians, from Governor John Patterson of Alabama to William Fulbright, is that whatever their rhetoric at the time, they were merely paying necessary obeisance to racist popular sentiment and, in reality, were working to moderate white responses and pave the way for inevitable racial change. As a black attorney ruefully noted to Calvin Trillin in 1960, if all the white politicians who said they were working backstage for racial justice actually were, "it must be pretty crowded there behind the scenes."²⁵

Southern liberal politicians were for the most part supporters of segregation after World War II. As David Chappell has pointed out, most southerners were. Few politicians publicly espoused the opposition to segregation that the radical New Dealers and labor leaders of the Southern Conference endorsed or that the academics and community leaders in the Southern Regional Council belatedly supported. But, as Chappell and Mills Thornton have reminded us, there are important gradations in the support of segregation which can dictate substantially different political action. Explicit racial appeals were not the stock in trade of the southern liberals. They did not always resist the temptation aggressively to use such appeals—Earl Long in 1939, Claude Pepper in 1944 were notable examples—but for the most part they eschewed violent racial appeals in favor of a pre-emptive strike to establish their segregationist credentials and then a rapid move on to advocacy of a substantive liberal economic agenda. On the whole they did not come from the black belt and they lacked the personal investment in status, the negative racial stereotypes, and the fear of a no-longer subservient black labor force that wedded black-belt whites to the determined maintenance of segregation.²⁶

What most liberals felt was a Jacksonian sense of fairness that blacks should neither suffer the inexcusable excesses of segregation, nor be denied the basic right to vote. Some had supported Claude Pepper campaign against the poll tax and backed federal legislation in 1942. Governors like McMath and Folsom resisted attempts by conservatives to reverse the effects of the *Smith v. Allwright* decision and appointed registrars committed to black voting rights. Earl Long sought to prevent New Orleans black voters being purged from the rolls—they were, he said, his niggers and he wanted their votes. Most Southerners who did not sign the Southern Manifesto in 1956 went on to support the Civil Rights Act of 1957, which they saw as a measure against voting discrimination, and, the younger ones went on to support the 1965 Voting Right Act.[27]

But the right to vote was intimately linked to education and economic growth. Education and economic opportunity was to be the key to gradual progress in racial matters. As Frank Smith said, "Large-scale economic progress was the only avenue likely to lead to a solution of the race problem in Mississippi." As he told Hodding Carter in 1949, outsiders had to understand "why the southern liberal or any southerner of progressive stripe must primarily concern himself with trying to improve the *economic* position of his people." Just as the solution to the region's racial problems lay in increasing prosperity for black and white southerners, so the region's economic problems could not be solved while southern blacks were mired in poverty. The keys to solving the region's racial problems were first, political rights for blacks to extend the electorate and make the system more responsive to the welfare needs of lower-income voters; second, federal economic assistance for the region to raise the living standards of both blacks and whites; third, education to enable African Americans in particular to take advantage of the economic opportunities created by liberal policies. Southern liberal governors saw federal aid to education as essential to meet this last objective. This policy was clearly prudential: it served the needs of the liberals' bi-racial coalition of supporters without driving a wedge in that alliance by raising the issue of segregation. But it also reflected a good deal of contemporary academic optimism that economic modernization would inevitably bring racial change, since segregation would be too inflexible and expensive for a modern society and higher incomes would lessen the competitive racism and insecurities of poor whites.[28]

It is this southern liberal agenda which Numan Bartley believes was undermined by the racial moralism and symbolic posturing of national liberals. It is easy to sympathize with Bartley's irritation at Truman's policy of "after the bang, the backtrack," the bold demand for legislation which embarrassed southern liberals but which he knew had no chance of passage. Demands for a permanent FEPC and the issue of the Powell amendment to proposals for federal aid to education were undoubtedly awkward for southern liberals. But I think that Bartley underestimates the extent to which social democratic redistributionist politics persisted among mainstream southern politicians into the 1950s. The popular front liberalism of the SCHW was not an economic reform program undermined by the imposition of a national civil rights agenda. The SCHW was race-baited and red-baited for its own indigenous racial radicalism. His argument that the targeting of de jure segregation, particularly segregated education, was misguided, seems to be me a little misplaced on two grounds. First, it assumes that tackling de jure segregation was somehow a goal that had nothing to do with the aspirations of southern blacks active in the voter-registration and union-organizing drives of the 1940s. Second, it assumes that a concentration on extending the franchise would not have aroused the same powerful opposition that desegregating the schools provoked. The violent resistance to extending voting rights in Mississippi throughout this period rather belies that assumption. As Jeff Norrell showed in Macon County, Alabama, black-belt leaders like Sam Engelhardt realized that school desegregation was probably inevitable. What they did not want to see was black voting. As Englehardt recalled, "Everybody has an angle when they get in [politics]. I was worried . . . about the tax assessor . . . because of all our holdings. That was my angle—to protect ourselves. Not only me, but my family. My aunts, uncles, and cousins owned land." Black voting would mean black tax assessors, "If you have a nigger tax assessor what would he do to you?" he asked a journalist in 1956.[29]

The gradualist liberal agenda presupposed a regional compromise on race: the South would put its own racial house in order, the federal government would back off its civil rights agenda. Harry Ashmore, the editor of the *Arkansas Gazette*, and liberal Arkansas representatives Brooks Hays and James Trimble, with William Fulbright's encouragement, attempted to establish the ground rules for this compromise in 1949. The South would make good its commitment to gradual racial change by eliminating lynching, removing the obstacles to full political participation by African Americans, and by striving for genuine equality in the provision of black education. In return the national government would be patient and back off counter-productive demands for immediate desegregation.[30]

The Arkansas Plan received little support in either the North or the South. Southern liberals may have espoused the necessity for gradual racial change, but they did little in the run-up to the Brown decision to lay out a strategy for achieving that gradual change. They continued piecemeal to protect black votes, fight for increased appropriations for black institutions and appoint some African Americans to government office and to state Democratic party positions. The coherent strategy in these years came from conservatives in Mississippi and South Carolina who mounted a massive drive genuinely to equalize school facilities in an effort to forestall a school desegregation decision. Liberal politicians were inhibited from that sort of program by the nagging realization that the Supreme Court would not necessarily protect separate but equal.

v

If the liberals anticipated *Brown,* which in retrospect most of them did, they did not share this knowledge with their constituents. Their standard response was that they thought that segregated schooling was the best for both races and that the Court had not ruled yet. In many ways they remained in control of the race issue in the years after 1950, even through 1955. Sid McMath attributed neither of his two defeats, for governor in 1952, for the senate in 1954, to the race issue—rather to McCarthyism and the issue of unions. His liberal protégé, Orval Faubus, won election as the racially moderate candidate in both 1954 and 1956. John Sparkman was re-elected in 1954 without significant opposition, just as Lister Hill had been in 1950. Jim Folsom secured a second term as governor with the highest first primary vote in Alabama history. He enjoyed unprecedented success with the state legislature in 1955. Earl Long was elected to a third term as governor in Louisiana in 1955. Earl Black indeed has noted how rarely race surfaced as a major issue in gubernatorial elections in the South as a whole, 1950–1954. Albert Gore was elected to the Senate in 1952 and Estes Kefauver re-elected in Tennessee in 1954 against conservative, segregationist opposition.[31]

Kerr Scott was elected to the Senate after the Brown decision in 1954 despite a last-minute racial smear by his opponent when eastern North Carolina was flooded with a forged advertisement in which a Winston-Salem black leader endorsed Scott for his stand on non-segregation. As Terry Sanford, his campaign manager recalled, the vicious race-baiting campaign against Frank Graham four years earlier had seared minds in North Carolina:

the lesson to those who would heed it, [was] that the race issue is a terrible weapon and can be used with overwhelming effectiveness . . .

I learned a great deal out of that. I started keeping a notebook of how to deal with the racist campaign. In fact, I kept that notebook in a bureau in my bedroom and everytime I'd have a little thought about how to gig somebody and get around the issue, I'd make a note of it . . . I may have had twenty-five or thirty pages of notes in there. But I learned one thing and that is don't ever let them off the defensive.

Sanford put that lesson to good effect in 1954. He exposed the fraud, called in the SBI and FBI, secured confessions from one of the perpetrators and gave every possible publicity to the tactic.[32]

But Scott's success in fighting off that smear illustrated the dilemma southern liberals faced after the Brown decision. Sanford's anger at the smear was not because the statement by the Winston-Salem black was false—it was not; the African American was a genuine supporter of Scott. The anger was at the implication that Scott was not a supporter of segregation. What Scott had said when Brown was announced was that "I have always opposed, and still am opposed, to Negro and white children going to school together." Scott, as did all southern liberals, called for compliance with the law of the land, but also made it clear that he did not intend to run against popular sentiment. Other liberals, like Albert Gore, endorsed the decision more explicitly, but were still careful to point out that advocating compliance did not mean that they approved of the decision. Lyndon Johnson and Estes Kefauver both argued that people of goodwill at the local level should best resolve the matter.[33]

In 1954 and 1955 the contradictions in these stances were not exposed. In 1956 the liberals found it harder to square the political circle. In 1954 and 1955 it may have been, as Albert Gore recalled, that white southerners still did not think that school desegregation would actually happen. By 1956 they could be under no such illusion. The *Brown II* implementation decree, the petitions of African American parents to local school boards, for example in Dallas County, Alabama, and the appearance of black plaintiffs in court, for example in Little Rock, indicated that desegregation would eventually get under way. Conservative leaders throughout the South moved to alert white southerners of the danger and to impose conformity in defense of segregation. Citizens' Council leaders attempted to coerce local dissenters into silence. Black Belt leaders in the state legislatures attempted to prevent any local school board from stepping out of line and voluntarily complying with court-ordered school desegregation.

The authors of the Southern Manifesto, notably Harry Byrd, Strom Thurmond and Richard Russell, aimed to impose a regional "unity of action" and force the five or six southerners in the senate who Russell lamented were prepared to agree with the *Brown* decision, to get off the fence and proclaim their determination to resist the Supreme Court.[34]

Most southern liberal politicians did run for cover. Lister Hill, facing opposition from right-wing zealot John Crommelin, almost fell over himself in the rush to sign the Southern Manifesto. Indeed, Fulbright claimed that Hill signed without even reading it. Sparkman and the Alabama congressional delegation followed suit. Sparkman was soon being praised by Citizens Council leader, Sam Engelhardt, for his part in bringing about "a unified effort . . . in Congress by all the Southerners to uphold our traditions of segregation." William Fulbright claimed to have signed more reluctantly after changes were made in the draft of the Manifesto. His aides, anxious to disassociate him from the intemperate document, drafted a statement explaining why he would not sign: the Manifesto held out the "false illusion" that the Supreme Court decision could be overturned and would merely alienate non-southerners and make the task of resisting forcible federal intervention more difficult. Fulbright rejected their advice and remained convinced "that I wouldn't have survived politically if I hadn't taken the course I did." Kerr Scott in North Carolina made the same move, even more reluctantly. He had been deluged with mail from the North Carolina Patriots in early 1956 and did "not intend to run counter to the majority of our people in North Carolina which is against integration." He changed his mind and attempted to take his name off the list of signers but he was too late. Brooks Hays, like Scott, regretted signing. He only signed when Faubus came to Washington and persuaded Hays and James Trimble, at Trimble's hospital bedside, to sign "if we did not do something along that line to quiet the people down, that we would find what he called the Ku Klux Klan and the extreme Citizens' Council groups taking over the political life of the state, and that the racists and the radicals would displace the moderates."[35]

It was a decisive move for men like Hill, Scott and Fulbright. Hill cut himself from contact with anybody that might taint him with racial liberalism. As his old campaign manager Richard Rives started making landmark decisions protecting black rights on the Fifth Circuit Court, so Hill disowned him. They had offices in the same federal building in Montgomery, yet Hill never talked to Rives from 1956 to the time he retired from the

Senate in 1968. He cut off all personal and public contact with Supreme Court justice Hugo Black, the man to whom Hill owed his senate seat. He even took a portrait of Black off the wall in his own home, lest any visitor suspect that he had any sympathy with the judge's views. Even as Virginia Durr voted for Hill in 1962, she noted sadly that she had not talked to her old family friend for eight years.[36]

Fulbright continued to appoint liberal staff who attempted to push him towards a more moderate stand on civil rights, but he refused to divert from his opposition to any federally-inspired racial change. During the Little Rock school crisis, Sid McMath pleaded with Fulbright to return to the state and make a television address to call for compliance with the law but he failed to do so. His staff urged him to return from an Interparliamentary Union meeting in London and make a statement but Fulbright used his absence in London as a justification for refusing to comment. He never abandoned his belief that hypocritical neo-abolitionists in the North were attempting to impose alien change on the South. He fully participated in the filibusters against civil rights legislation in 1964 and 1965 and voted against the open housing act in 1968. He did this despite the fact that his assistants believed in 1964 that they had persuaded him to vote for a closure motion to end the filibuster. He did this despite LBJ's entreaties. He did this despite the mounting evidence that business interests and even conservative religious groups in Arkansas by the mid-1960s were prepared to accept the desegregation of public accommodations and the protection of black voting.[37]

Kerr Scott's aide, Bill Cochrane, was always sad that he had not been able to take the Senator's name off the list of signers of the Manifesto. Scott, he recalled, never believed in that kind of "strong stuff." But North Carolina leaders had brought forward the Pearsall Plan, the state's own version of massive resistance which would allow local schools to close rather than desegregate. The state's leaders aimed to stir up segregationist sentiment, to persuade whites in eastern North Carolina that school desegregation could be avoided in the foreseeable future. Scott endorsed the Pearsall plan. His protégé Terry Sanford would continue to support the plan right through 1964. North Carolina's resistance succeeded so well that fewer African American children were attending white schools in 1964 than in any other southern state.[38]

Liberals who took a bolder line nevertheless offered a precisely circumscribed alternative. Sid McMath recalled "there were people, intelligent and educated people, and people in positions of leadership that knew it [desegregation] was inevitable." People in Little Rock were prepared, he said, to accept the Blossom plan for school desegregation in 1957. "The Virgil Blossom plan, if Faubus had stayed out of it, would have gone in and worked . . . if they'd had proper leadership at the time the Central High school thing never would have happened." But McMath himself admits that the Little Rock crisis caught him unawares: too late did he and Winthrop Rockefeller go round to see Faubus to try and dissuade him from his strategy of defiance. Community leaders in Little Rock had co-operated with Blossom in winning over elite opinion: they had made no effort to win over the support of lower-income whites whose children would attend Central High. It was as if they thought that if they kept quiet school desegregation would slip in without arousing mass white out-rage.[39]

Similarly in Alabama Folsom proved incapable of devising a successful strategy to confront the three challenges he faced in 1956: the barrage of anti-desegregation measures that were going to pass the state legislature, what to do about the bus boycott in his own state capital, and what to do about the court-ordered entry of Autherine Lucy to the University of Alabama. He might denounce the legislature's interposition resolution as futile but he persisted in his public belief that you could maintain segre-gation *and* uphold the Supreme Court decision and advanced no alterna-tive strategy for facilitating gradual desegregation. In Montgomery, secret meetings with black leaders seemed to convince him of their steadfast intent, indeed, he may have encouraged them to step up their demands to call for the complete dismantling of segregation on the buses. But his call for a biracial commission to solve the problem was irrelevant and inef-fectual when white leaders were simply not prepared to negotiate. As the mob gathered determined to prevent Lucy from enrolling at the Univer-sity, Folsom was on a drinking and fishing spree. By the time he sobered up and rang his office from a payphone in a country store, the mob had won. It would take another seven years of increasingly racist politics before the federal courts would finally end Alabama's massive resistance.[40]

The congressmen who refused to sign the Southern Manifesto also offered a cautious strategy for racial change. What they wanted was token compliance whereby the issue of school desegregation could be left to local men and women of goodwill of both races. This was an important argument against the massive resisters who were determined not to let local school boards have the discretion to desegregate. But there was a substantial element of wishful thinking in the liberals' approach. The moderate strategy begged the question of what would happen if local white men and women of goodwill would not agree to desegregate, because the liberals had also set their face firmly against what they called "forced integration." Their faith that economic growth would produce gradual racial change also involved a good deal of wishful thinking. Southern business leaders, as Jim Cobb has shown, were prepared for the longest time to believe that they could have economic modernization and preserve traditional patterns of race relations at the same time. They were prepared to tolerate very considerable damage to the region and their communities before they decided that the cost of resistance was too high. Finally, southern liberal politicians, like southern conservatives, could not really envisage African Americans dictating the timetable of racial change. It was not surprising that Albert Gore, Jim Wright and Dante Fascell could refuse to sign the Southern Manifesto, vote for the 1957 and 1965 Civil Rights Acts which dealt with the right to vote, but voted against the 1964 Civil Rights Act.[41]

VI

Did the white southern liberal politicians have to be so cautious? Did they have to be so deferential defer to white segregationists sentiment?

A historian should not lightly second-guess the conclusions of a Frank Smith, a Carl Elliott or a Hale Boggs from Deep South states who decided that they could not afford to take a public stand in favor of black civil rights or school desegregation. The fate of two North Carolinian non-signers of the Southern Manifesto, Charles Deane and Thurmond Chatham, particularly the conscientious constituency servant Deane, shows that the perils of electoral retribution were real enough. It is difficult to see that there was much room for maneuver in Mississippi, South Carolina, and perhaps in Louisiana. But the survival of Estes Kefauver and Albert Gore in Tennessee suggests that liberals could survive where a significant part of the state political leadership defined the parameters for debate in such a way that racial moderates earned a measure of protection.[42]

In Arkansas, where his own brother-in-law had presided over school desegregation in Fayetteville, it is difficult to see that William Fulbright had to be so cautious. Fulbright's chief assistant liked to drive off potential opposition by depriving possible candidates of any sources of campaign funds in the fall before a re-election year. When Fulbright signed the Manifesto in 1956 he was already assured of the backing of the single most powerful source of funds in the state. Witt Stephens was firmly behind Fulbright because of the senator's support for the Arkansas Louisiana Gas Company. Fulbright was still on close terms with the Faubus administration.[43] In Alabama, where the state's three leading elected politicians were all liberals and where the state House delegation was the most liberal in the South, it seems that politicians could have afforded a more moderate racial stance. Hill faced no serious opposition in 1950. In 1956 his supporters assured him that he had nothing to worry about. Sparkman admitted that the "only really hard" campaign he ever had was in his first race for the House of Representatives in the 1930s. Subsequently he was never forced into a run-off in the whole of his political career.[44]

Closet moderates justified their racial caution by maintaining that they needed to stay in office to reserve their influence for racial moderation and economic liberalism. Yet they faced more and more right-wing segregationist opponents, some of whom would see to Frank Smith and Carl Elliott's defeats in 1962. And increasingly they had to moderate their economic liberalism as their constituents responded more and more favorably to the anti-government rhetoric of the segregationists.[45]

Most southern liberal politicians found it difficult to envisage the ending of segregation. Even those who believed that segregation was wrong were understandably in no hurry to give up the privileges that the system brought to them as whites. Some, like Charles Deane, had undoubtedly come to the conclusion that segregation was wrong from a Christian and moral point of view, at least once the Supreme Court had pointed the way. Such decisions were, on the whole, guarded and individual: they secured support from state and regional church groups, but much less often from local congregations. Most put a premium on obedience to the law. But such views were not likely to lead politicians to risk a crusade or campaign for compliance with school desegregation in the 1950s as long as they believed that the mass of white sentiment was opposed to racial change.

But, as David Chappell points out, staunch segregationists were by no means equally convinced that the majority of whites were zealously determined to defend segregation. Most liberal politicians believed that whites were so stirred up on the race issue that politicians had either to retreat and become "closet moderates" or adopt a stealth-like approach to racial change. Conservative leaders, by contrast, feared that public opinion was insufficiently aroused on the race issue, that most southerners were too likely to accept the inevitability of compliance with the Supreme Court. The difference was that conservatives, passionately committed in the 1950s to segregation, were prepared to mount a righteous crusade to convince white southerners that desegregation was not inevitable, that white supremacy could be protected. Liberal and moderate politicians, personally much less passionate about the issue of desegregation, were not prepared to take their case to the people. In a battle between politicians prepared to take their case for massive resistance to the people and politicians who were reluctant to campaign for gradualism, there could only be one winner.[46]

One reason why southern liberal politicians were so resigned was that they much more attuned to the passions of their white constituents than to the impatience of their black supporters. White liberals were unable to penetrate the ritual of condescension and deference that characterized their relations with black leaders. Their relationships with the African American community were conducted at a distance. We do not yet know enough about how politicians secured black support in the politics of the 1940s and 1950s. They rarely campaigned directly for black support. Instead they approached, usually through intermediaries, local leaders in the black community who delivered their community's vote as a bloc. Kerr Scott used a funeral director in Winston-Salem and a janitor at East Carolina Teacher's College. Folsom used his chauffeur, Winston Craig. When Charles Deane, perhaps the most liberal southern congressman, faced a tough primary battle after refusing to sign the Southern Manifesto, he had to write to James Taylor at North Carolina College in Durham to check out the names of African Americans in his own district he could contact. To no avail, the black vote in Rockingham was delivered to his opponent by the sheriff's contacts in the black community. Revealingly, Sid McMath, when interviewed by John Egerton, could barely remember the names of the African American leaders he dealt with. When Terry Sanford ran for governor in 1960, he claims to have turned down the offer of the black vote in Durham in the first primary. Instead he arranged for the vote to go to another candidate. He knew he was going to need a second primary and he did not want his opponent to be able to identify him as a recipient of the black bloc vote. By contrast, when a younger politician like Dante Fascell ran for Congress in 1954 he recalled that he was the first candidate in Miami to campaign for the black vote "in daylight."[47]

African American leaders understood the system and the limitations of their leverage. In 1950 when Strom Thurmond ran against Olin Johnston for the Senate, the Rev. I. DeQuincy Newman explained that "It was a matter of choosing between a rattler and a moccasin." Johnston campaigned by attacking Thurmond for appointing a black doctor, a "nigger physician" said Johnston, to the state medical board. But African Americans remembered, as Modjeska Simkins put it, that "Strom vilified Negroes in 1948 . . . and we swore vengeance." An estimated 50,000 African Americans voted overwhelmingly for Johnston, who won by less than 28,000 votes. Sometimes politicians unexpectedly came up against undiluted African American sentiment. Ed Dunaway recalls taking Sid McMath in 1949 to a meeting of the Urban League in Little Rock. Harry Bass gave the secretary's report. According to Dunaway, "he got up there and started haranguing and waving his arms and he said that there—this had nothing to do with any report of activities—he said 'there is absolutely nothing wrong with intermarriage between Blacks and whites' . . . Well, I thought Sid was very uneasy as you can imagine, and I was absolutely, almost purple and finally said, he just kept on, finally Sid said, 'Ed, I can't sit here and listen to this.' So we got up and walked out of the damn meeting."[48]

But more often prudent black leaders, "racial diplomats" as Numan Bartley describes them, told white politicians what they thought the white politicians wanted to hear. In 1956, for example, I. S. McLinton in Arkansas assured Fulbright's aide that the black community recognized that the Arkansas senator had no alternative but to sign the Southern Manifesto. Most white politicians were shielded from the growing sense of grievance in the black community: they did not have the same personal feel for the humiliations and impatience of the black community that they had for the fears of the white community.[49]

As a result this first post-war system of bi-racial politics simply could not satisfy the demands of black voters. Montgomery provided an early example of how politics failed to yield results and pushed African Americans into direct action. As Mills Thornton showed, black voters constituted 7.5% of the electorate and held the balance of power between two white factions. They used this leverage to secure concessions from white politicians on the appointment of black policemen, representatives on the parks board, and better treatment on the buses. When Mrs. Parks was arrested, black leaders intended to use the boycott simply as a temporary method of increasing that leverage. It was the intransigence of the white community that negated that form of political negotiation and drove the black leaders to the courts to seek the complete overthrow of bus segregation and a sustained boycott. By contrast in Mobile Joseph Langan actively solicited black support in his race for the state legislature in 1946 and worked closely with NAACP leader John LeFlore, protected black voters and worked to equalize teachers' salaries. In 1953 he was elected to the city commission with black support which he publicly welcomed. In office he worked with LeFlore and the Non-Partisan Voters' League to secure urban renewal, desegregate public accommodations, schools, and the University of South Alabama. Because the system was responsive, African Americans in Mobile eschewed direct action protest. [50]

In most communities, however, biracial politics in its 1950s variant increasingly could not deliver the changes in segregation that black community leaders and their supporters wanted. Direct action, rather than electoral politics and negotiation, and demands for the immediate, rather than gradual, end of segregation increasingly became the tactics of the black community.

This is a process of racial protest and political change that is rather different from that outlined by Michael Klarman and David Chappell. Klarman sees the violent white supremacist backlash after Brown producing ultimate federal intervention. Chappell sees the divisions in the white community over the best way to defend segregation being shrewdly exploited by the civil rights movement. My interpretation is that white conservative aggression and white liberal fatalism ensured that the system of biracial politics failed to deliver the changes that African Americans wanted. African Americans, rather than exploiting white divisions, were forced into direct action tactics by white unity. The white backlash to these protests generated the political dynamic of the 1960s where federal intervention mandated racial change and whites had to come to terms, belatedly, with the implications of inevitable racial change.

VII

No white southerner could dictate the timetable of racial change in the 1960s. The civil rights movement from below and the federal government from outside executed a squeeze play on the South. One southern liberal was, however, a key player in this exercise, Lyndon B. Johnson. In moves that brought joy to his old radical New Deal friends from the South, Aubrey Williams and Virginia Durr, Johnson secured the passage of coercive federal legislation, rather than voluntary local agreements, to provide for immediate, rather than gradual, change in public accommodations and voting in the Civil Rights Acts of 1964 and 1965. Johnson's Great Society also produced the economic and welfare reforms that southern liberals had been pushing for in the 1940s and federal aid to education, another southern liberal article of faith. Kerr Scott's former campaign manager, Terry Sanford, saw his creation, the North Carolina Fund, serve as both a model and an ally of the War on Poverty.[51]

In the politics produced by civil rights protest on the one hand and white backlash on the other the white southern liberal politicians had little role to play. The dominant figures of the 1960s were the good ol' boy segregationists and business leaders.[52]

The short-term consequence of the failure of the system of biracial politics was that the lower-income whites who potentially supported liberal candidates on economic issues, increasingly supported segregationists in the late 1950s and 1960 who combined a "common man good ol' boy appeal" with the staunchest rhetorical defense of white supremacy, men like Orval Faubus, Ross Barnett, Lester Maddox and pre-eminently, George Wallace. The attempts by old southern liberals—McMath and Folsom in 1962, Carl Elliott and Ellis Arnall in 1966—to halt the tide were doomed.[53]

The leaders who finally recognized the inevitability of federally-imposed racial change were business leaders who belatedly recognized the damage to their community's economies that massive resistance was causing. As Jim Cobb showed almost twenty years ago, southern business leaders moved to help their communities to take the first steps towards integration. As Sanford Brookshire, President of the Chamber of Commerce and then Mayor of Charlotte recalled, "It seems odd now that . . . I, and I think the rest of the white community throughout the South were overlooking the legal and moral aspects of the problem . . . the Chamber was aware and concerned about the boycotts and disruption of business in [other cities], apprehensive that Charlotte might suffer in a like manner unless the protest movement could be contained here." As Harry Golden acidly noted, Charlotte's business leaders "would elect Martin Luther

King or Malcolm X mayor if somehow one of them could give them a guarantee of no labor unions and no minimum wage for laundry workers." Two white leaders were crucial in negotiating a settlement to the racial crisis in Birmingham in 1963. One was the reform mayor Albert Boutwell, elected after David Vann and other young professionals had swept out the old city commission government. The other was Sid Smyer of the Senior Citizens Committee. What had these two leaders been doing when liberal Jim Folsom was confronting the racial crisis in Alabama in 1956? Boutwell had been the mastermind behind the massive resistance in the state legislature. Sid Smyer, a leading former Dixiecrat, was busy in the North Alabama Methodist Conference. He was making sure that the Conference did not unite with another jurisdiction that was integrated and he was orchestrating lay pressure on any Methodist minister who showed signs of departing from racial orthodoxy.[54]

The passage of the 1965 Voting Rights Act and the dramatic extension of black voter registration led to a biracial coalition very different from the lower-income alliance that southern liberal politicians had put together in the 1940s and 50s. Now affluent whites and blacks formed a cross-class biracial coalition based on shared interests in peaceful racial change. In the 1970s there were new young faces adept at coalition building— moderate enough on racial issues to satisfy their black constituency, conservative enough on social and economic issues to appeal to white voters. Racial moderation was allied to business progressivism. That combination was too powerful for William Fulbright. When Dale Bumpers challenged the senator in 1974 the 125,000 registered black voters in Arkansas blacks voted 4 to 1 to retire Fulbright from office.[55]

But alongside the bright New South politicians and the transmogrification of old-style segregationists like Wallace and Thurmond who now had to adjust to the reality of African American voting, there was another shift, a shift that put the final nail in the southern liberal coffin. Lower-income white voters who had been conservative and anti-government on race now became conservative and anti-government on economic issues as well.

Whites in eastern North Carolina had been the backbone of the liberal wing of the Democratic Party in the state since the New Deal. In 1964 whites in eastern Carolina resisted the blandishments of Barry Goldwater, no doubt because of the threat he posed to tobacco price supports. African American assertiveness had not yet impinged on their daily lives. But after 1964 school desegregation finally came to the East, albeit in token form. It was one thing for the affluent whites of the Piedmont to tolerate racial change when they could retreat to their white suburbs or send their children to private schools. These options were not open to whites in eastern Carolina. African American assertiveness was even more threatening in areas where large black populations would be competing with whites for scarce economic resources. White taxpayers lost sympathy with the redistributionist spending and welfare programs of the Great Society, which seemed to them to reward lawlessness and rioting. They saw traditional cultural and religious values undermined by rioters, privileged students at Chapel Hill who protested the Vietnam War and burned the flag, and a Supreme Court which banned school prayer, opposed segregated schools, yet sanctioned pornography and protected the rights of criminals. The whites confronted these changes when the tobacco economy they depended on was being revolutionized by mechanization. Driven from the land, they had to adjust to new work disciplines in low-wage sewing factories, pickle plants and poultry-processing facilities. As Linda Flowers noted, "That they were all the victims of an utterly impersonal concentration of trends and forces, of history in fact, was not so satisfying an explanation as that somebody was in charge and caused the bottom to drop out." The scapegoats were easy to find: a liberal federal government, the national Democratic Party, and blacks.[56]

    The first response was to join the Klan. Between 1964 and 1967 North Carolina had the largest Klan outside of Alabama and Mississippi. In 1968 they would vote for George Wallace. But no man was better positioned to tap their anger at the liberal media, communists in Chapel Hill, and Martin Luther King than Jesse Helms who had been addressing their concerns daily first on the radio, then on WRAL TV 5. As Frank Rouse, Helms ally in the Republican Party noted, these eastern North Carolina Democrats were "rednecks . . . country . . . rural . . . extremely honest . . . plainspoken and ultraconservative . . . if not religious on a day to day basis . . . he would be inherent Southern Baptist . . . he may not go to church and Sunday School every week and go to choir practice on Thursday night, but because of his environment and because of his family, he would be religious." These rednecks compromised their political morality a bit by voting for Wallace in 1968, said Rouse, and that broke the bond. By 1972 they were ready to vote for Jesse Helms. That religious conservatism and economic insecurity was but a forerunner of what would happen in the South as whole with the rise of the Christian Right and the economic insecurities of ordinary whites whose median income declined from the 1970s.[57]

So Jesse Helms, the supporter of the liberal Kerr Scott who had fostered a coalition of lower-income whites and blacks in the 1940s, had become the lily-white conservative Republican of the 1970s.

VII

Texas-born political scientist V. O. Key had confidently predicted that the collapse of the main institutional supports of conservative power, which duly took place, and the extension of political participation and competition, which also duly took place, would substitute the politics of economics for the politics of race. The forces of southern liberalism would be greatly strengthened and the "have-nots" who lost out in traditional southern politics would at last receive tangible benefits from the distribution of government largesse.

The politics of race did not disappear. The extension of political participation and competition did not in the long run produce the liberal, class-based, biracial coalition of lower-income blacks and whites that Key expected. Instead it produced a political system which pitted an all-white Republican party against a Democratic party that secures 90% of the African-American vote but which to win sufficient white support to gain power has to espouse conservative economic policies.[58]

This polarization, as Numan Bartley strongly and rightly asserts, did not come about because in some immutable fashion "the font of southern racism was [always] poor and working-class whites." It came about because confronted by the pressure for racial change in the 1950s, conservative leaders in the South were determined to convince ordinary southern whites that segregation could be preserved. White liberal politicians by contrast were paralyzed by their belief that mass white segregationist sentiment was overwhelming. Because their own commitment to racial change was so limited and their awareness of African American demands so second-hand, they could not devise a strategy for gradual racial change that could deliver substantive change to the African Americans who supported them in the 1950s variant of bi-racial politics.[59]

African Americans eschewed politics therefore for direct action. The pincer movement of the civil rights movement from below and the federal government from above imposed immediate and rapid racial change on the South. The calm with which the South reacted to these changes gave the lie to the dire warnings of the segregationists. It was, of course, lower-income whites who bore the brunt of the physical reality of desegregation on a day-to-day basis in the South and they did not face it in a major way until the late 1960s, when their own economic future was uncertain. Their frustration with a government that imposed racial change and failed to halt cultural change spilled over into a hostility to government intervention in the economic sphere.

The dream of a liberal biracial politics was over.

The Struggle Against Equality

Conservative Intellectuals in the Civil Rights Era, 1954–1975

RICHARD H. KING

If any single issue has "belonged" to post-World War II American liberalism, it is race. In domestic politics, the Democratic Party became the party of racial liberalism and the home base of African Americans, while the Republican Party, once the party of Lincoln and abolitionism, saw its black support all but disappear by the end of the 1960s. Indeed, post-war liberalism, particularly in the South, was defined largely in terms of its civil rights commitment. Internationally, the post-war, moral-legal consensus on race and ethnicity represented a triumph for what might be called liberal universalism in the aftermath of the Holocaust and in response to decolonization of the Third World.[1]

With this post-war consensus in mind, I want to examine the way that conservative thinkers engaged with issues of race and civil rights as an important, but neglected, chapter in the intellectual and moral history of American conservatism in the first three decades after World War II with an emphasis upon the two decades that followed the 1954 *Brown v. Board of Education* decision handed down by the Supreme Court in May of that year. My analysis will focus less on the positions conservative intellectuals took on specific issues—though that will inevitably be part of the story—and more on the way their responses to issues and events were shaped by conservative principles distilled from more systematic conservative ideologies. The bulk of the paper will explore various meanings of equality as a way of understanding American conservative thought on the issues of race and civil rights.[2]

SETTING THE SCENE

Despite the desire of many conservative intellectuals such as T. S. Eliot to revitalize a "Christian" culture after World War II, a not inconsiderable bit of moral impertinence in its own right, post-war American conserva-

113

tive thinkers largely eschewed blatant or even subtle anti-Semitism. The founder of *National Review* (1956) and impresario of post-war intellectual conservatism, William F. Buckley, rejected his own father's anti-Semitism and brought together a healthy mix of Jews and Gentiles (Protestant and Catholics) as contributors to the magazine and as members of its editorial board.

As the Cold War unfolded there was a good bit of sympathy for the Federal Republic of Germany in conservative circles. Eugene Davidson, the second editor of the conservative journal, *Modern Age*, wrote a history of the German resistance to Hitler that sought to rehabilitate the reputation of a certain type of German conservative who had opposed Hitler. And though *National Review* could tread close to the anti-Semitic line in occasional comments on the state of Israel before 1967, liberal journals as well reacted with a certain skepticism to Israel's decision, for instance, to put Adolph Eichmann on trial in 1961.[3] In general, American conservatives were not fellow-travelers, after the fact, of European fascism, much less of Nazism, though the two authoritarian regimes on the Iberian peninsula were generally treated with leniency. If nothing else, anti-communism consumed too large a proportion of conservative energies to allow room for anti-Semitism.

Nor were all conservative intellectuals racists just because most of them were militant critics of Supreme Court decisions on desegregation, of Congressional legislation dealing with civil rights, and of liberal attitudes toward race and civil rights in general. Though George Nash's judgement is, I think, overly generous, it can stand as a rough, first approximation to the truth. Writing about *National Review*, Nash observes:

> Many prominent right-wing intellectuals had been critics of the civil rights movement from the beginning. *National Review* persistently and forcefully challenged the integrationists' tactics and ultimate goals, despite the initially adverse climate of opinion. The conservative leadership strenuously abjured any notions of innate black inferiority.[4]

One factor which shaped the conservative intellectuals' position on racial matters was that by the early 1970s the Republican Party in particular and conservatism in general had found a popular/populist voice of its own. This was of course helped along mightily by "white backlash" against the civil rights revolution itself which was originally triggered off by George Wallace's emergence as a national figure in the 1960s. This political development presented a problem and an opportunity for conservative think-ers. On the one hand, intellectual conservatism had always included a certain distaste for mass democratic politics. Yet, it now found itself the "(white) people's" champions on race and civil rights, while remaining high-minded defenders of educational and cultural standards, which racial integration allegedly threatened. In the wake of the 1960s, conser-vatism became the respectable ideology of white particularism and thus partially transcended class, ethnic or regional boundaries within the white population.

But what was the ideology of conservatism? A definition of conserva-tism, like that of liberalism, is extremely hard to settle on. Alan Brinkley certainly captures a certain truth about American conservatism when he describes it as more a motley cluster of values, attitudes, beliefs, and ideo-logical fragments than a unified ideology. But he is on much less certain ground with his claim that the basic principles of American conservatism "are not readily distinguishable from the liberal tradition."[5] This would arguably be correct for the libertarian tradition, articulated by economist Milton Friedman and Austrian Friedrich Hayek, in which ideas of nega-tive liberty and individualism play a prominent role. Similarly, there are parallels, though nothing approaching an exact fit, between the conserva-tive universalism of the natural law/natural rights position developed by Leo Strauss and his followers, and the liberal rights "talk" which enjoyed a revival in the 1960s. Brinkley is on most firm footing in reference to several of the founding figures of post-1970 neo-conservatism, especially Daniel Patrick Moynihan, Daniel Bell and Nathan Glazer. If communism was described as "liberalism in a hurry" in the Popular Front of the 1930s, neo-conservatism, a crucial element in the post-1960s Popular Front of the Right, was liberalism "with the brakes on." Or, as Irving Kristol once quipped "a neo-conservative is a liberal who had been mugged by real-ity."[6] Indeed, since the Reagan Revolution, even a bit before, Moynihan, Bell and Glazer have moved back toward their natural liberal home.

But Brinkley's claim fails to accommodate traditionalist conservatism, especially in its southern incarnations. This traditionalist conservatism has historically valued social and cultural hierarchy, an organic conception of society, a commitment to religious principles, support for traditional val-ues and the values of tradition, and an emphasis upon responsibilities not rights. Beyond that, and not surprisingly, southern conservative intellec-tuals seemed less troubled than their northern counterparts with the white racial ideology that continued to justify opposition to desegregation. Traditionalist conservatism was—and is—also deeply suspicious of social sciences and of the modern worship of technology. Overall, traditionalist conservatism has rejected the "modernist project" of progress through reason as applied to the natural and human world. Such a cluster of positions would seem to stand considerably at odds with the settled principles of American liberalism.

Among conservative intellectuals, political theorists and philosophers, literary and cultural critics generally outnumbered social scientists, except perhaps for economists, in the first quarter century after the end of World War II. Two separate, though related, factors explain this. First, since the Enlightenment, the conservative tradition has been deeply suspicious of the intellectual and political implications of the social sciences. In Straussian terms, the modern social sciences are grounded in the fact-value distinction, which implies a "value free" stance toward social and political arrangements. "Objective" political and social science are thus seen as agnostic about the best political regime. Furthermore, the application of so-called scientific concepts to human affairs instrumentalizes human beings and relativizes and historicizes basic values. On this view, social and political science were themselves part of the problem not the solution to the malaise of modernity.[7]

Second, after 1945 and until the early 1970s, the social sciences in America were dominated by broadly liberal ideas and assumptions, particularly on race. As both cause and effect of this sea change, Gunnar Myrdal's *An American Dilemma* (1944) was a species of universalist social science, and the Myrdalism paradigm reigned supreme well into the 1960s. This meant that relatively few conservatives worked at the cutting edge of the social sciences in the three decades after World War II, especially not in educational psychology and the study of race.[8] Thus, conservatives were placed very much at a disadvantage when arguing about matters of racial equality in scientific terms. Indeed, the most surprising thing about the post-war conservative intellectuals was their general attempt to steer clear of explicit arguments for white racial superiority— though here northern and southern conservatives tend to part company. But even James J. Kilpatrick, editor of the *Richmond News-Leader* and leading publicist against school desegregation, agreed that "whether the Negro's shortcomings are innate" was irrelevant, while some social scientists defended racial differences vigorously yet were at pains to deny that they were racists.[9]

ANTI-MODERNISTS ALL!

What southern conservative M. E. Bradford said of one-time Agrarian Andrew Lytle—"his reiterative subject is declension"—was true of practically all forms of post-war conservatism.[10] At its most sanguine, the conservative grand narrative placed conflict at the center of historical process, with the forces of decline and decadence generally having the upper hand. Fellow southern conservative Richard Weaver located the fateful turning point in the history of the West in the nominalism controversy of the fourteenth century when the unity of spirit and matter, the transcendent and the real, was rent asunder. Eric Voegelin, a refugee German philosopher who taught at LSU in the 1940s and 1950s and was one of the spiritual fathers of post-war conservatism, traced the origins of modernity back to the thirteenth century where he found it in Joachim of Flores' vision of history as divided into three ages or empires. The twentieth century manifestations of this vision of history and politics were most obviously Nazism, and its vision of "The Third Reich," and Marxism-Leninism which posits the end of history with the emergence of a classless society. The basic impulse behind the spirit of modernity which Voegelin called "gnosticism" was the attempt to "immanentize the eschaton," Voegelinian lingo for the effort to bring about "a change in the nature of man and the establishment of a transfigured society." For the German-Jewish, refugee political philosopher, Leo Strauss, the spiritual history of the West reached a point of crisis in the thought of Hobbes and Machiavelli and, more recently, with Nietzsche and Weber; while for Friedrich Hayek, not only the Bolshevik Revolution but also the British welfare state was a way station on the "road to serfdom." Other conservatives such as T. S. Eliot identified a "dissociation of sensibility" in the seventeenth century, while the father of modern conservatism, Edmund Burke, located the beginning the French Revolution as the beginning of the end. For neo-conservative intellectuals, it was the 1960s which represented the beginning of the end of modernity. For conservative thinkers, then, decline was not just an incidental or all too common fact of modern life; it was inherent in the nature of modernity.[11]

Accompanying this narrative of decline was the belief that most, if not all, of the spiritual/moral crises of modernity derived from the attempt to subject human society and human nature to rational transformation. The sources of Ronald Reagan's characterization of the Soviet Union under the ideological sway of Marxism-Leninism as the "evil empire" can be found in this early post-war conservative political theology. Though it is tempting to read conservative anti-communism as the expression of its infatuation with capitalism, things are more complicated than that. Southern conservatives such Weaver and Bradford, not to mention the original Vanderbilt Agrarians, tended to see socialism and finance capitalism as twin, not unrelated, evils. In Bradford's words: "atomistic or impersonal corporate business and the omnicompetent state" are "two faces of one phenomenon."[12] The southern distaste for "abstraction" often just meant opposition to social change imposed from the outside in the form of social engineering. In indicting "rationalism in politics," English political philosopher Michael Oakeshott observed wryly of Hayek's swinging attack on state planning in *The Road to Serfdom*: "A plan to resist all planning may be better than its opposite, but it belongs to the same style of politics." And while most conservatives concentrated their moral fire on communism, Voegelin's *New Science of Politics* (1952) reminded its readers that "the German Revolution," with its traits of "economic materialism, racist biology, corrupt psychology, scientism and technological ruthlessness," was a prime example of "modernity without restraint."[13] Voegelin identified the sources of Nazism not in conservatism but in the revolutionary tradition of the Right so strong in Germany. Similarly, southern conservative intellectuals such as William Alexander Percy and Weaver offered a class analysis of the origins of Nazism, their dominant assumption being that the best check on the rise of such plebeian, mass movements would have been to maintain the aristocracy in Europe in power.

Such change as did come should arise organically out of the workings of society (the traditionalist position) or of the market (the libertarian tradition) rather than being spearheaded by State action. Armed with a theo-politics and grand narrative of decline, post-war America conservative thinkers tended to demonize the ideologies of planned change, such as liberalism and socialism, in particularly virulent terms. Parallel to the McCarthyite assault on liberal politics, Voegelin, for instance, engaged in some theo-political red-baiting of his own: ". . . if liberalism is understood as the immanent salvation of man and society, communism certainly is its most radical expression; it is an evolution that was already anticipated by

John Stuart Mill's faith in the ultimate advent of communism for mankind."[14] Andrew Lytle offered his own down-home demonization when, with apparent seriousness, he claimed that "liberal democracy is a part of the Christian drama, but it represents the devil."[15]

Moreover, for philosophically inclined conservatives, the liberal State was the institutional agent of the gnostic impulse. From this perspective, the civil rights movement was the usually unwitting agent of State efforts at massive social engineering to impose black rights and usher in a new millennium of compulsory equality. Indeed, because conservatives could only see southern society as a white society, southern culture as the culture of whites alone, the largely black movement for political and civil rights appeared as an artificial rather than as an organic force for change in the South.

Overall, then, the theo-politics of many European-born or -influenced conservative thinkers, what might be called the "decline of the West" school, seems in retrospect, as it did to some at the time, like theoretical overkill. If American liberalism had ever been in an anti-utopian, anti-gnostic phase, counter-millennialist phase, it was in the period between 1945 and the early 1960s. Daniel Bell's classic "The End of Ideology in the West"(1959) explicitly put paid to "chiliastic hopes, to millennarianism, to apocalyptic movements—and to ideology," while Arthur M. Schlesinger's *The Vital Center* (1949) preached the Niebuhrian gospel of limited expectations and tragic limits.[16] With the revival of radical political and counter-cultural movements in the 1960s, more radical manifestations of what conservative philosophers so feared did begin to surface. But in general, the thrust of the post-World War II conservative "reading" of American liberalism was exceedingly crude, the right-wing equivalent of left-wing claims that fascism was the inevitable destination of conservatism. More importantly, the tone-deafness of conservative intellectuals to the civil rights movement, their belief that it was simply the activist wing of American liberalism, led them to consistently misunderstand what it was about.

MORAL-CONSTITUTIONAL (IN-)EQUALITY

Post-war American conservatism was deeply committed to the idea that equality was a pernicious idea; and it was around the issue of equality that much of the conservative discussion of the race and civil rights turned. As M. E. Bradford asserted in 1975: "Equality as a moral or political imperative, pursued as an end in itself—Equality with the Capital E—is the antonym of every legitimate conservative principle."[17] One principle shared by conservatives of almost every stripe was that the distribution of power in a well-ordered society should mirror the distribution of talent, merit and virtue among its population. From this it followed that the maintenance of the existing order, so central to the thought of conservative Wilmoore Kendall and the young Garry Wills, was crucial. Kendall, for instance, severely criticized any conservatism that sought to destroy existing institutions in the name of resurrecting past institutions. True conservatives, he asserted, "are defending an established order against those who seek to undermine or transform it . . . in the absence of urgent express reasons to the contrary." In the late 1970s, Wills still described himself as a believer in the "convenient state" rather than a state bent on realizing any one purpose or condition—such as equal justice.[18]

But for Kendall, a man who made even Thorstein Veblen seem "academically domesticated,"[19] the primacy of consensual political order entailed a political culture that privileged order over equality as it was understood by liberal advocates of civil rights. In "Equality and the American Political Tradition"(1964), Kendall contended that the central question of the American political tradition was whether the Declaration of Independence, specifically the idea of equal inalienable rights, stood at the heart of the American political tradition, as Jefferson, Lincoln and more recently Gunnar Myrdal had asserted? Or was it the Constitution, which "did not so much as mention the topic of equality,"[20] along with the Federalist Papers and the Bill of Rights, documents which were also silent on equality, that established the basic moral point of the political system—the maintenance of order through balancing power and interests? For Kendall the answer was clearly the latter.

Specifically, Kendall claimed that the civil rights movement raised a crucial question about the "equal protection" clause of the 14th Amendment. Like the Supreme Court in the school desegregation cases, Kendall was concerned with the original intentions behind the 14th Amendment; and like the Court he despaired of recovering those original intentions. This undecidability, however, allowed Kendall to frame the issue as follows: did the authors of the 14th Amendment mean for equal protection to refer to "impartial enforcement of existing laws," however unequal their effects might be? Or did they intend that equality should provide "a standard—nay the standard—by which existing laws may be tested and—where they fail to meet the test—set aside."[21] Though feigning even-handedness, Kendall clearly preferred the first sense of equality, which in turn suggested the priority of the 10th Amendment over what had become the liberals' favorite Amendment—the 14th.

Finally, the central issue, raised by the civil rights "revolution," as Kendall saw it, was whether the civil rights forces would win by force or through "persuasion." It was an article of faith with Kendall that political change, particularly controversial change, should be implemented after, not before, a national consensus had been achieved. He concluded his article forthrightly: "I concede" that "Conservatives drag their feet on what are unfashionably called civil liberties, equal representation, desegregation." But he continued:

> either the Liberals pull in their horns and decide to do it the hard way, that is, by persuading Us the American people over to their point of view; or, second, the Liberals will continue their present strategy . . . to impose the new interpretation by sheer fiat of the Supreme Court.[22]

Thus what bothered Kendall was that, contrary the notion of shared consensus, the civil rights movement, with the moral impetus of the Declaration and the 14th Amendment behind it, "understands itself as a revolution" and "will not take no for an answer." As a result "preservation by discussion" and thus "government by consensus" were hardly possible any longer.[23]

Yet, it is difficult to credit Kendall's celebration of the politics of consensus-formation when a sizable number of black southerners were denied the right to participate in that consensus-building discussion altogether. But he shrewdly identified a couple of possible reactions to the 1964 Civil Rights bill in his 1964 article and re-iterated them three years later when he revisited his 1964 prediction of impending crisis. First, he suggested that passage of the 1964 bill might make the movement dependent upon the "system," thus taming its revolutionary ambitions. He also noted that the acceptance by the movement of the Public Accommodations Act was likely to create "great pockets of irredentism" made up of radical irreconcilables.[24]

By 1967, Kendall noted with some glee that the civil rights movement had come to "choke on" success. Though it had achieved the passage of two highly desired pieces of legislation, it had failed to obtain authorization for a much needed program of economic assistance and had become the "prisoner of consensus politics." Indeed, one could see the whole course of events as a "great Conservative victory."[25] In the end, Kendall, the canny political analyst, could claim that the course of events had confirmed the centrality of consensus to the proper working of the system. For Kendall, the civil rights movement had proved to be right in the American grain, which is to say, not revolutionary at all.

Yet, Kendall's story of the moral origins of the American political tradition did not go unchallenged within the conservative camp. On his "left," historian Harry Jaffa, a student of Leo Strauss, had been arguing in season and out for the central place of the Declaration of Independence—not the Constitution—in the American political tradition. On this view, Lincoln became the central figure in the American story of equality, since he had re-interpreted what was only potential in the Declaration at the moment of its writing—that equality of rights "is a condition toward which men have a duty ever to strive," a goal to be realized in creating a just polity. Writing in 1958, Jaffa explicitly agreed with Myrdal on the nature of the American Creed and thus the essence of the American "political religion." In offering a principled opposition to slavery against Stephen Douglas, Lincoln drew upon both the Enlightenment and the Puritan traditions, upon both "revealed religion" and "secular political rationalism."[26] Later Jaffa explicitly attacked Kendall's work as "utterly stultified by his refusal to condemn American slavery."[27] In making political consensus the final test of the wisdom or viability of legislation, Kendall's position was, to Jaffa's way of thinking, the modern-day equivalent of Douglas's populist, moral indifferentism to slavery.

But all this was like a red rag to a bull. In the first half of the 1970s, M. E. Bradford joined the fray. Bradford's position was saturated with southern animus—he described Jaffa's conservatism as "Old Liberalism hidden under a Union battle flag." On Bradford's reading, the Declaration was not a "piece of reasoning or systematic faith." It was an expression of "mores majorum." Anything that smacked of appeals to "higher law" or to the "goddess Reason" was anathema.[28] According to Bradford, the rights declared in 1776 derived from the historical rights of Englishmen not the natural rights of man in general. More importantly, the Declaration was a statement of the rights of sovereign states in forming a federal union, not an assertion of the rights of individuals as they constructed a polity.

Though Bradford agreed with Jaffa (and disagreed with Kendall) about the continuity between the Declaration and the Constitution, he disagreed violently with Jaffa as to the nature of the rights spoken of in Jefferson's Declaration.

Jaffa's Lincoln (or almost anybody else's Lincoln for that matter) stood for everything Bradford found to be pernicious. Lincoln had fundamentally misunderstood the Declaration to be a "deferred promise of equality;" and, as a kind of "Illinois Cromwell," Lincoln re-created a gnostic vision of a nation united by a civil religion. Bradford concurred with Edmund Wilson's comparison of Lincoln to Bismarck and Lenin, but then proceeded to strain the reader's intellectual credulity—and his own moral credibility—by suggesting Hitler as a "useful analogue" to Lincoln. Both men were, among other things, "higher law men."[29] Jaffa was hardly a leveler to say the least, but Bradford considered his attempt to place moral equality, and hence the condemnation of slavery, at the heart of the American tradition utterly mistaken. Overall, then, not only did conservatives differ on the nature of moral and constitutional equality, their opinions on the Second Reconstruction clearly influenced the way they viewed the First and Second American Revolutions.

RACIAL AND MORAL (IN-)EQUALITY

Not all conservative discussions of race and civil rights were carried on so obliquely. As noted by George Nash, even northern conservative intellectuals such as William Buckley, himself the son of two southern Catholic parents, opposed practically all of the Court decisions on civil rights issues and civil rights legislation after *Brown*. On one level, the conservative position was thoroughly shopworn, basically a reprise of the official southern states' rights doctrines. As an early 1956 editorial in *The National Review*, probably penned by William Buckley, stated: "desegregated schooling is not the issue" but whether "a central or local authority should make that decision."[30] This was the straightforward version of the modern conservative position opposition to the *Brown* decision and to all federal attempts to dismantle the Jim Crow system in the South.

But if that were Buckley playing it straight, another Buckley turned up in a 1957 *National Review* editorial entitled "Why the South Must Prevail." There Buckley unleashed an attack against black political participation and based his broadside on alleged cultural differences between the

two races. This position was one which lurked behind much of the constitutional rhetoric of conservatives. Writing in the midst of the massive
resistance crisis, Buckley now identified the central question as: "whether
the White Community in the South is entitled to take such measures as
are necessary to prevail, politically and culturally, in areas in which it does
not predominate numerically?" His answer was a resounding "yes," since
"for the time being, it is the advanced race." Indeed, it must and can
"assert[ing] the right to impose superior mores for whatever period it
takes to effect a genuine cultural equality between the races."[31]

Buckley's argument—that the need to maintain their "superior" culture
justified southern officials in preventing black voting by practically any
means necessary—was too much for Brent Bozell, Buckley's brother-in-
law and also a staff member at *National Review*. According to Bozell,
Buckley's editorial "calls up the question of how serious *National Review*
takes the law and the Constitution," since the 15th Amendment was pretty
unambiguous about discrimination in voting. In his response to Bozell,
and then later when he revisited the issue in *Up from Liberalism* (1961),
Buckley insisted that there was no "absolute right of universal suffrage,"
as though that were the issue. He did allow that the South "should prove
its own bona fides by applying voting qualifications impartially, to black
and white . . ." But he added: "There are no scientific grounds for assuming congenital Negro disabilities. The problem is not biological, but cultural and educational."[32]

This disclaimer on innate black inferiority, along with his belated call
for even-handed disfranchisement does, I suppose, fit with George Nash's
contention that the conservative intellectuals at *National Review* avoided
crude racist arguments, even as they opposed desegregation. But only
barely. It also needs mentioning that Buckley attacked African home rule
in *Up From Liberalism*, since home rule required a "politically mature
people"; and he later referred to the Congolese as "semi-civilized sav-
ages." Over the years, *National Review* was filled with a steady drumbeat
of articles opposing decolonization in Africa and lending strong support
to colonial/white regimes in Angola, Rhodesia, Mozambique, the Congo
and South Africa.[33] It is hard not to conclude that the difference between
the cultural and the biological argument against equality was (and is) not
all that great. The cultural inferiority argument was all the more suspect,
since in both cases—Africa and the United States—the group whose cultural achievement and intelligence were placed in question was black.

Thus, arguments against decolonization in Africa sounded for all the world like cover versions of arguments against desegregation in America. In light of all this, perhaps a different category such as "political-legal racism" would be appropriate to apply to the kind of conservative intellectual who judges political and legal issues on the basis of putative group characteristics, though those characteristics are not seen as biologically determined.

By the end of the 1960s, Buckley was still backing and filling on racial equality. For instance, he took note in April 1969 of the explosive new work of Arthur Jensen, an educational psychologist at Berkeley. Jensen's controversial work claimed that there was a significant genetic component to the differences in intelligence and school achievement between black and white students. Buckley was surprisingly critical of Jensen's claims and suggested the readers of *National Review* consult the essay by Ernest van den Haag, which had appeared in the magazine in December, 1964, for a more nuanced view of such matters. Buckley also blamed liberals for creating the situation whereby intelligence had become the chief, even sole, criterion in discussions of racial equality. Later, in October 1969, Buckley returned to the topic of Jensen, now accusing liberals of trying to rule out of order any studies linking race and intellectual ability. Suddenly a First Amendment absolutist, Buckley asserted that "the truth should be pursued wherever it might lead."[34] Again, he blamed liberals for stressing intelligence as the sole determinant of equality. Clearly, Buckley was trying to have it both ways. One should question inherent racial differences, on the one hand; yet maintain an "open mind" on the matter and favorably review books that leaned toward racial explanations of differences between the races, on the other.

Van den Haag's *National Review* piece of 1964 was itself problematic in much the same way. Cast as a Q. and A. dialogue in which van den Haag took both parts, the NYU sociologist and psychoanalyst, shuttled between agnosticism on the question of innate racial differences and strong suspicion that those differences actually existed. As an example of his ability to keep his readers wondering, there is the following: "our inability to prove native inferiority or superiority is, of course, no proof of native equality." Though van den Haag could only suggest "the possibility of differences in innate difference . . . among ethnic groups,"[35] the basic drift of such a statement was clearly toward accepting that possibility.

Van den Haag's next move was a quite common one among "enlightened" conservative intellectuals. He contended that, regardless of whether genes or the environment was decisive in determining academic performance, black children as a whole needed more help than white children and thus "mixed education" would impair the scholastic achievement of children of both races. Nor was it at all clear that the separation of the two races impaired the performance of black children, since the evidence put forward by psychologist Kenneth Clark for the psychic damage caused by segregation was contradictory and thus untenable.[36] Indeed, it was when children of one race were mixed, against their will, with those of another that psychological damage, as well as physical conflicts, developed. Finally, van den Haag argued that intellectual inferiority/superiority did not signify per se that an individual or group was inferior/ superior to another group in all other aspects.

Undeniably, van den Haag was a very hard target to hit squarely. Indeed, some of his arguments were pretty convincing; for instance, that Kenneth Clark's own evidence from some of his earlier studies contradicted his testimony before the courts in the school cases. Van den Haag readily granted that blacks might be angered or even insulted by segregation. That was entirely understandable. But such reactions did not prove that any lasting personality damage would take place. Nor did it demonstrate that the segregation affected academic performance in a negative fashion; otherwise, as Bruno Bettelheim noted in a review of one of Kenneth Clark's books in *Commentary* in 1956, European Jews would have languished intellectually and culturally, and that had manifestly not been the case.[37] Overall, then, van den Haag insisted that one should not confuse black intelligence/achievement and black self-esteem. This position was in turn related to the issue of institutional intentions. For, as van den Haag noted in an article in *The Modern Age* in 1964–65, the courts would soon have to decide whether it was the fact of segregation or the intention to segregate that "causes the alleged injury."[38] In more familiar language: was de facto segregation as well as de jure segregation to be ruled illegal since the former was an insult, as well, to black Americans?

But other of his positions were considerably more shaky. Though van den Haag readily granted that, even if blacks scored lower on the average than whites on academic tests, a large percentage of white and black children would overlap, he still preferred that these black children be segregated from their white counterparts. Just as dubious was van den Haag's claim that forced "congregation" was as damaging to the whites who objected to it as forced "segregation" was to black children. Such an argument ignored the larger social context in which whites were a dominant majority and also confused damage to black self-esteem with damage to white arrogance, a distinction that a psychoanalyst should surely have been able to make. Van den Haag also seemed to accept the controversial claim made by Hannah Arendt in her article on Little Rock that because "schools are social institutions," their student enrollment can properly be determined by parental choice rather than decided according to the principle of equal protection enforced by federal action. Another problematic, though prophetic "guess," was that preferential treatment of blacks, just then beginning to be debated among intellectuals in the mid-1960s, would mean that their "self-esteem" would be "likely to suffer." The anecdotal evidence on this issue allows no firm conclusion.[39]

Finally, van den Haag's solution to the school desegregation issue was one heard in many conservative circles, particularly libertarian ones. Segregated schools should be available to whites and blacks who preferred them, while integrated facilities should be offered for those who wanted to attend them. But it was not clear why most conservatives, much less libertarians, would be willing to pay taxes to support a tri-partite school system when the South had not supported, and still could not adequately support, one, much less two, school systems adequately. If financial support for such a scheme was supposed to come from private sources, the economic and social differences within, and between, both races would become so obvious as to make the situation scandalous.

Most dubious theoretically were van den Haag's views on the provenance of prejudice itself. In typically elusive, even slippery, fashion, van den Haag concluded his *Modern Age* article with the assertion that the answer to the question "whence comes the preference for one's own ethnic and national group" was "beyond the scope of this essay." But after this typical feint toward modesty, he proceeded to answer the question anyway: "this preference is so deeply rooted–in culturally elaborated biological differences-that mere mixing of groups is most unlikely to extinguish it."[40] No footnote referred the reader to anthropological or ethnological studies which confirmed a biological explanation for prejudice, in large part because the existing consensus on race had cast considerable doubt on the existence of such an impulse. Even van den Haag went on to suggest that such instinctual prejudice could be blunted, even neutralized, though claiming with some plausibility that State coercion would not do the trick.

The question remains whether there can be a principled, conservative defense of moral and racial equality. One problem was that school desegregation forced scholastic achievement and IQ to the forefront of concern. That aside, the only kind of American conservative intellectuals who would explicitly defend moral equality in principle seem to have been the Straussians. Very briefly, the Straussian position was that all human beings dispose over rational speech as a "definitive human characteristic." This means that "the making of moral distinctions," the pursuit of the good life and the best polity are uniquely human characteristics. In terms of these fundamental human propensities, then, all human beings are all morally equal.[41]

But this did not mean, for Harry Jaffa, that all cultures were equal. As he observed in his *Crisis of the House Divided*, the "great tragedy" of the Negro was that "Negroes did come from an 'inferior civilization,' that is, from a civilization in which there was no recognition of the universal rights of man."[42] Jaffa went on to observe, however, that there were also European countries circa 1861 where such rights were not recognized. Since the South refused such recognition to its slaves, its despotism over those slaves was a moral outrage and the peculiar institution justifiably condemned to perish. With passage of the 14th Amendment, all former slaves became citizens and thus constitutional equality was also to be guaranteed them as citizens. On that there could be no equivocation.

Moreover, the Straussian position offered firm grounds for rejecting intelligence or scholastic achievement as criteria for determining moral and civil equality. Even to suggest that empirical tests could settle the issue was to succumb to the positivist, fact/value dichotomy, though there was nothing in the Straussian position to forbid the use of tests in the appropriate context. (It is another matter to ask what such tests measure and how the categories such as "white" and "black" are defined and determined.) In retrospect, if more conservative thinkers had been willing to state clearly that slavery and segregation were wrong because they made alleged intellectual and cultural achievement the pre-requisite for moral and political equality, conservatives might have been on firmer grounds to make distinctions in other areas.[43]

Overall, then, on issues of racial equality and cultural differences, American conservatives were ambiguous and ambivalent. Over the course of the 1960s Gary Wills and Brent Bozell may have helped push Buckley toward the center on racial issues and away from a hardcore southern position,[44] but southern conservative intellectuals, especially Jack Kilpatrick and Richard Weaver (before his death in 1963), remained mainstays of Buckley's journal, while two of the older, fire-eating Agrarians, Andrew Lytle and Donald Davidson, also contributed to *National Review* in its first decade of publication.

Not surprisingly, conservatives strongly condemned urban rioting by blacks in the mid- and late 1960s and stressed that the first priority was the restoration of order, no matter what liberties had to be curtailed. Above all, conservatives called for liberals to cease raising black expectations which were impossible to fulfill, while refusing to concede the genuine progress that had been made. Since poverty was increasingly seen as a black problem, conservative arguments against welfare as demoralizing to its recipients and as a waste of taxpayers' money found increased resonance throughout white society. Nor, needless to say, did conservatives accept Kerner Commission claims that white racism lay at the root of the nation's racial agonies. Some conservatives did see the need for economic development, job training and better education in black urban areas,[45] though they often coupled general approval of such programs with demands that the minimum wage and the closed shop be abolished. But for many conservatives the descent into near anarchy of many of America's larger cities confirmed doubts about the capacity—or willingness—of white liberals and black radicals, and their followers, to deal with America's racial dilemmas.

THE STATE AND SOCIAL (IN-)EQUALITY

Daniel Patrick Moynihan, Nathan Glazer and Daniel Bell were such a godsend to intellectual conservatism just because they were card-carrying liberals and social democrats, not eastern European irredentists bent on liberating the captive nations nor belligerent southern conservatives spoiling to refight the Civil War. They were also trained as social scientists rather than as historians, political theorists or litterateurs; and a figure such as Pat Moynihan actually had experience in public policy deliberations at the highest level.[46]

Fundamentally, the neo-conservative position reflected a disillusionment with the capacity of liberal measures to improve the social and economic position of African Americans, particularly in northern urban areas. Neo-conservatives came to agree with paleo-conservatives that the liberal political and intellectual elites had oversold the Johnson War on Poverty. Best known, and certainly most controversial, was Moynihan's discovery over the first half of the 1960s that the status of a certain sector of the African American population was not improving and that conventional liberal welfare policies seemed helpless in remedying that fact.

In contrast with most liberals, Moynihan's politics was grounded in a tradition of Catholic social thought which focused on the family as the key institution of social coherence and personal advancement.[47] Specifically, Moynihan identified the black family as the site of, even the cause of, black difficulties. As he later acknowledged, poverty was linked with "female headed families" of both races. But he insisted that this connection was "most pronounced among blacks and other 'new arrivals' in the city. . . ."[48] Most jarringly, his internal Labor Department memorandum of 1965, which was leaked and then became known as the Moynihan Report, characterized urban black life as a "tangle of pathology"(Kenneth Clark's phrase) and talked candidly of the problems of black illegitimacy and "female-headed" households. As Moynihan reflected upon the 1965 controversy a couple of years later: "This country is not fair to Negroes and will exploit any weaknesses they display. Hence they simply cannot afford the luxury of having a large lower class that is at once deviant and dependent."[49] Such views hardly ingratiated Moynihan with liberal social policy specialists or with the more militant black leadership—and he knew it. But whatever calculation was involved, they did ingratiate Moynihan with conservatives, though clearly their reading of Moynihan and others was highly selective.

Other conservative academics began to link questions of black culture to what seemed to be the failure of African Americans to advance economically and socially. In his *The Unheavenly City* (1970), political scientist Edward Banfield noted that there was much confusion between racial prejudice and distaste for certain types of behavior associated with class-based attitudes and behaviors, i.e. what Banfield referred to as "class-culture," which was in turn different from "ethnic-culture." "Prejudice," he boldly pronounced, "is no longer the obstacle."[50] The position developed by Banfield was to gather considerable support over the next decade or so. For it suggested that neither racial differences or the negative effects of capitalism and the free market were responsible for the black failure to

make more social progress. It was rather their cultural values and attitudes that was the operative cause of their failure to advance more rapidly. Moreover, it was precisely government interference in the workings
of the market that re-enforced and confirmed the values so deleterious to
African Americans.

Another concern of neo-conservative intellectuals—and others as
well—was what they saw as an imminent collapse of cultural values in the
wake of the counter-cultural revolt of the 1960s among America's youth
and the propensity of the cultural avant-garde to push modernist culture
to its limits—and beyond. Daniel Bell spoke in *The Cultural Contradictions of Capitalism* (1976) of a "culture of sensation," while Irving Howe,
far from the neo-conservatives politically, spoke of cultural situation dominated by "the psychology of unobstructed need." Cultural apocalypse
seemed imminent.[51]

But it was left to the sociologist Philip Rieff to make explicit the link
between the collapse of modern culture and the situation of African
Americans. According to Rieff, black Americans had historically come to
be associated with images and values of cultural "remissiveness." He suggested that black militants were "dishonoured by their assignments as the
storm troops" of cultural revolution by their white allies and fellow travelling intellectuals. Moreover, the cult which had grown up by the early
1970s around Frantz Fanon, the late Martinican analyst of colonial revolt,
violated Fanon's own best insights. He had, Rieff observed, "understood
perfectly the pathological connection between the phallic myth of the
black and murderous racism, on either side of the colored mirror-image."
In a not-so-oblique reference to Eldridge Cleaver, Rieff could only
observe: "Rapists grow didactic."[52]

Finally, it is no small irony that Moynihan was one of the writers of
President Johnson's speech at Howard University in June, 1965. On that
occasion, Johnson contrasted "equality of opportunity" and "equality of
results" and suggested that social policy dealing with poverty, particularly
African American poverty, should shift from the former to the latter principle. The irony lies in the fact that by the early 1970s Daniel Bell and
much of the older liberal intellectual establishment, along with their
newly found paleo-conservative support, saw this shift in the meaning of
equality as of great political and moral significance in providing the ratio-
nale for what was to become affirmative action. Not only did it re-define
the goal of government-sponsored social policy, it re-defined the meaning

of equality as such. Thus by the early 1970s, many mainstream liberals had became neo-conservatives, while many paleo-conservatives, eager for once to be on the side of the angels, had found considerable merit in equal opportunity that they had hardly noticed before.[53]

But the differences between neo-conservative intellectuals and post-war southern conservative intellectuals on the issue of equality were striking. Southern conservatives were not disillusioned with State action; they had never recognized its validity or efficacy in the first place. For a figure such as Bradford in "The Heresy of Equality"(1975): "equality of opportunity and equal rights lead, a fortiori, to a final demand for equality of condition."[54] "Equality of opportunity" was not opposed to "equality of condition" (the rough equivalent of "equality of results"). Rather, it stood at the crest of a slippery slope leading inexorably to the decline of standards and the destruction of differences between the sections and races. More generally, post-war southern conservative intellectuals were simply unable to discuss equality without fulminating against "leveling" in social terms and "mixing" in racial terms. Similarly, any notion of rights implying that their writ ran beyond the most narrow of communal boundaries could simply not be entertained.

Also striking, though predictable, was the failure of post-war southern conservative intellectuals to acknowledge the existence of a black southern (sub-) culture or, more generally, to consider black southerners as anything but a massive "problem." Telling here is Richard Weaver's work. Almost everyone's choice as the outstanding post-Agrarian conservative intellectual and known to some as "the South's Aquinas," this reputation is, in some respects, well-deserved. Weaver did have a wider range and more philosophical cast of mind than many of his fellow southern conservatives. Unlike them, he was not ashamed of the life of the mind and he rued the absence of an analytical capacity in the mind of the South. Alone among southern conservatives, he discussed the relationship between the southern ideology and Nazism during the war. He saw the difference as one of historical provenance—Nazism was a reaction against modern mass society from within that society, while southern conservatism had emerged organically out of a traditional, aristocratically dominated, pre-modern society. But by no means did he try to disguise the affinities between the southern tradition and the *Blut und Boden* ideology, including their romantic tendencies, their distaste for the materialistic, the rational and the mechanical, and yearning for the challenges of a certain hard muscularity.[55]

Still, there were distinct limits to his sympathies and to the range of Weaver's intellectual and moral concerns. His *The Southern Tradition at Bay*, originally his dissertation under Cleanth Brooks at LSU in the late 1940s but not published until 1968, five years after his death, displayed a certain interest in, but little sympathy for, the situation of black southerners in the post-Civil War South. Weaver presents former slaves in the most stereotypical of terms. Several of his anecdotes emphasize the devotion of former slaves to their erstwhile masters but then seem to belittle them for it: "The Negro was an exceedingly pliable being" and displayed an "unwillingness . . . to work regularly."[56] Weaver is also fond of recounting examples of black incompetence, the textual equivalent of racial jokes, and falls back on the hoariest of cliches concerning the "outbreaks of crimes against women" and asserts that "their[the former slaves] best friends were to be found among the people who had owned them." On black culture more generally, he writes of the "tendency of Christianity to become Africanized" and comments on the propensity to "addiction to heathen religions" and "voodooism"[57] on the part of blacks.

Later, in *Ideas Have Consequences* (1948), Weaver revealed a distinct blind spot regarding the positive contribution of jazz, "the clearest of all signs of our age's deep-seated predilection for barbarism." The word jazz itself "signified an elementary animal function," as though human beings never engaged in sexual relations at all. Echoing the Nietzschean dichotomy between the Appollonian and Dionysian impulses, Weaver describes jazz as a "music not of dreams . . . but of drunkenness."[58] So much for jazz, one of the major contributions of African Americans to the southern tradition, to American music, and to the culture of modernity in general.

Weaver, as already noted, was a regular contributor to *National Review* up to his death in 1963. Of particular interest for an understanding of his concept of society and culture was his *National Review* essay "The Regime of the South"(1959). There Weaver sought to develop the notion of "regime" as a counter to modern "anomie," a variation on the contrast he often drew between "society" and "mass." By "regime" Weaver referred to "a complex of law, custom and idiomatic social behavior . . . a system of sustaining forms" which impart a much needed "sense of inclusive ordering."[59] It is what might be called the texture of a culture.

But besides this quick lesson in southern meta-sociology—clearly

Weaver was describing the ideal type of a rural, small town South vs. modern, urban northern society—, Weaver also offered an ontological justification for southern resistance to outside (liberal) attempts to transform its regime. Just as a regime implies inclusion, so is it also a "principle of exclusion."[60] Put another way, a "regime therefore cannot be liberal about itself," that is, it cannot raise "the question of whether it ought to continue." That liberal orders can raise such questions only demonstrates their failure to be authentic regimes. Ultimately, what underlies southern distinctiveness is a sense of the "aristocratic" as a "structural form of society", a "receptivity to the idea of transcendence;" a "preservation of history" which allows it to "conserve and stabilize." But—and here entered the issue of race—this southern order was not perfect since it was involved in "accommodating a large minority distinct in race and culture."[61] African Americans seem a problematic "other" whom Weaver can not bring himself to name.

Clearly Weaver and Bradford himself provide a graphic illustration of Bradford's own observation that whenever race was at issue, Americans—and by extension southerners—lose all sense of proportion. No better example of a kind of hysterical over-intellectualizing of the civil rights movement exists than Bradford's "Fire Bell in the Night"(1973). Speaking to American historians, Bradford proposed that the civil rights movement and its more radical aftermath exemplified gnostic, millennialist politics at its most pernicious. Most pointedly, the civil rights era had provided "the occasion of our first (and unlike Lincoln's) positive commitment to equality of condition qua mandatory brotherhood." As such it was a species of "indigenous millennialism" and thus "to be discouraged," since "the mechanical elevation of racial minorities is the most dangerous of all reformist undertakings."[62] Theo-political terminology such as "gnosticism," "rationalism in politics" and "millennialism" was liberally strewn throughout the article. In addition, Bradford's skillful use of rhetoric should be noted. He characterizes the goals of the movement as a "positive" commitment as opposed, one supposes, to a "negative" desire simply to remove restrictions. Civil rights laws, informed by the demands of the movement, are bent on the legal imposition of "mandatory brotherhood." And the use of the adjective "mechanical" obviously refers to the nature of State action as opposed to the "organic" social change so dear to conservatives' hearts.

Finally, the point is not so much that Bradford, as a representative, if extreme, southern conservative intellectual, disapproved of the changes wrought by the civil rights revolution. It is that he could scarcely conceive of the fact that a predominantly black movement had initiated them. They were, rather, the brainchild of the liberal State and represented the destructive essence of modernity, which had been, and still was, undermining the society and the tradition of the fathers.

SUMMARY

What, overall, is there to say of the efforts of intellectual conservatives to confront issues dealing with race and civil rights in the years after World War II? Specifically, how does it reflect or reveal anything important about the conservative intellectual tradition?

1. European-inspired theorizing of the State was largely wrong and certainly wrong-headed as applied to the civil rights movement and the issues of race. It produced analyses that imposed the totalitarian experience of the State in Europe upon an American experience that bore little resemblance to that experience. The (evil and all pervasive) totalitarian State was not the (inefficient) State of libertarian thought nor was it the (remote and out-of-touch) State so pilloried in the constitutional doctrines of states' rights southerners. Nor was it the liberal (bureaucratic, welfare) State. Yet, conservative intellectuals almost always implied that the various notions of the State amounted to the same thing. Indeed, most conservative political theorists easily forgot that the laws and statutes passed by state governments were State actions and not the issue of organic social processes per se. Thus, "stateways" did change "folkways" and it was disingenuous for conservatives/southerners to pretend otherwise.

2. This intellectual demonization of the State and the apotheosizing of (white) society in turn helped blind conservative intellectuals to African American social and cultural reality. Conservatives could not believe that a predominantly black movement for political and social change could arise from within white southern society without prompting by outside, liberal forces and aided by State power. They could not see this because they did not see black southerners as an integral part of that society.

This failure of understanding was a failure to acknowledge the reality of black life as a lived experience, to take it as a valid form of life. Of the many articles I have read on race and civil rights in *National Review* and *Modern Age*, practically the only one that showed a (then) conservative intellectual respond directly to a piece of black writing on its own terms was Garry Wills' "What Color is God?"(1964), a review essay of James Baldwin's *The Fire Next Time*. In it, Wills clearly gave evidence that he had listened to Baldwin's indictment of American and Western Christian culture. A former Catholic seminarian, Wills was clearly shocked—and moved—by that indictment and sought to answer back. His pained response did Baldwin the honor of taking his charges seriously rather than falling back onto puerile name-calling as most conservatives did when the work of a writer such as Baldwin was at issue.[63]

3. On the issue of equality, conservative intellectuals did no better than they did with the concept of the State. They continually conflated two or more of the distinctive meanings of equality—moral equality, constitutional equality, political equality, civil rights or equal protection, social equality, equal capacities, equality of opportunity, equality of results, and equality of condition. They confused their philosophical support for a pluralist ontology, an ontology of difference according to Bradford, with a defense of inequality. The result was that conservatives too easily reacted to black southern demands for one of these forms of equality as though it were a demand for all of them. This issue was the one upon which it was most tempting for conservatives to demagogue.

4. My final overall point is a civic humanist one. The most obvious failure of conservative thinking about race and civil rights arose from a failure of historical-political imagination. In a modern republic, the political morality implied by a two-tier concept of citizenship is simply unacceptable. There neither can nor should be first- and second-class citizens, what Hannah Arendt once referred to as "over-" and "underprivileged" citizens qua citizens. If one segment of the citizen-body of a republic—in this case African Americans—is regularly branded as inferior, dangerous or a problem, then the political loyalty of that group can hardly be demanded or expected. But analogously, liberals, as Daryl Scott has emphasized, should not have been trapped into justifying constitutional equality by emphasizing the psychological damage that social inequality or institutional exclusion causes—if it does. Political and constitutional equality are fundamentally matters of political morality and should never be dependent upon the results of empirical tests or speculation about psychological conditions.

I wish to thank Bill McClay, Steve Whitfield, Kevin Yuill and Joel Revill for their helpful readings of early drafts of this chapter.

Jim Johnson of Arkansas

Segregationist Prototype

ELIZABETH JACOWAY

In Arkansas they called him Justice Jim. He was the last of a long line of colorful Arkansas political characters, displaced in an era of television by the more bland and sophisticated David Pryors, Dale Bumpers's and Bill Clintons. His Mama gave him the middle name Douglas, because as he says "she was in love with Douglas Fairbanks"; and some of the movie star's aura clung to the boy from Crossett who blew into Arkansas politics on the charged winds of the Dixiecrat movement.[1]

In 1948 Jim Johnson was twenty-three and a newly-established lawyer in his home town in south Arkansas, not far from the Louisiana line. One of his political heroes, former Governor Ben Laney of neighboring Camden, had been among those southern bolters to walk out of the Democratic Party convention and form the National States' Rights Party, or the Dixiecrats; under Laney's tutelage, Johnson became the south Arkansas manager of Strom Thurmond's presidential campaign. In that heady experience Johnson cut his political teeth on the conservative issues that had been the hallmarks of the southern political tradition: small government, states' rights, and white supremacy; and he would spend the next fifty years promoting those issues with a consistency that spoke to his sincerity, if not his ability to accommodate himself to changing political fashions.[2]

Johnson's defining moment came in his 1956 campaign for governor against the incumbent Orval Faubus. The young lawyer had arrived on the political scene amid the birth pangs of the segregationist crusade, and he had a much firmer grasp of the racial fears of white southerners than did the then-liberal Governor Faubus. Johnson had spent the preceding eight years building a following by employing the defiant segregationist rhetoric of the states' rights and Citizens' Councils movements, and he forced Faubus in that campaign to move to the right in order to parry his blows and survive the segregationist onslaught. As he would say later in reflecting on Faubus' 1957 maneuvers: "He took my nickel and hit the jackpot!"[3]

Over the years, political commentators in Arkansas and beyond (most notably the Arkansas Gazette) have branded Johnson with an assortment of derogatory and value-laden labels such as "diehard segregationist," "redneck . . . and rabble rouser" or one of the forces of "organized racism," designations which have had the intended effect of causing more moderate observers to want to distance themselves from him and to discount his brand of thinking.[4] He has also been the butt of many a political joke as one who was out of touch with the political realities of a modernized, industrialized, sanitized South; George Fisher's cartoons in the Arkansas Gazette regularly placed him in the Old Guard Rest Home along with Orval Faubus and the other kingmakers of an old-style Arkansas politics. The annual political roast put on by the Arkansas Bar Association, the Gridiron Show, for years included a segment that parodied Johnson's message as well as its delivery: "Stand uup fer Ar-kin-saw, and stand uup fer whut's riiit—faar riiit!"[5]

Johnson has been an easy target. His slow Arkansas drawl and his emotional, stump-style delivery seemed to fit him perfectly for a skit on Saturday Night Live; his endless flood of hand-written letters (usually in pencil) and his outrageous spelling seemed to suggest that he was nothing more than a country-bumpkin with no claims on the respect of more sophisticated types such as the image-conscious, upwardly-mobile denizens of the region's new political and economic elite.[6] Unappealing as he may have been, however, to the boosters of a hopeful new Sunbelt South, and distasteful as his ideas may now seem to the academic and political commentators who attempt to reconstruct the milieu of his heyday in the 1950s and 60s, contemporary students of southern history and the civil rights movement will proceed at their peril if they refuse to listen carefully to Jim Johnson's voice, for he was the spokesman for a significant element of the populace, and the era, they are seeking to understand.

Much as a later generation may now wish it were otherwise, in his passionate denunciation of the political and media "insiders," the communist infiltrators, and the "un-American" and "un-Christian" infidels abroad in the land in the South of the 50s and 60s, Jim Johnson spoke the language of the hard-working, God-fearing, rural people of the traditional South. These were people who had struggled through the agricultural depression of the Twenties, the Great Depression of the Thirties, the Second World War of the Forties, the mechanization of agriculture with its attendant displacements of the Fifties; these were people who, for the most part, had

had neither the benefits of higher education nor of comfortable living, but who believed as passionately in the American Dream as any urban Horatio Alger. These were people who made up in hard work and hard praying for what they lacked in book-learning and sophistication, people who felt intense pride in their country and the traditions of their region, people who had suffered long and patiently as the dispossessed of the earth and who did not take kindly to being toyed with or talked down to. Jim Johnson was their kind of folks, and in speaking their language he has much to teach us about a cardinal element of the southern experience.

James Douglas Johnson came into this world in 1924 in the Arkansas Black Belt town of Crossett, the third son of a small-town grocer. His was a rowdy sawmill town, a company town that was "owned" by the bosses of the Crossett Lumber Company. Significantly for Johnson's future, his father despised the system that made his neighbors the virtual slaves of the company; they were paid in scrip which they could then redeem at the company store in a pernicious system that was reminiscent of arrangements throughout the industrializing as well as the plantation South. Jim Johnson's daddy operated an independent grocery on the edge of town, often forcing prices down at the company store through the competitive processes of the open market.[7]

Young Jim heard a lot about freedom in his household, and the dangers of outside control; his mother (whose maiden name was Long and who thought herself to be related to the legendary Huey—another one of young Jim's political heroes) complained bitterly about the pennies in sales tax "the government" forced her to assess and then record; and his father preached daily about the virtues of being free to work for a fair wage and then to spend one's wages in a free and open market.[8] These early lessons about freedom and control hit their mark with the boy who was learning as captain of the football team and president of the student body that he had the gift of leadership, and they were themes that would emerge time and again in a political career spent fighting the intractable forces of an expanding national government. In these early years of living "beyond the pale" in a company town Johnson also forged a conception of himself as an outsider, a self-image he would carry into politics, and one that would serve him well with a constituency that increasingly felt itself to be outside the main currents of American thought.[9]

Johnson remembers vividly his introduction to the world of politics and government. He was the first boy from Crossett to be invited to attend Arkansas Boys' State, and when he got off the bus in Little Rock at the end of Capitol Avenue and gazed down that broad vista at the majestic capitol building at the other end, he knew that his life had changed; it put chill bumps on him then and the thought of that experience still does. So awed was he by the beauty of that building and everything it represented that was fine and good, he later proposed to his wife in the backseat of a taxicab stopped just outside the Arkansas State Capitol. For good measure, he and Virginia celebrated their Fiftieth Anniversary in the old Supreme Court chambers in that very same building. Surely few politicians have a more colorful story to tell of their devotion to state government.[10]

Johnson's entry into the political arena in 1948 placed him in the vanguard of a movement that its supporters felt to be nothing less than a righteous crusade—a quest to save the "southern way of life" from the myriad forces of darkness abroad in the land. His work for Strom Thurmond brought him to the attention of such traditional southern leaders as Senator Richard Russell of Georgia, Senator James Eastland of Mississippi, journalist James J. Kilpatrick of the *Richmond News Leader*, and conservative thinker Dean Clarence Manion of the Notre Dame Law School (and the Manion Forum). Conversely, being welcomed into the inner councils of these respected leaders was heady stuff for a twenty-three-year-old just a couple of years out of law school; Johnson had foregone an undergraduate education when he was accepted into Cumberland University Law School, and consequently the aforementioned conservative political thinkers were to have a shaping influence on his development.[11]

Johnson came back to Arkansas and ran for the state legislature, securing a seat in 1950 as the youngest state senator in Arkansas history. At the end of his two terms in that office, the then-President of the Arkansas State Senate stated that Johnson "had introduced and sponsored more constructive and progressive legislation than any senator in his memory."[12] Having built his contacts and his understanding of the legislative and electoral processes, by 1954 Johnson felt ready to run for state-wide office, standing for election as Attorney General; despite his loss he made a good showing, and he began to be touted as a coming force in Arkansas politics. He had maintained his association with the Deep South politicians who were mounting a defense against the threat of desegregation, especially Senator Eastland. When the United States Supreme Court handed down the 1954 *Brown* decision outlawing segregation in public schools, Johnson was ready to swing into battle mode.

Jim Johnson had learned from his states' rights compatriots the language of resistance. Added now to the litany of evils of the intrusive federal government, the corrupt manipulation of the northern Negro vote, and the growing communist conspiracy would be the Supreme Court's usurpation of legislative power with its "unconstitutional" 1954 decision. As Johnson's mentor Senator Eastland had stated defiantly: The South "will not abide by or obey this legislative decision by a political court," and any effort to integrate southern schools would lead to "great strife and turmoil." The line had now been drawn in the sand across all parts of the South.[13]

Orval Eugene Faubus assumed power as governor of Arkansas in January of 1955. A former member of the liberal administration of Governor Sid McMath, Faubus grew up in a poor, Ozark household with a Socialist father (the Eugene in the new governor's name was in honor of the old Socialist Party candidate Eugene V. Debs).[14] When Faubus's campaign had run into trouble over the issue of his attendance at supposedly-communist Commonwealth College in Mena, Arkansas, Harry Ashmore, the liberal editor of the Arkansas Gazette and the consummate "insider" in Arkansas politics had written the speech that put him over the top in the Democratic primary.[15] Everyone expected Faubus to be a moderate on the race issue, and when he failed to mention segregation in his inaugural address, Jim Johnson detected a fatal flaw in the new governor's armor.

Understanding implicitly (because he shared them himself) the depth of Black Belt Arkansans' fears about racial amalgamation, which segregationists thought to be the inevitable outcome of integration, Johnson set about in the early months of 1955 forging the weapons he would use to assail Orval Faubus in the next gubernatorial campaign. Having neither a large following nor a large war chest, he launched a crusade that would supply him with both (or at least with adequate funding to make the race.)

Johnson began by allying himself with a man who came to him and offered his services as a political consultant.[16] Curt Copeland was a questionable character with a checkered past, most recently employed (before being run out of town) as the editor of a "recklessly libelous periodical" called the *Hot Springs Rubdown*.[17] Together they launched an Arkansas chapter of the South-wide Citizens' Council movement which they entitled the White Citizens' Council of Arkansas; they also created the official organ of their Council, a scurrilous publication dubbed, significantly, *Arkansas Faith*. The first issue of *Arkansas Faith* carried a picture of Jesus Christ on the cover, and its pages were filled with anti-black, anti-communist, anti-government diatribes of every stripe.[18] As Johnson would comment in a televised broadcast several months later: "Don't you know that the communist plan for more than fifty years has been to destroy southern civilization, one of the last patriotic and Christian strongholds, by mongrelization, and our negroes are being exploited by them to affect [sic] their purposes."[19]

Johnson spent much of 1955 travelling across the state speaking at rallies designed to increase membership in his organization (and of course to draw attention to himself).[20] He found his stride in that campaign, and he cultivated a speaking style that would win him a growing following. As Orval Faubus' biographer Roy Reed has described the young campaigner: "Capital reporters who had known him only as a somewhat reform-minded young senator began to notice that he had a genuine talent on the stump. He was fast on his feet. He established instant affinity with an audience. His public style was Old Testament: thunder, lightning, and dark warnings. . . . He was altogether the most effective wielder of the language that Arkansas had seen in many years."[21]

The usual pattern was for Curt Copeland to warm up the audience with an emotional and generally racist presentation, followed by the playing of one of several recordings of various NAACP leaders speaking in behalf of black civil rights, and then concluding with Johnson's analysis in rich stentorian tones of the "unconstitutional" decisions of a "tyrannous" Supreme Court.[22] Communism, Christianity and the Constitution were always a part of the recipe, but the active ingredient was a heaping portion of fear of miscegenation with its consequent loss of Anglo-Saxon purity and culture. The use of the word "forced" before "integration" played effectively on individualistic southerners' fears of a loss of control, especially to the still-hated Yankee and the seemingly insatiable federal government.

In the early autumn of 1955, Johnson found the issue with which to undermine Orval Faubus. The school board in tiny Hoxie, Arkansas, which had paid for years to bus its small number of black children to attend the neighboring Jonesboro schools, voted in an economy measure to integrate its own public schools. Unfortunately for the success of the venture, *Life* magazine decided to cover the story and publicized it in a three-page spread in an article entitled "A 'Morally Right' Decision."[23] Within days of the release of the magazine, white supremacist organizations from all over the South had targeted the little north Arkansas community as a place where the line had to be held; all of the Arkansas Citizens' Councils, including Johnson's, converged on Hoxie. Local segregationists at this point began to find their voices and called for the resignation of the school board. In a desperation measure, the besieged Hoxie board closed its schools two weeks early for the annual fall break cotton harvest.[24]

Johnson and Copeland went back to Hoxie for a massive rally while the schools were still closed. Before a cheering crowd they urged the white people of Hoxie to "stand up against forced integration, mongrelization of the races, a treasonous Supreme Court, and the Communist plan to destroy the southern way of life." Then they blasted Faubus for failing to join them in that noble crusade.[25] Faubus the liberal was still trying to steer a course of moderation between the competing forces of the past and the future, and he was maneuvering mightily to keep from having to assume responsibility for integration in his state. It would be another two years before Johnson would be able to force Faubus to move in defense of segregation; and by the time he did, the wily governor would rob Johnson of his political base.

A federal judge at length enjoined Johnson and Copeland from further interference in the Hoxie affair, but Johnson had now found a weapon with which to hammer away at the governor's Achilles' Heel.[26] Relentlessly he would proclaim the governor's apostasy—one of the recordings he played at Citizens' Council rallies even had a Professor Roosevelt Williams, purportedly of Howard University, spelling out the promises Faubus had supposedly made to Arkansas blacks in order to win their votes.[27] By January of 1956, the moderate Faubus found himself declaring: "I cannot be a party to any attempt to force acceptance of a change to which the people are so overwhelmingly opposed."[28]

One outcome of the Hoxie imbroglio was that all of the Arkansas Citizens' Councils united under Johnson's command.[29] Another was the recognition across the South of his titular leadership of the massive resistance forces in Arkansas, and the consequent invitation for him to join the governing board of the newly-formed Federation for Constitutional Government. The brainchild of Senator Eastland, the Federation was designed "to serve as the central agency for a broad states' rights movement, a clearing house to direct massive resistance."[30] As Eastland explained it: "It will be a peoples' organization . . . to fight the Court, to fight the CIO, to fight the NAACP and to fight all the conscienceless pressure groups who are attempting our destruction. . . . We are about to embark upon a great crusade to restore Americanism and return the control of our government to the people." Furthermore, Eastland predicted: "Defeat means death, the death of Southern culture and our aspirations as an Anglo-Saxon people. . . . Generations of Southerners yet unborn will cherish our memory because they will realize that the fight we now wage will have preserved for them their untainted racial heritage, their culture and the institutions of the Anglo-Saxon race."[31]

Federation membership included an impressive roster of southern leaders, from senators and congressmen to governors and other state and federal office-holders, top officials of the state Democratic parties, leaders of a variety of white supremacy organizations, and former Dixiecrats.[32] Johnson's inclusion in this august body, since he held no elective office and played no official role in his state's Democratic Party, was a tribute both to his organizational ability and his friendship with Senator Eastland. The indefatigable Eastland had taken Johnson under his wing during the Dixiecrat crusade and had played an instrumental role in the development of his political career ever since. Johnson's writings and speeches customarily reflected the Eastland influence, especially in their always-visible seam of paranoia.[33]

As chairman of the Senate Internal Security Subcommittee, Eastland gave full vent to his fear of a vast communist conspiracy. In his view the South had a vital role to play in defending against communist subversion. As the historian of massive resistance Numan V. Bartley has written, quoting Eastland: ". . . so squarely did states' rights, the most important bulwark against communist subversion, rest upon a southern foundation that 'when state sovereignty falls in the South, it automatically falls elsewhere.' Obviously, any threat to the 'southern way of life' struck at the very heart of America's national integrity. The *Brown* decision, assaulting both Anglo-Saxon culture and states' rights, was a body blow to the Republic."[34]

Under Eastland's guidance, Johnson now joined the South-wide forces that were engaged in drafting legislation to "interpose" the power of the states between their local school officials and the federal courts. Following the lead of Richmond's James Jackson Kilpatrick, Johnson committed himself throughout the winter of 1955–56 to drafting an interposition amendment to the Arkansas constitution and then getting that amendment onto the November, 1956 ballot. Not incidentally, he also set his sights on toppling Orval Faubus in the August, 1956 gubernatorial primary. Told that in order to secure a spot on the ballot for his amendment, under the provisions of the Arkansas statutes regarding an initiated vote he would have to secure the names of 33,000 registered voters on petitions, Johnson replied that his organization and other pro-segregation groups could get 300,000 signatures.[35] Clearly he believed that Arkansas' incumbent governor was vulnerable, and Faubus himself began to take notice of the threat from south Arkansas.[36]

If passed, the Johnson Amendment would direct the Arkansas General Assembly, at its January, 1957 session, to "take appropriate action and pass laws" nullifying the *Brown* decision; it also would order the state legislature to enact laws to enforce segregation, and it would subject to criminal prosecution any state officials who failed to carry out the laws. Johnson's amendment stated further that the legislature should evade the Supreme Court rulings on racial segregation as "encroachments upon rights and powers not delegated to the United States nor prohibited to the states by the Constitution . . ." Jim Johnson commented that "When this amendment is approved, it will absolutely guarantee continued segregation in the public schools of Arkansas and in other phases of Arkansas society."[37]

Although considerable ambiguity clouded the debates over interposition in the various southern states, the arguments employed in Arkansas and Mississippi showed a marked consistency, reflecting once again the Eastland influence on the Arkansan's thinking.[38] As Johnson would comment to Faubus biographer Roy Reed years later: "That amendment was damned near a declaration of war against the United States. It'd kill corn knee-high. It was strong. Actually, too strong for me."[39]

Clearly, Johnson was being swept along by forces much greater than himself: his segregationist and states' rights mentors needed Arkansas to hold the line with other upper South and border states in order to diminish or delay the threat of integration in the Deep South.[40] Similarly, his ally Curt Copeland was writing unabashedly racist articles in their publication *Arkansas Faith*, which Orval Faubus would describe as "one of the vilest, most dissolute, neo-pornographic publications it has ever been my disgust to see."[41] Johnson commented recently that he regrets now some

of the tactics he employed in the campaign to get the Johnson Amendment passed, but he felt at the time that those things were necessary in
order to get out the rural voters who were not controlled by the traditional
political machines in their counties.[42] The *Arkansas Gazette* would never
let him—or the people of Arkansas—forget the *Arkansas Faith* component of the 1956 campaign, and he would carry the burden of that choice
for the rest of his political career.[43]

On April 30th, 1956, Jim Johnson made his gubernatorial candidacy
official in what Roy Reed has described as "a triumph of theatricality." At
a rally of two thousand people in Little Rock's largest auditorium, with
former governor Ben Laney as master of ceremonies, the crowd cheered
enthusiastically "as it heard repeated cries against the communistic, athe-
istic, integrationist threat." After a twenty minute demonstration during
which supporters tossed money into the orchestra pit to pay his filing fee,
Johnson declared his candidacy and the race was on.[44]

Orval Faubus was a master of political maneuvering. As Roy Reed has
explained: "The more substantial leaders of the Arkansas low country had
not jumped on the resistance bandwagon that was careering across the
rest of the Deep South. They opposed integration, but, unlike their peers
in most of the rest of the Black Belt, they had little respect for the arri-
vistes running the Citizens Councils. . . . These traditional leaders wanted
no tampering with the customary power structures in the delta." Consequently, when Faubus decided he would have to move to the right on the
race issue, "he went over the heads of the council hotheads and reached
out to the established leadership."[45]

In February Faubus had appointed some of the delta's most respected
citizens to a study committee that he charged with devising a plan of resistance based on the work that was currently being done in Virginia. The
"Faubus plan" that grew out of this committee's work included both a
pupil-assignment program and a resolution of interposition.[46] Hoping that
these measures would help him to maintain his centrist position in the
increasingly charged atmosphere of the massive resistance movement,
Faubus found that in the wake of the southern congressional delegation's
abdication of leadership with the "Southern Manifesto" and a Johnson
campaign that Numan Bartley has described as "blisteringly racist," the
center was crumbling under his feet.[47]

By July 9th Faubus found himself saying "No school district will be
forced to mix the races as long as I am governor of Arkansas."[48] Faubus

also lashed out at Johnson, describing him as "a purveyor of hate," and
describing *Arkansas Faith* in equally uncompromising terms: "This opposition candidate for governor readily and willingly supplements the filth
contained in this publication with hate-filled mouthings of intolerance,
suggestions of violence, totalitarian proposal of changes in our methods of
government, and an advocacy of mob rule."[49] Faubus carried the day in
the Democratic primary and defeated Johnson by more than 2 to 1, but
as Numan Bartley has written, ". . . it was the challenger who set the tone
of the campaign, defined the issues (or to a large extent the issue), and
dominated the election in spirit if not in ballots."[50]

Johnson's loss was a reflection of two political realities. First, Orval
Faubus had by this time—through patronage appointments and careful
attention to the courting of the traditional county bosses—established
himself as the party leader and the master of the Democratic Party
machinery. Second, Arkansas' division into two distinct regions, one
mountain and one low country, meant that only half of the state would
care deeply about the race issue; and Faubus had appealed to these east
Arkansas voters with his pupil placement plan and his proposed interposition resolution. One can hardly dispute Bartley's argument that Faubus
and his advisors must have learned from this election that "the path to
political success in Arkansas" did not lie "along the path of racial extrem-
ism."[51] Jim Johnson is convinced, however, that with the passage of both
the Johnson Amendment and Faubus' milder interposition resolution in
the November election, Faubus took note of "the will of the people" and
thus was predisposed to play to the segregationists by closing the schools
to blacks the next fall.[52] Whatever his motivation, Faubus did follow a
course until September of 1957 that allowed him to support local officials—even when they pursued a policy of desegregation—while promising to prevent "forced integration."

Roy Reed spun out an intriguing scenario of what would have happened if Jim Johnson had been elected governor of Arkansas, either in
1956 or 1958:

> Governor Johnson would have had little interest in day-to-day govern-
> ing or in the compromises and negotiations required to push a program
> through the legislature. His interests were broader. He was dancing at
> the edge of revolution, and with the governorship of a state to propel
> and support him, he would have become overnight the commanding

general of the southern resistance. George Wallace that year was still an obscure minor official in Alabama. He would not become governor until 1963. With four years' head start, Jim Johnson would have made George Wallace's southern leadership unnecessary. He was just as intelligent as Wallace and just as ruthless. He was better with words and better at speaking them. He was good-looking in a dark, menacing way; Wallace was merely pug-nosed and threatening. And one other thing: Wallace was held back from the precipice by some restraining hand, cowardice, perhaps, or just simple caution. Jim Johnson was not built for restraint. As governor of Arkansas, he would have carried the fight to the bitter and certain end. The feds might have had to take him by force, along with whatever fellows of fortune who had elected to go down with him. One could see him running for president from his prison cell in the manner of Eugene Debs, or some Guatemalan insurgent. And back home, Arkansas would have had to climb out of the abyss once again, much as it had done after the Civil War. Who knows: the reformer selected to clean up the mess might have been calm, reasonable Orval Faubus.[53]

Johnson was convinced that the forces of liberalism in this country, realizing that they could not persuade the Congress to mandate the kinds of social and cultural changes they desired, had turned to the Supreme Court to engineer the social revolution spelled out in the *Brown* decision. In his mind there was no question but that the Court had overstepped its bounds in Brown, and that the 1954 decision was a direct violation of the tenth amendment. Johnson's interposition amendment was an attempt to create such an impasse ("there wouldn't have been enough jails to hold all of the resisters!") that Congress would have been forced to submit to the states an amendment stating clearly what he felt the *Brown* decision implied—that the states no longer had any rights with regard to the education of children. He believed that such an amendment if passed and then ratified would resolve all differences, so that no one could say "No, that's not the law"; although he might have been willing to go to jail as a part of an effort to force Congress to act, he claims that if three fourths of the states had ratified such an amendment then he would no longer have felt that he had the constitutional grounds to resist. Of course he knew that such an amendment was not a viable political option for the Congress, and he believed then and now that it was easier to discredit the

Jim Johnsons of the South by calling them "haters" than it was to address squarely the merits of their constitutional arguments.[54]

Jim Johnson had to watch from the sidelines as Governor Faubus appropriated his issue and his following in the 1957 desegregation crisis in Little Rock. Johnson's only contribution to that cause—and it was a contribution that gave Orval Faubus political cover, if only temporarily— was his orchestration of a telephone campaign that threatened both Faubus and Superintendent of Schools Virgil Blossom with violence at Central High if school desegregation were to proceed as scheduled. These threats were the explanation Faubus offered for his decision to call out the Arkansas National Guard and station them around Central High School.[55]

In the 1958 political season Jim Johnson did not tip his hand until the last minute, filing at the eleventh hour for a seat on the Arkansas Supreme Court and handily defeating a highly-respected and long-time member of that body, Justice Minor Millwee. Upon learning that he had won the election, he commented to his wife: "Well Virginia, we've won it—now what're we going to do with it?"[56] His frosty reception by the other Justices persuaded him that he would have to earn his spurs, and in the next six years he served in an impartial and color-blind manner that even the *Arkansas Gazette* could not fault.[57] Johnson claims that at the end of his Supreme Court service he got a call from Wiley Branton, the black NAACP attorney who had represented the Little Rock plaintiffs in *Cooper v. Aaron*, the landmark Supreme Court case that grew out of the Little Rock crisis, congratulating him on his fairness and his dedicated service.[58]

In 1964, while still on the Court, Johnson openly supported the Republican presidential nominee, Barry Goldwater; he remembers as "one of the great moments of my life" his appearance in a South-wide telecast with Goldwater and Jimmy Byrnes of South Carolina.[59] In 1966 he won the Democratic gubernatorial primary the first time that Orval Faubus declined to run; his opponent in the general election was the new Arkansan Winthrop Rockefeller, who was the standard-bearer of a recently-resurrected Arkansas Republican Party. Rockefeller embodied the hopes of many Arkansans for a new kind of Arkansas politics—one freed from the machinations, and the taint, of the Faubus years—and at any rate the campaign chest of the New York millionaire was an insurmountable obstacle for Johnson and the Democrats.

In 1968, still burdened with the debts from his failed gubernatorial race, Johnson allowed himself to be persuaded to run against J. William

Fulbright for the United States Senate. A member of Governor Ronald Reagan's "kitchen cabinet" who had helped to put Reagan in the statehouse in California, Henry Salvatore appeared in Johnson's office one day with a fat dossier of information about Johnson and informed his surprised listener that powerful conservative forces had decided that Jim Johnson could beat Bill Fulbright in the upcoming Senate race, and that they had committed themselves to providing the financing. Johnson had never had adequate financing before, and this seemed too good to be true. It was.[60]

Johnson actually thought that his Arkansas supporters were more interested in the governor's office than a Senate seat, so Salvatore persuaded him to ask his wife Virginia to run for governor and let him run for the Senate. Johnson did not have the least doubt that they could win. In his words "Virginia was one of the most beautiful women on earth," she had always been his primary campaigner, she frequently appeared in his stead at campaign functions in head-to-head encounters with other candidates and "she would always clean their plow." In short, Johnson allowed himself to be run as the front man for a group of Reagan Republicans. Unhappily for the Johnsons, Winthrop Rockefeller and his people with their strong inroads in the national Republican apparatus were able to, in Johnson's words, "pull the teeth of the Salvatore effort. It took the connections of Chase Manhattan Bank to put a stop to this, but their argument was 'We don't have to have substitute Republicans any more, we can have real Republicans such as Winthrop Rockefeller.' " [61]

In the same year that Johnson and Johnson were running for their state's most coveted electoral positions, they also promoted the campaign for President of American Independent Party candidate George Corley Wallace. Johnson remembers the work he did for "that little bastard," borrowing money to rent Barton Coliseum, extra chairs, a piano, etc.; the Wallace campaign team departed from Little Rock with literally trunkloads of money, and they left Johnson holding the bag for all the expenses. In the ensuing election, Arkansans defied all political logic by casting their votes for the Republican Winthrop Rockefeller for Governor, the liberal Democrat J. William Fulbright for Senator, and the maverick Independent George Wallace for President.[62]

In the 1980s Johnson was an enthusiastic Ronald Reagan supporter and a vigorous opponent of Bill Clinton. Today he thinks of himself as an anti-Clinton southern Democrat. As he explains it, "we considered ourselves to be Democrats even in the Dixiecrat movement; any leaving of the party was done on the part of the national Democrats, not the southerners." In reflecting on the incongruity of calling himself a Democrat in a Bill Clinton world, Johnson comments that "the old breed of Southern Democrats were a lot unto themselves; maybe they're all dead now and I just don't know it." The conservatives infuriate him because "they would rather fight and even disembowel each other than fight a common enemy." The liberals seem to be able to accommodate their differences, and as a result he catches himself "being so ultra-critical of the conservatives who fail to live up to my expectations that I feel a personal disgust for the Republicans. I think 'I don't have anything in common with these people,' and I wouldn't hesitate to support a Democrat tomorrow."[63] The career of Jim Johnson speaks volumes about the travail of the conservative southerner in the changed political terrain of the post-World War II world.

When the Supreme Court handed down the *Brown* decision in 1954, the southern world of the Jim Johnsons turned upside down. For True Believers in the ideology of white supremacy, this necessitated a response that was beyond politics, one that was in the old religious sense a Crusade—a quest to reclaim the threatened verities of Christianity, Americanism, and Anglo-Saxon superiority. All of these old certainties had been under siege for a decade: from the changed values and perspectives the veterans had brought home from the war, from the dislocations associated with the mechanization of agriculture, from the new materialism of the post-war, post-Depression spending, from the increasing assertiveness of black southerners, from the Cold War imperatives of improving the treatment of black Americans. Casting about for explanations for the frightening new realities, Americans of all regions and classes found themselves swept away by the communist hysteria of the McCarthy movement. Subversion of traditional institutions and verities seemed to be exactly what was happening in America; and how much easier it was to blame an evil, unseen culprit than to grasp the shadowy and elusive "forces" that were producing the change. What is more, there truly were communist and subversive elements involved in the civil rights struggle at all stages, so the claims of some of the defenders of the "southern way of life" were not completely outrageous.

Jim Johnson's paranoia was not confined just to the communists. He has told a story many times about the night he stayed as a guest at Senator Eastland's home in Ruleville, Mississippi, and when he folded his trousers over the hanger an important key slipped out of his pocket unnoticed. Upon arriving home in Crossett he called Eastland and reported his loss; when the Senator returned to Washington, a member of an Army intelligence unit (the CIC) popped his head into Eastland's office door and asked: "Did you find Jim Johnson's key?" This kind of experience would make anyone paranoid, and it is difficult to say where rational thought patterns begin and end in such a situation.[64]

Thirty years ago historian Sheldon Hackney enumerated all the things that the rest of the nation has imposed upon a recalcitrant South, right down to Daylight Savings Time.[65] From the segregationist perspective, the *Brown* decision was simply the most heinous episode in this long and inglorious history of strong-arming the South into swallowing bitter medicine, and it was the deciding factor in alienating the Jim Johnsons of the region from their fragile sense of community with the rest of the country. The trouble with the Jim Johnsons of the world was that they believed the things they said about integration leading inevitably to miscegenation, and they believed that what was at stake was the integrity of their culture. George Wallace may have been playing politics with race, as his biographer Dan Carter has so richly demonstrated, but Jim Johnson was not playing games.[66] At this very moment he has a floor mat in front of the fireplace in his den that proclaims his homestead to be named "Whitehaven"; at least in his own home he has found a haven of safety from what he perceives to be the continuing threat of black defilement.

One of the foremost historians of American race relations, George Fredrickson, has catalogued the ideology of white supremacy; between at least 1830 and 1914, he claims, almost all white Americans (and not simply southerners) shared a belief in the following propositions:

1. Blacks are physically, intellectually, and temperamentally different from whites.

2. Blacks are also inferior to whites in at least some of the fundamental qualities wherein the races differ, especially in intelligence and in the temperamental basis of enterprise or initiative.

3. Such differences and differentials are either permanent or subject to change only by a very slow process of development or evolution.

4. Because of these permanent or deep-seated differences, miscegenation, especially in the form of intermarriage, is to be discour-

aged (to put it as mildly as possible), because the crossing of such diverse types leads either to a short-lived and unprolific breed or to a type that even if permanent is inferior to the whites in those innate qualities giving Caucasian civilization its progressive and creative characteristics.

5. Racial prejudice or antipathy is a natural and inevitable white response to blacks when the latter are free from legalized subordination and aspiring to equal status. Its power is such that it will not in the foreseeable future permit blacks to attain full equality, unless one believes, like some abolitionists, in the impending triumph of a millenarian Christianity capable of obliterating all sense of divisive human differences.

6. It follows from the above propositions that a biracial equalitarian (or "integrated") society is either completely impossible, now and forever, or can be achieved only in some remote and almost inconceivable future. For all practical purposes the destiny of the blacks in America is either continued subordination—slavery or some form of caste discrimination—or their elimination as an element of the population.[67]

This ideology of white supremacy apparently remained fairly constant in the South until the 1950s, for historian Neil McMillen found most of the same propositions in place in his study of the Citizens' Councils.[68] Despite the findings in the early twentieth century of scholars such as anthropologist Franz Boas that led American academics to a more optimistic view of racial differences, the rank and file of southern whites never heard of Franz Boas, and before the 1950s they had had few challenges to their racial paradigm. An occasional Lillian Smith or James McBride Dabbs might stray from the fold, but so rare was this occurrence in the era of segregation that southern literary critic Fred Hobson subtitles his book on the subject "The White Southern Racial Conversion Narrative"—suggesting that it took the force of a religious epiphany for white southerners to break through the intellectual construct of white supremacy.[69]

The ideology of white supremacy was not the only force holding southern racial patterns in place. The Supreme Court decision of *Plessy v. Ferguson* had been the law of the land for two generations by 1954, and as the historian of the *Brown* decision has made abundantly clear, seven of the nine Justices of the Supreme Court had to be persuaded over a period of several years that the *Plessy* decision was bad law—not bad sociology, or bad psychology, but bad law.[70] Once the Justices were persuaded, the assumption seemed to be that somehow the South would fall into line. But as historian Richard Kluger has written: "Law in a democracy must contend with reality. It has to persuade. It has to induce compliance by its appeal to shared human values and social goals."[71] Of course Kluger was writing here in celebration of the passage of the *Brown* decision, but his test of good law can be applied as well to the opponents of that decision. No effort was made to persuade them; somehow they were expected to choke down the bitter pill and abandon a time-hallowed thought pattern that offered myriad social, economic, and psychological benefits. In their refusal to do so they met with the vilification and scorn of the nation, a scenario in which they had had many rehearsals.

Jim Johnson recently wrote a letter to the editor of the *Arkansas Democrat-Gazette*, Paul Greenberg, questioning the reasoning the Jewish Greenberg had employed in an editorial in which he expressed his desire for his children to marry within his faith. In the characteristically dismissive tone that the *Arkansas Democrat-Gazette* (and its predecessor, the *Arkansas Gazette*) has always employed in dealing with Johnson, Greenberg replied, in the newspaper: ". . . that was an interesting story you told about the Jew who was asked, What would you think if your daughter married a black? He said he didn't care whom she married so long as the boy was Jewish. I can identify with that. Because I want any grandchildren of mine, God willing, to share the covenant He made with me at Sinai. Not because I believe my faith is superior to that of others, . . . but because it is mine." What is more, Greenberg continued, "Race is not identity, and it's certainly not faith. . . . So I care not what my grandchildren look like—they can be black but comely, as the song of songs says, or Cherokee or Chinese, or as fine-speckled as the prettiest trout—so long as they're Jewish." Finally, "We all have our priorities in this life, and race is irrelevant to mine. But you take issue with what I see as the irrelevance of race. Can that be the essential difference between us on this issue, that I worship the Lord God and you worship race? Peace, A fellow sinner."[72]

Johnson's son David answered the Greenberg insult because, as his father had explained his decision not to write a response himself: "there's none so blind as those who refuse to see." But David could not let it pass. In his published response he wrote: ". . . let me say that a careful reading of Greenberg's letter would make a blind man see that his professed unwavering loyalty to his faith makes his claimed belief in the 'irrelevance of race' the height of duplicity. Therefore, the question as to whether Greenberg cares if his grandchildren are 'speckled' is irrelevant. The real question is whether he has the arrogant right to impose that lot on the rest of us and our grandchildren."[73] It was the same question the segregationists were asking in 1954, and it is one they will be asking in 2054 if Americans cannot find a way to construct a shared community of values.

Jim Johnson was the prototypical segregationist. An "outsider" from birth, he and other rural southerners had been baptized in a litany of southern exclusion at least since the Civil War. A proud individualist, he revered the southern traditions of local control and maximum freedom for the responsible citizen. A student of the constitution, he revered the traditions of American and Anglo-Saxon jurisprudence that sanctioned a federal rather than a national system of governance, and that protected citizens against the dangers to liberty of a strong central government.

In its essence the states' rights campaign was about freedom and control, freedom for the highly individualistic white southerner, and control—not only over the black population he felt threatened everything he held dear, but over the institutions of government that regulated his daily behavior. Consequently, the states' rights movement was a rebellion primarily against the imposition of outside control or force, and the segregationists' use of the terms "forced integration" and "forced bussing" was a coded language of resistance that communicated a continued commitment to the threatened older values.

In their failure to persuade the Jim Johnson's of this nation—and the Wallace phenomenon certainly demonstrated that the segregationist mentality stretched far beyond the South—and in choosing to force rather than persuade recalcitrant Americans to accede to a modernized code of legalities and racial etiquette, the collective forces of liberalism in this country may have undermined the civil rights movement they were seeking to promote, and they certainly weakened the cohesiveness of the larger body politic. The shared sense of devotion to a larger good has fallen by the wayside as the fragile cohesiveness of democracy has been rent asunder, once again, by the issue of race. Only when Americans learn to communicate with each other with respect, leaving aside such hurtful epithets as "redneck"—as well as "nigger"—can this country rediscover the path toward a renewed American quest for democracy.

Doubtless Sincere

New Characters in the Civil Rights Cast

LAUREN F. WINNER

With each new book on civil rights, the movement's dramatis personae grows larger. The old cast of black heroes still has center stage, but supporting actors who used to be walk-ons now have speaking parts. We know about gentleman segregationists like James J. Kilpatrick and Ku Kluxers like Sam Bowers. We can read about white liberal black sheep like Virginia Durr and moderate ministers like Episcopal Bishop Charles Carpenter.[1] Scholars, in other words, recognize that to speak of "the white experience" of the civil rights movement is absurd; "the white South," after all, comprised George Wallace and Casey Hayden and everything in between. But when it comes to the decade after Brown, we still too often fall unthinkingly into that lazy and inaccurate catch phrase "the black experience": The black church. The black middle-class. The black community. To white Americans, scholars readily attribute lots of experiences, lots of churches, lots of politics, and, usually, lots of middle-classes. But black Americans have only one of each.

The literature on the early and middle decades of Jim Crow has begun to challenge the portrayal of a monolithic "black community." To cite just two examples: Glenda Gilmore, writing about the progressive era, has recently reminded scholars to be cautious about "either mythologizing African American solidarity or applying notions of class formation based upon white experience." Adam Fairclough's nuanced portrait of black teachers "in the Age of Jim Crow" reveals teachers who tousled with ministers and other leaders in black communities; and demonstrates that "education—-and the lack of it—became sources of . . . class tension" among African Americans.[2] This essay suggests simply that black southerners during the era of civil cights were no more homogenous than their parents and grandparents. In 1943 Carter G. Woodson acknowledged that "There are a few [Negro] defenders of segregation who are doubtless sincere." Almost sixty years later, we should follow Woodson's lead and begin to study those black defenders of segregation.[3]

Black southerners responded to the civil rights movement in a variety of ways. Many risked their lives to support the freedom struggle, but others distanced themselves from the activists. There were those who opposed the movement because they were terrified of economic intimidation and violence. Anne Moody's mother, for example, was probably acting out of fear when she tried to forbid Moody to attend an NAACP convention in Jackson. Voter registration reports in the early '60s described "That prohibitive kind of fear which binds the minds of the people here, especially the Negroes . . . [An] appalling, nebulous fear." Other African Americans eschewed the movement because they believed that black leaders should be spending their time not on integrating lunch-counters, but, as one Greensboro, North Carolina resident put it, on cracking down on teens' "guzzling" alcohol, extramarital sex "practiced right under our noses on every ill-lighted stairway," and other symptoms of moral decay. Still other black southerners were among the so-called gradualists. Either too dignified or too up-tight to embrace the demonstrations and marches, the sit-ins, and the pray-ins, these African Americans urged even the leaders of SCLC—who, by the end of the movement, would be considered gradualists themselves by some of the younger, more radical activists—to take it slow.[4]

Finally there were those who rejected integration outright. A 1966 study by Donald Matthews and James Protho found that one in three "Negroes is not committed to the goal of racial integration," with 16% favoring "strict segregation" and 15% favoring "Something in between" strict segregation and integration.[5] Black nationalists who abhorred Jim Crow but sought an alternative more radical than integration constituted part of that 16%. But according to Matthews and Protho's study, most of the African Americans favoring segregation were not "potential black nationalists," but "old style 'Uncle Toms.' "[6] Black defenders of segregation look, at first blush, very much like black nationalists, especially in their preference for all-black institutions; but black defenders of segregation differ from nationalists in two key ways. First, while both groups criticize NAACP-style integration, nationalists articulate a third alternative to integration and Jim Crow, while segregationists preferred to stick with the status quo. Second, absent from black defenders of segregation's political vocabulary was the demand for self-determination. They called for all-black institutions, but not autonomous all-black institutions; indeed, some

defenders of segregation asserted that black people needed white pater-
nalism and oversight in order to thrive. As Joseph F. Albright, a Jackson,
Mississippi, "public relations consultant" and journalist, told the "swarm
of 'saviors' that have come with dubious intent," "I don't want to be
'saved' from the continuous adoring association my own desirable women,
some of the earth's loveliest creatures"; from black churches, those "per-
petual guiding lights," illumining the "path of righteousness"; from black
fraternal organizations, or black newspapers; from "my own great educational institutions without which it would have been a sorry day for Negro
progress." But most of all, Albright did not want to be saved from "my
friendship and encouragement that I receive daily from that long and
splendid list of white Mississippians without whose generous, sympathetic aid I could never walk successfully down that high road of progress."[7]

Albright and his fellow travelers, it is important to remember, were
defending segregation, not Jim Crow. The most enterprising researcher
will have trouble coming up with black southerners actively arguing that
African Americans should be disenfranchised or denied courtesy titles.
Zora Neale Hurston's widely circulated letter-to-the-editor of the *Orlando
Sentinel* is illustrative. She was "not delighted," she said, with *Brown*. The
logic behind the decision was no more than "old white mare business"
(an unrestrained mule, common wisdom goes, "will automatically follow
a white mule"): the Supreme Court's decision, "insulting rather than honoring to my race," merely perpetuated the myth that "there is no greater
delight to Negroes than physical association with whites." Separate
schools, Hurston suggests, are not inherently unequal: the notion that
black children begin to think of themselves as inferior beings after a few
months in segregated schools, put forth by witnesses by the NAACP and
embraced by the Warren Court, was condescending hogwash, and the
notion that black children are missing out by not being able to rub elbows
with white kids during recess no better. "I can see no tragedy in being
too dark to be invited to a white school social affair."[8]

Hurston vociferously denounced the NAACP's strategy of integration,
and she in turn was vociferously denounced by Ralph Ellison, Richard
Wright, Roy Wilkins and other black intellectuals and activists, who
accused her of "accomodationism." However sympathetic today's readers
may be to her critics, it is crucial to note what, exactly, Hurston was
accommodating: segregated schools, not the entire political order of the

mid-century South. She was critical of condescension, and wary of the NAACP's strategy; she was not disdainful of citizenship and equality. To the contrary, disgust with Negro-vote buying led Hurston to write "I Saw Negro Votes Pedaled," in which she urged black Floridians to take their voting responsibilities seriously.[9]

If historians have neglected the likes of Albright and Hurston, white segregationists of the 1950s ballyhooed them. Stunned that "their people" were turning on them—marching in the streets, sassing employers in the kitchen, integrating classrooms in the public schools—white segs searched for reliable Negroes who would prop up the idea that black southerners liked things just fine the way they were before outside agitators had come south and stirred up trouble. White segregationists had a hard time finding black allies. Hard, but not impossible; when southern politicians did find them, they crowed, and cultivated the black spokesmen for segregation. In August 1959, for example, Zack J. Van Landingham sent a memo to the director of Mississippi's State Sovereignty Commission. Van Landingham had just come from a meeting with Needham Jones, a school principal in Wiggins, Mississippi, and the president of the South Mississippi Association of Negro Teachers. Jones opposed the integration of Mississippi schools, and denounced the outside agitators stirring up trouble in the state. After sending the head of the Sovereignty Commission a detailed report of his meeting with Jones, Van Landingham suggested that Jones "can be of valuable help in maintaining segregation and keeping down racial tension in the southern part of the State of Mississippi. He should be further visited and developed along this line." When attorney Lewis L. Scott, an NAACP attorney who "resigned because of recent actions by the NAACP," wrote to Georgia attorney general Eugene Cook to declare that he was "openly, avowedly and unalterably opposed to desegregation," Cook sent out a press release about Scott's suggestion that the state make Fort Valley State, Savannah State, and Albany State, Georgia's three public black colleges, part of the University of Georgia. That way, wrote Scott, "any student clamoring for admission into the University of Georgia may be readily admitted," and sent to one of the three black schools. Southern newspapers gleefully reprinted letters like Hurston's, and governors and their staffs passed around those scraps of newspaper like they were holy writ.[10]

Nor did civil rights activists ignore black defenders of Jim Crow. To the contrary, they spared little in vilifying men and women they saw as selfish traitors. Roy Wilkins castigated them as the "hat-in-hand variety" of Negro. Selma civics teacher John Shields challenged his students to wonder "If your leaders are leading, where are they leading?" Black leaders, according to Shields, were "part of the problem . . . The wealthiest black people, the funeral directors and the doctors, had their connections with the white power structure. If a black person got killed, the police chief could turn the body over to whichever funeral home he wanted. So the funeral directors were always sending a turkey to the chief or the mayor on their birthdays. None of them was trying to work any changes for the black race."[11]

Many black defenders of segregation were members of the bourgeoisie and had an obvious stake in the system: the doctors and dentists, who, in Pat Watters and Reese Cleghorn's phrase, "being relatively prosperous and comfortable," made little time for civil rights; the "few middle-class Negroes who," according to Martin Luther King, Jr., "because of a degree of academic and economic security and because in some ways they profit from segregation, have become insensitive to the problems of the masses." The Negroes who "actually favored segregation," wrote Myrlie Evers, were those who "had so ingratiated themselves with whites that they had been rewarded with the better jobs, the better acres of land, or the better chance to escape the unequal justice of the state." In the same boat with those groveling Uncle Toms were the "Negroes who served as spies in the Negro community for the white political powers, those obsequious traitors to their people who sold bits and pieces of information for the crumbs of privilege such intelligence was considered to be worth." (Evers knew whereof she spoke—as the recently opened papers of Mississippi's Sovereignty Commission make clear, not a few well-placed black civil rights workers in Mississippi were on the Commission's payroll.) Black segregationists also "included sometimes a Negro school principal or college president, a Department of Agriculture county agent or a minister, whose reward for helping to keep their people down was to be raised above the important or powerful whites"—those to whom local Negroes "turned to for help in time of need."[12]

Chief among those prosperous and comfortable black southerners were ministers. Many preachers, of course, supported the civil rights movement—without them there would probably have been no civil rights movement. But there were also ministers who opposed the movement:

not simply those who preached caution, tried to prevent their congregants from adopting the "unrespectable" tactics of sit-ins and marches, or urged keeping the peace while simultaneously funneling money to the NAACP; not the ministers who wanted the movement to move more slowly, those who wanted it not to move at all.

These ministers were the ones who sought money when the black church needed a new roof (and they usually got that roof built). They were the ones John Shields targeted when he described clergy who "play[ed] a role in the exploitation and repression of their own people. . . . [They] were like the straw bosses in the black settlements in slavery times who helped the masters keep the black people subservient and reconciled to slavery while the straw boss got a little authority and a few other scraps from the white man's table. [They were] selling us out . . . preaching in the pulpits that their congregation would get their reward in the afterlife." They were the ones whom Charles Evers characterized as "the cautious Uncle Tom preacher who obeyed the commandments, had a cozy house, maybe a little field. Whites greeted him on the street. He couldn't bear to risk losing all that. So he ignored civil rights and took the white man's crumbs. He wouldn't pay the price. . . . Most black preachers accepted beatings, lynchings, and black poverty. They promised their flock heaven in the sweet by-and-by and asked them to live like dogs here on earth." They were the ones who sold out their congregants in order to maintain their own privileged position, building their most modest of mansions upon the backs of black lynchees. These "by-and-by" preachers, promising their parishioners pie-in-the-sky-when-you-die, echoed Ralph Abernathy, thought desegregation either "frivolous or threatening." Those ministers, said Abernathy, proved to be the "chief stumbling blocks in the way of progress when the civil rights movement developed."[13]

Black ministers had been preaching about heavenly rewards for earthly suffering long before the civil rights movement. In the 1930s, Benjamin Mays found that southern black clergy tend to "encourage Negroes to feel that God will see to it that things work out all right; if not in this world, certainly in the world to come. They make God influential chiefly in the beyond, in preparing a home . . . where His suffering servants will be free of the trials and tribulations which beset them on Earth." Gunnar Myrdal made a similar point, noting that "the Negro preacher" delivered "other-worldly" sermons, while maintaining very this-worldly ties to white businessmen and politicians.[14]

Even after 1954, some black ministers preached avowedly seg sermons, taught explicitly seg Sunday School lessons, and never hesitated to read Scripture through a segregationist scrim. Scriptural-citing seg preachers pointed to the Tower of Babel (God graciously gave people different languages to different races wouldn't communicate or socialize with one another) and the Bible's prohibitions of "interracial mixing" and intermarriage. The Reverend M. L. Young of Memphis was president of the Mutual Association of Colored People in the South. Young, one of the "Negro clergymen who championed segregation," did not mind that his position earned him the vitriol of black civil rights leaders. In the words of Reed Sarratt, Young "supported his position by saying 'The Bible is right regardless of the stand anyone may take.'" Theological educator Collier P. Clay formed the Negro Improvement Association of Alabama, Inc., a group that "seeks equalization of Negro facilities rather than integration" and was in "avowed opposition to the 'outside troublemakers' of the National Association for the Advancement of Colored People." Dallas's Reverend W. R. Farley, who declared in June 1955 that "most Negroes" were peace-loving bearers of goodwill, who wanted black and white each to "hold [to] his distinctive place in life." True, there were some "sore sports," and wrongs had been done to Negroes in the past. But those wrongs were being corrected: "Negroes are getting better wages, better schools, better churches, and better and more recreational facilities." Whatever the "sore spots," integration was not "the solution of the race problem. God made a distinction between races, so why should mere man try to change it?"[15]

Black ministers, of course, had something to lose from integration. Not that the Supreme Court was threatening to integrate the churches that were the institutional heart of black southern communities—as the cliché goes, 11 o'clock on Sunday morning remains the South's most segregated hour. But integration threatened the delicate choreography that lifted up the local black minister as the spokesman of the community. Ministers and other designated go-betweens spoke eloquently of that community. In a widely circulated editorial, Percy Greene, editor of *The Jackson Advocate*, denounced the "new crop of Negro leaders." The new leaders, he said, branded as an Uncle Tom anyone who "seeks to maintain a friendly and respectful attitude toward the responsible white people of the community." Black southerners didn't need freedom on the NAACP's terms—they needed segregation and white patronage, patronage that decades of leaders like Greene had worked to cultivate, patronage that could be maintained by "manners, and [an] attitude of respect toward the responsible white leaders." Indeed, the Mutual Association of Colored People South published a list of ten tips for "Get[ting] Along With People." It urged the well-mannered reader to keep promises, no matter what; "Keep skid chains on your tongue"; avoid gossip, and refrain from making jokes "at the other fellows expense." Above all, "Do your work be patient and keep your disposition sweet, forget self and you will be rewarded." Manners, not marches, would help the Negro.[16]

If ministers had something to lose through integration, so did businessmen. Davis Lee, a New Jersey newspaperman who took over the *Orangeburg Herald*, a black newspaper in South Carolina, was among the most articulate African American defenders of segregation. Lee, who has been described as "a staunch enemy of the civil rights movement," attacked the movement in editorials and in court. He filed suits against the Anderson County branch of the NAACP and filed a motion to intervene on behalf of the state to prevent the forced integration of state parks between 1961 and 1963. Under his leadership, the *Herald* painted a positive picture of black life in the Palmetto State, and especially emphasized the many business opportunities open to African Americans in the state's urban areas. No love was lost between Lee and other black leaders in the state—Roy Wilkins blasted him in his weekly column—but working-class black Carolinians continued to read his paper through the early 1970s, when it folded.[17]

Lee was one of many spokesmen who believed that black businesses in the South would crumble if segregation ended. "The whites with the South stay with their own and the Negroes do likewise," he wrote. "This one fact has been the economic salvation of the Negro in the South. . . . Negroes [in Atlanta] own and control millions of dollars worth of business. All of the Negro business in New Jersey will not amount to as much as our race has in one city in Georgia." Black businessmen, Lee warned, simply could not make it in an integrated setting. Lee wasn't the only black spokesman to worry about Atlanta's fate. W. R. Farley pointed to Atlanta as evidence that "There's no place in the world, where the Negro owns and controls as much as he does in the South. . . . I would say without question that Atlanta is the Negro capital of the world. It is thought by many to be the center of education and culture, finance and business." What would Atlanta be like 50 years from now, asked Farley. If the integrationists have their way, black Atlantans would be no better off than black New Yorkers. The Mutual Association of Colored People South reminded readers that "Negroes can't eat integration. They need jobs," and they had more job opportunities in the segregated South than anywhere else. "The South is the only section of this nation that offers [Negroes] opportunities. If these liberals and agitators are the Negroes' friends and the Southern whites are his enemies, then someone needs to protect him from his friends."[18]

Teachers, some black defenders of segregation argued, were also sure to lose out in the new integrated order. "[A] Negro can attend most of the schools in the north and get a fair education," wrote W. R. Farley, "but few of the Northern states which educate him will hire him as a teacher. The State of Connecticut does not have 235 Negro teachers." Georgia, in contrast, employed 7,313 black teachers. In Georgia, one high school principal who made it clear that he had no patience for voter registration drives may have been more representative. A student leader who needed the principal's recommendation for college dropped out of the registration movement; the basketball coach threatened to drop any members of the team who flirted with SNCC; a lunchroom employee, who was also the mother of a student, was fired after she participated in a small demonstration. (This was nothing new: Teachers and school administrators had long voiced support for segregated schools. In 1934, for example, a black principal in Houston objected to black and white people sitting together "on the same benches in a Negro-owned auditorium. The whites themselves raised no such objection.")[19]

Those teachers who opposed school desegregation figure prominently in activists' attacks of Uncle Toms. The *Brown* decision, after all, was the emblem of the movement, and to dissent from its wisdom was seen as heresy. Mrs. Nanie Tubbs of Indianola, Mississippi, complained that "The white racists are bad enough, but the Uncle Toms are even worse . . . . Uncle Tom principals do just what the white folks want them to do; they're supposed to be our leaders, but they're holding us back, holding back the progress of Negro children." Black teachers from across the South worried that they would lose their jobs in an integrated school system, and, indeed, many were right. As one caustic civil rights leader wrote in 1967, some black teachers "actually feared an eventual desegregation of schools. It was at least conceivable to them, that the state might someday permit some Negro students to attend white schools; it was inconceivable that Negro teachers would be allowed to teach in those schools."[20]

That may have been the reasoning of the three black members of Governor William Umstead's "Governor's Special Advisory Committee on Education," North Carolina A&T president Ferdinand Bluford, Edgecombe County, North Carolina, home demonstration agent Hazel Parker, and J. W. Seabrook, president of Fayetteville State Teachers college. In December, 1954, the committee unanimously advised that North Carolina "not . . . attempt" school desegregation. They suggested the legislature give local school boards control of pupil assignment. Or the reasoning of Freeman Burns, Negro Superintendent of the Rehobeth school district, who, shortly after *Brown*, spoke at the Fairfax, Alabama, Kiwanis Club meeting. Disturbed by the prospect of school integration, Burns advocated "voluntary segregation." Burns offered four reasons that "vast majority of my people" would embrace his plan: "the natural desire of the Negro . . . to be associated with one another"; state government's increased allocations for black schools; the commitment of "patient" Negroes to racial harmony; and "the pride we have in our institutions. Integration would finally mean the death of the Negro college," Burns said, echoing Davis Lee, "and of all Negro institutions as we know them."[21] Nanie Tubbs would have had no time for Burns.

Not all the black defenders of segregation were middle-class community leaders. Matthews and Protho found that most of the African Americans who were critical of integration in 1966 were "blue-collar workers with a grade-school education at best and with a family income of less than $2,000 a year." Many of those blue-collar workers were maids. Why would domestic workers, who hardly benefited from segregation, defend it? Myrlie Evers explained in her memoir that the maid who preferred segregation to the civil rights movement was the loyal retainer who had worked for the same family for thirty years, earning the family's loyalty and consequently their protection from the worst ravages of Jim Crow—the maid who knew her employer would always get her husband out of jail or pay her medical bills in a pinch.[22]

Although Evers is right that some domestic servants criticized the civil rights movement, her explanation of why is too narrow. There were surely those who preferred the patronage and protection of their employer (the Devil they knew) to the uncertainties of the civil rights movement. But that preference was born out of specific criticisms of the movement, not out of a naïve romanticization of domestic service in the segregated South. Maids' criticisms were two-fold. First, they, like Hurston, criticized what they perceived to be an emphasis on space, not power. "We knew what integration was like long before it came to the rest," said Mary Simmons, a black maid from North Carolina. "We knew it was not going to be the great good everyone thought it would be." Making a point that many historians still have not grasped, Simmons added: "We were all living close together and sharing stores and houses during slavery times, and that was not heaven on earth."[23]

Second, a handful of maids criticized the place that consumerism occupied in the pantheon of civil rights goals. As several recent studies have suggested, the civil rights movement was, in part, a revolution in consuming.[24] Civil rights came to be construed not only as voting and equal educational resources, but as entitlement to the supposed benefits of consumer society. Especially for women in the movement, being able to shop anywhere and be treated with dignity was a central goal of the movement. The hostile attitudes of white sales' clerks who spoke "frostily" to black female customers and would not allow black women to try on clothing or hats were understood as being every bit as galling as being spurned by a voting registrar. For Charles Evers, the issue was that "Negroes in Mississippi had never been able to sit down and enjoy a milk shake. The best we could do was to buy one at a drug-store take-out stand." His sister-in-law recounted going shopping on Saturday nights with her husband, Medgar. Medgar, Myrlie Evers wrote, "would point out a plantation owner huddled with the storekeeper as the sharecroppers made their weekly purchases of meal and flour and lard. 'You don't need that, Willie,' the owner would tell a ragged Negro, pushing aside a box of cookies or a pound of bacon. 'This is enough for you.' And the Negro would meekly accept the command, taking, in effect, what he was permitted to take, feeding his family what the plantation owner decided he should feed them." Some domestic workers questioned the benefits that would accrue to them should the middle-class Everses get their dream. As maid Sarah Peters put it: "I might be allowed in a shop, but that won't do me much good if I'm not making any money to spend there."[25]

This essay introduces a cast of characters about whom more needs to be known. A full understanding of black defenders of segregation will require a detailed social and economic cartography of individuals and their communities. When a black preacher tells his congregation that the Bible teaches segregation, we want to know where his church was, who owned the building, who held the mortgage, where his family worked. The minister whose church building is free and clear is in a different situation from the minister whose church could be foreclosed tomorrow.

The arguments of the ministers and maids, the teachers and business-men, deserve careful analysis from intellectual historians. Some of their arguments will be illuminating. Black businessmen, for example, were not stooges, and they were not merely victims. Put differently, they were not only, as Carter Woodson allowed, sincere, they were also shrewd. Some businessmen believed that having a captive market or a geographically delimited community was in their interest—they would never have a white client, and if black people could go to any lawyer in town, they might never have a black client either. Others believed that having a pro-tected market was the only way that black people could advance. Black businessmen's logic was nothing less than a civil rights-era reiteration of strategies for protecting infant industries that date to Jefferson and Hamil-ton. Davis Lee was right that integration would hurt black businesses. Although the black middle-class is much larger today than it was 50 years ago, it is not the same middle class, as the boarded up buildings in Vine City and East Hargett and other formerly flourishing black business dis-tricts make clear. The absentee-owned or franchised convenience stores and currency exchanges are the only things left where once there was a small but solid petit bourgeoisie of proud shopkeepers.

Other defenses of segregation, like Hurston's arguments about min-gling with white people, may prove lacking. Huston's emphasis on prox-imity, rather than power, did presage some of the limitations of the NAACP's strategy of desegregation. But it also caricatures that strategy. True enough, the arguments in *Brown* suggest that the real essence of the thing is that black people have to be next to white people. But no one took to the Pettus Bridge because they wanted to hobnob with white folks.

So too, the arguments of the maids may be wanting. Consider their crit-icism of the NAACP's focus on consumption. Sarah Peters raised a point with which we must grapple: some young activists were indeed too gung-ho about lunch counters (to wit Julian Bond's admission that he and some of his contemporaries, during the heady days of the sit-ins, were com-pletely puzzled when Ella Baker pointed out that the whole world wasn't about a hamburger). But consumption, it must be recognized, played a role in civil rights strategy for good reason: in the post–World War II era, issues of consumption and ability to consume in public places increasingly carried the social weight of the rights of citizenship. As Americans evacuated class as a political question by collapsing everybody into a single class that was defined by how people lived; it is no surprise that people who were denied the right to live that way readily assimilated lifestyle and consumption to questions that are more traditionally political.

As our historiography makes room for black defenders of segregation, we would do well to remember a lesson Eugene Genovese taught 30 years ago. The normal desire of human beings is to live a life and have a routine with as much dignity, and as little unnecessary exposure to harm, as they can manage. Most people will make the compromises they need to make most of the time to lead a quiet life. That desire is understandable, but it needs to be understood against the backdrop of a recognition that though people may be free to decide that they are going to recreate a routine that keeps their heads down, they may have no power to decide the contours of the world that constrains their choices. The civil rights activists of whom Hurston, Peters, and other black defenders of segregation were so critical understood that when one person is holding another person hostage, only in the narrowest possible sense does the captive have an interest that coincides with the captor. The larger interest of the captive is in not being held captive any longer.

Many thanks to the people who read—and re-read—versions of "Doubtless Sincere": Tony Badger, Joseph Crespino, Barbara Jeanne Fields, Eric Foner, Grace Elizabeth Hale, Paul Harvey, Michael O'Brien, Ted Ownby, Gerald Smith and, especially, David Chappell.

Notes

Notes to NIEBUHRISMS AND MYRDALERIES: THE INTELLECTUAL ROOTS OF
THE CIVIL RIGHTS MOVEMENT RECONSIDERED
by David L. Chappell

1. This is particularly evident in Stephan and Abigail Thernstrom, *America in Black
and White* (New York: Simon and Schuster, 1999), and Dinesh D'Souza, *The End of Racism* (New York: Free Press, 1995), which credit the erosion of discrimination before the
mid-1960s to a blend of natural economic progress and limited liberal reformism. Gavin
Wright, *Old South, New South* (New York: Basic, 1986), has a somewhat different emphasis on government policy and pressure from protesters together liberating the labor market so that it could realize its natural tendency to break down artificial distinctions such
as race. John Egerton, *Speak Now against the Day: The Generation before the Civil Rights
Movement in the South* (New York: Knopf, 1994), sees the South moving inexorably away
from tradition towards a more modern system of race relations. Patricia Sullivan, *Days of
Hope: Race and Democracy in the New Deal Era* (Chapel Hill: University of North Carolina Press, 1996), somewhat more moderately sees antiracist "implications" in the general
trend of the New Deal. All these have in common a belief that moving forward through
time means moving away from a racist past.
    2. Tension between liberalism and Christianity is a major theme of the history of lib-
eralism. Many studies, from J.B. Bury's *A History of Freedom of Thought* (New York:
Henry Holt, 1913) to Guido de Ruggiero's *History of European Liberalism* (Oxford:
Oxford University Press, 1927) to Pierre Manent's *An Intellectual History of Liberalism*
(Princeton: Princeton University Press, 1997), see the history of liberalism as essentially
anti-Christian. A different tradition, from Christopher Dawson's *The Judgment of Nations*
(New York: Sheed and Ward, 1942) to William Aylott Orton's *The Liberal Tradition* (New
Haven: Yale University Press, 1945), sees liberalism as deriving from a specific kind of
Christianity, while noting that liberals denied or were unaware of their Christian roots.
    3. There are other ways to see liberalism. Peter Berkowitz, for example, in *Virtue and
the Making of Modern Liberalism* (Princeton: Princeton University Press, 1999), ambi-
tiously attempts to rescue liberalism from post-Rawls critics who claim it takes for granted
and/or contributes to the atrophy of virtues and obligations on which a humane and
decent life depends. Berkowitz establishes that what he calls "extraliberal" virtues were
in fact on the minds of the great liberal thinkers. Far from defending liberalism against
charges of shallow short- sightedness, however, he proves that the best liberals always
understood they had to look outside liberalism for whatever qualities may redeem liberalism.
    4. The prophetic tradition is elaborated in H. Richard Niebuhr, *The Kingdom of God
in America* (New York, 1937), and in Norman Cohn, *The Pursuit of the Millennium* (London, 1957).
    5. Richard Fox, *Reinhold Niebuhr: a Biography* (New York: Pantheon, 1985).
    6. See notes 29 and 30, below.
    7. John Kirby's *Black Americans in the Roosevelt Era* (Knoxville: University of Ten-
nessee Press, 1980), along with Harold Cruse's old warhorse, *The Crisis of the Negro
Intellectual* (New York: Morrow, 1967), are useful correctives to the treatments of the
1930s by Pat Sullivan and John Egerton, cited above, note 1, who seem to me to view the
New Deal era too whiggishly as a period of advance *towards* a true confrontation with
racial issues.
    8. Alan Brinkley's *The End of Reform* (New York: Knopf, 1995) makes this point about
post-World War II liberalism, though he sees bold hopes begin to ebb after 1937. Richard

Hofstadter observed in 1948 that liberals had been in a "rudderless and demoralized state" since FDR's death. *The American Political Tradition* (New York: Knopf, 1948), vii.

9. Even then, individual rights more often meant civil liberties—the largely self-interested defense of open political debate against right wing attack—than the kind of individual rights whose guarantee would have structural economic consequences in the South and many of the major cities. R. Alan Lawson, *The Failure of Independent Liberalism* (New York: Putnam, 1971), 172; Brinkley, *The End of Reform*.

10. Liberals always understood their program to be based on faith that human reason could solve the "problems" of human society. Yet the deepest believers in reason sensed that reason was not enough. The Pragmatist philosopher who gave American Liberalism its distinctive cast in the Progressive Era, William James, memorably expressed the need for an irrational crusade to inspire the sacrifices that reason could not inspire in "The Moral Equivalent of War" (1910). James, the scientific thinker who had suffered a nervous breakdown, was echoing the patron saint of modern English-speaking liberalism, John Stuart Mill, who suffered a similar breakdown in the early-19th century. Mill's famous breakdown came with the revelation that, if all his desires for personal and social reform came true, as measured by the rationalistic, "utilitarian" calculations of his father's great system, he would still not be happy. Thus began Mill's search in the unscientific flights and irrational urges of Romanticism for the missing elements of liberalism. See Mill, *Autobiography* (London: Longman's, 1873).

11. See especially Dewey, *The Quest for Certainty* (1929) and *A Common Faith* (1934); R.A. Lawson, *The Failure of Independent Liberalism* (New York: Putnam, 1971), Robert Westbrook, *John Dewey and American Democracy* (Ithaca: Cornell University Press, 1991), 419–25, 448, and Alan Ryan, *John Dewey and the High Tide of American Liberalism* (New York: Norton, 1995), 234–5, 241–2, 262–76.

12. Despair over the loss of faith is most powerfully developed in Joseph Wood Krutch, *The Modern Temper* (New York: Harcourt Brace, 1929), and Walter Lippmann, *Preface to Morals* (New York: Macmillan, 1929).

The prominent New Deal thinker Thurman Arnold discussed the need for faith more optimistically than Dewey and Ross, but with equal emphasis on the importance of it. "A new creed called psychiatry is dimly understood by millions of people. . . . . . . A conception of an adult personality is bringing a new sense of tolerance and common sense to replace the notion of the great man who lived and died for moral and rational purposes. . . . . . . In medieval times nations were holy and kings led crusades to dramatize that idea. In modern times governments act in the image of great businessmen. . . . . . . It is true that there is little in the present conduct of the governments of the world which can by any stretch of the imagination be called adult. . . . . . . Fanatical devotion to principle on the part of the public still compels intelligent leaders to commit themselves, for political reasons, to all sorts of disorderly nonsense. So long as the public holds preconceived faiths about the fundamental principles of government, they will persecute and denounce new ideas . . . . and orators will prevail over technicians. . . . Nevertheless one who desires to be effective in society must be permitted to hope. . . . . . . The writer has faith that a new public attitude toward the ideals of law and economics is slowly appearing to create an atmosphere where the fanatical alignments between opposing political principles may disappear and a competent, practical, opportunistic governing class may rise to power." Arnold, *The Symbols of Government* (New York: Harcourt, 1935), 270–1. Arnold developed this emphasis on the need to correct the animating faith of society in his best-seller, *The Folklore of Capitalism* (New Haven: Yale University Press, 1937).

A hunger after missing faith also drove the most influential liberal critic of the New Deal. Walter Lippmann defended liberalism, "the philosophy of [the] industrial revolution," against what he saw as the "collectivism" of the New Deal and "Totalitarian" states of the left and right. He urged true liberals to provide society not just new structures of law and organization, but the "cultural equipment that men must have if they are to live effectively, and at ease with themselves, in an interdependent [i.e., modern industrial]

Great Society." He found liberals stymied by "the science" they inherited; they are "unable to carry forward their science." Lippmann clearly envied the "collectivists," who have "the zest for progress, the sympathy for the poor, the burning sense of wrong, the impulse for great deeds which have been lacking in latter-day liberalism." The premise of Lippmann's attack on the New Deal was that a deep liberal "faith" in individual freedom had been lost. The loss was a necessary consequence of the new division of labor brought by industrial development (Lippmann thought concentration of corporate power was merely a "secondary" concern). Lippmann was the most militant of liberals in his resignation to the "realities" of modern capitalism: "men may have to pass through a terrible ordeal before they find again the central truths they have forgotten." Lippmann, *The Good Society* (1937; reprint, New York: Grossett & Dunlap, 1943), 237, 236, 204, 40–1.

The idea that modern (often a synonym for liberal) man's loss of faith was dangerous may have come into liberal discourse in the 1930s via one of the great Jeremiads of the prophetic tradition, Robert and Helen Lynd's best-selling sociological analysis of urban society *Middletown* (New York: Harcourt Brace, 1929). Richard Pells takes the Lynds' work as a starting point for his observation that "the recurring desire for some sort of group ethos, the insistence on new forms of cultural adjustment, the assumption that social change in America had to mean more than political reform would all become major themes in [the 1930s] as well." Pells, *Radical Visions and American Dreams: Culture and Thought in the Depression Years* (New York: Harper, 1973), 27. Richard Fox interprets the Lynds' work as part of the American tradition of Jeremiad in "Epitaph for Middletown," in *The Culture of Consumption*, ed. Richard Fox and Jackson Lears (New York: Pantheon, 1983).

13. Malcolm Ross, *Death of a Yale Man* (NY: Farrar & Rinehart, 1939), 59–63.

14. Ann Douglas, *The Feminization of American Culture* (New York: Doubleday, 1977).

15. Donald Richberg, looking back on the 1930s, wrote that the task of a man of affairs was "the maintenance of a simple faith in the reason and purpose of living, a guiding star that, often lost to view yet ever shining, will save him again and again from the emptiness of despair and a struggle that has no meaning and no end." For some, this could come from "old-time religion," for some it came from egotism or instinct, but it was vital, and it was missing. Donald Richberg, *My Hero: Indiscreet Memoirs of an Eventful but Unheroic Life* (New York: Putnam, 1954), 5–6.

16. All quotations from Trilling's preface to *The Liberal Imagination* (NY: Viking, 1949).

17. Arthur M. Schlesinger, Jr., *Vital Center* (Boston: Houghton-Mifflin, 1949), 166.

18. Schlesinger tried to fit Niebuhr into a special brand of *American* pessimism, which held that "power, unless checked by accountability, would corrupt its possessor." The Doughface progressive, Schlesinger said, has "rejected the pragmatic tradition of the men who, from the Jacksonians to the New Dealers, learned the facts of life through the exercise of power under conditions of accountability. He has rejected the pessimistic tradition of those who, from Hawthorne to Reinhold Niebuhr, warned that power, unless checked by accountability, would corrupt its predecessor." *Vital Center*, 36–7. He doesn't realize this is not pessimistic, or Niebuhrian, at all: A pessimist does not need that "unless checked by accountability" clause. Niebuhr's rejection of liberal optimism was more wholehearted than Schlesinger could see: Niebuhr believed, in the classical and Christian fashion, that power *always* corrupts. Jane Tompkins suggests that the tough-minded Hawthorne is in any case a discovery (or an invention) of the twentieth century: in his own day, Hawthorne was lauded in the same language as female sentimental novelists were lauded, and for the same qualities. Jane Tompkins, *Sensational Designs: The Cultural Work of American Fiction, 1790–1860* (New York: Oxford, 1985).

19. Niebuhr, *Moral Man and Immoral Society* (New York: Scribner's, 1932), xxi, xvii.

20. Schlesinger, *Vital Center*, xx; previous quotation p. 4. It may be objected that Schlesinger was making a reasonable compromise, that complete pessimism about human nature is as unrealistic as optimism, and at any rate would be an impractical basis for a political program. But Niebuhr himself was a compromise. Niebuhr insisted he was not

neo-orthodox; he rejected Karl Barth's pessimism, Barth's Augustinian rejection of this world. Niebuhr sought to engage in political conflict, to fight oppression, and "to mitigate the brutalities" of modern life, even while he insisted that complete success in such efforts was impossible. Niebuhr's biographers and other students of his work now emphasize that Niebuhr greatly exaggerated his own rejection of liberal theology. He was really criticizing liberalism from within, seeking to curb its excesses but not rejecting its engagement with and efforts to reform this world. Donald Meyer, *The Protestant Search for Political Realism* (1960; reprint, Middleton: Wesleyan, 1988). Richard Fox rightly identifies Paul Tillich's "non-Barthian" influence as far more important in Niebuhr's development than Barth's influence in *Reinhold Niebuhr: A Biography* (New York: Pantheon, 1985), 160–2. Fox focuses on Niebuhr's (and his more conservative brother, H. Richard Niebuhr's) reaffirmation of "a fundamentally liberal, modernist commitment" demonstrating "the continued potency of liberal Protestantism in the mid-twentieth century—a time when it was supposedly in decline and disarray," in "The Niebuhr Brothers and the Liberal Protestant Heritage," in *Religion and Twentieth-Century American Intellectual Life*, ed. Michael J. Lacey (Cambridge: Cambridge University Press, 1989), 94–115. In the latter essay, Fox points out that William Hutchison stressed the continuity of the Niebuhrs with the social gospellers back in 1963, in "Liberal Protestantism and the 'End of Innocence,'" *American Quarterly* 15 (1963), 126–36.

   21. Niebuhr's prophetic remarks on race and nonviolent action are in *Moral Man and Immoral Society*, 252–5. He says, "There is no problem of political life to which religious imagination can make a larger contribution than this problem of developing non-violent resistance." For all his Machiavellian emphasis on the practicality of nonviolent force, he says "secular imagination," is just "not capable" of developing the "attitudes or repentance which recognize that the evil in the foe is also in the self" and the "impulses of love which claim kinship with all men in spite of social conflict," things he elsewhere identifies with "prophetic Christianity," require, "a sublime madness which disregards immediate appearances and emphasizes profound and ultimate unities. It is no accident of history that the spirit of non-violence has been introduced into contemporary politics by a religious leader of the orient." He returns to the indictment of racism in *The Children of Light and the Children of Darkness* (1944), 139–42.

   22. Schlesinger on Gandhi, *Vital Center*, 7. After denouncing the arrogance of nonviolence, Schlesinger somewhat incoherently went on to say that we must defend and strengthen our "free society" against the one power that would *not* be susceptible to Gandhian tactics, the Soviet Union, but we must do it short of war, because war would destroy freedom almost as surely as surrender to totalitarianism, *Vital Center*, 10, 156. Schlesinger's certainty of America's virtues, bordering on arrogance, far exceeded Niebuhr's, even at the height of Niebuhr's "us or them" attacks on the Soviet Union in the Cold War. On Schlesinger's certainty of American virtues, *Vital Center*, 146–7, 166. Niebuhr's more melancholy, more Churchillian defense of the West—it isn't so great but it's usually better than the alternative—is expressed in *The Children of Light and the Children of Darkness* (1944). Niebuhr defends democracy as apparently the most effective check on human excesses, but insists that democracy, which exerts a communal control over the individual, cannot be equated with liberalism or freedom, let alone individualism. Schlesinger altogether ignores the distinction, using democracy interchangeably with freedom, liberalism, and individualism.

   23. Schlesinger, *Vital Center*, 190, 230. Niebuhr, for his part, specifically questioned whether any "disinherited group, such as the Negroes," would ever win justice by accommodating and negotiating with the dominant group. *Moral Man*, xvii, 252–3.

   24. Considering staying in power the *sine qua non* of all liberal hopes, including those for racial equality, liberals took great pains to avoid alienating southern Democrats. They had seen their party almost fall apart over a strong civil rights plank introduced in 1948 (echo of FDR's failure in 1938). In 1948, about one third of the ADA chapters in the country wanted to throw their support to Eisenhower, who was thought to be liberal on

many issues, though he opposed desegregation of the military and federal compulsion of states on civil rights. The main thing for the liberals was that Truman looked like a loser and Eisenhower's popularity rivaled that of the late FDR. Only two chapters out of 47 wanted to back the incumbent Truman. The liberals joined in introducing the radical civil rights plank, partly because they were sure Truman was going to lose anyway, and they might as well try to overpower the southern wing of their party. Truman won, but the party was badly injured. Some liberals had defected to Wallace (a few defected to the GOP) and many southerners defected to Strom Thurmond's Dixiecrats. Liberals did not want to repeat their mistake in 1952 and 1956, when they believed a Democrat had a real chance of winning. So they backed away from Truman's commitment to civil rights.

Schlesinger and other postwar liberals were as conscious as FDR had been that any action on civil rights would divide the Democratic Party, which they saw as the only viable vehicle for long-term liberalism. Visiting Chattanooga in 1950 to investigate the possibilities for establishing ADA chapters in the South, Schlesinger found that the civil rights issue was the liberals' "main obstacle in recruiting and organizing." Southern liberals, he found, did not "want ADA to modify its stand" on civil rights (which was not very strong at that point), but anything that would make the ADA "seem exclusively or largely concerned with the civil rights issue" would only make their lives more difficult. Accordingly, Schlesinger suggested that "It might help our organizing in the South if something could be done to make the ADA seem something else than another Yankee liberal outfit." It was especially important that "ADA seem in the South much less a personal machine for the civil rights program of Hubert Humphrey." Schlesinger quoted in Gillon, *Politics and Vision*, 62–3.

Liberals' willingness to support (and ultimate enthusiasm for) Democratic candidate Adlai Stevenson in 1952 and 1956 also illustrates that civil rights was not vital to them. John Frederick Martin observed, Stevenson "simply did not understand the civil rights issue." Martin, *Civil Rights and the Crisis of Liberalism* (Boulder: Westview, 1979), 96. Stevenson said civil rights were the responsibility of the states and that the federal government should not "put the South completely over a barrel." He seemed to think it relevant to add, "You know, I've got southern blood in me." Stevenson quoted in Steven Gillon, *Politics and Vision*, 84–5. See also, Herbert Parmet, *The Democrats* (New York: Macmillan, 1976), 99–100. This is especially clear in 1956, when there were clear civil rights supporters in the field of Democratic candidates (Harriman and Kefauver). Steven Gillon, the most thorough student of liberal attitudes on race in these years, says that the liberals' "indifference to Kefauver's candidacy" is "difficult to explain." But the difficulty disappears with Gillon's assumption that liberals by nature supported civil rights, as a principle, more than they opposed southerners, as political and cultural pariahs. Kefauver was an ardent supporter, not only of civil rights, but of the New Deal and Fair Deal. Kefauver's "folksy, neopopulist southern style made him anathema to the ADA's brand of urbane liberalism." Gillon suggests that Kefauver's effort to walk between sectional factions was "more important" than his populist southern style (Gillon, *Politics and Vision*, 85–6), but this is doubtful, since Stevenson was trying to walk the same "narrow path"— and for Stevenson walking that path meant greater concessions to the southern wing than Kefauver would ever make. Kefauver is one of the few southern politicians who risked his position in the Senate by standing up to the segregationists. (Lyndon Johnson was another, yet like Kefauver, Johnson failed to get significant support from northern liberals. Liberals liked John Sparkman and Lister Hill, if they liked anybody from the South, and they later grew fond of Fulbright and Ervin. But all four of those signed the Southern Manifesto and made regular campaign pledges to support white supremacy.) Gillon's explanation is doubtful from another angle: the next two Democratic nominees, Kennedy and Johnson, like the previous two, Roosevelt and Truman, also tried to walk the "narrow path" between North and South. Kefauver's liability was that northern liberals had an aversion to him as a southerner, and that southerners hated him for his treachery on civil rights.

25. In the major histories of Myrdal's project, both sympathetic, Myrdal comes across as dogmatic in his insistence on his optimistic thesis, with which many collaborators did not agree. He apparently fixated upon his notion of an American creed without much reflection or study, before coming to America, then clung to it and tried to impose it on his collaborators. See David Southern, *Gunnar Myrdal and Black-White Relations: The Use and Abuse of An American Dilemma, 1944–1969* (Baton Rouge: Louisiana State University Press, 1987), esp. 32–3. Southern focuses more on the reception and influence of the Myrdal report. Walter Jackson focuses more on Myrdal, the production and publication of the research, and the way Myrdal's own life intertwined with the subsequent history of the report, in *Gunnar Myrdal and America's Conscience* (Chapel Hill: University of North Carolina Press, 1990). The two overlap some, but present two distinct narratives, Jackson's offering I think a more nuanced and plausible (not at all unsympathetic) view of Myrdal's motives and preconceptions. But Southern is indispensable for the way Americans received the study.

26. A few critics of Myrdal's book complained that it was too optimistic, but for the most part these criticisms did not catch on until a general disillusionment with the limits of civil rights took root in the 1960s, when radical and conservative critics indicted Myrdal for the limitations of the civil rights movement, which they mistakenly believed he initiated. The most important such criticism was probably Ralph Ellison's review, originally slated for publication in the *Antioch Review* shortly after the release of Myrdal's book in 1944, but for some reason never appearing until Ellison's collection, *Shadow and Act*, was published in 1962. Though Niebuhr could not have been more diametrically opposed to Myrdal's approach—Niebuhr said the basic liberal "creed," which stressed that education and progress could overcome social problems, including group conflicts and inequality, was "sentimental" (*Children of Light and Children of Darkness* [1944], 33)—he actually gave Myrdal a favorable review.

On fatalism in America, see Tony Badger, "Fatalism, not Gradualism: The Crisis of Southern Liberalism, 1945–65," in Brian Ward and Tony Badger, eds., *The Making of Martin Luther King and the Civil Rights Movement* (New York: New York University Press, 1996): 67–95.

27. The greatest mistake liberals made, Niebuhr said, was to think that collectives, even nations, could be compelled to act on the basis of moral rules. In fact, they only acted on the interests their constituents. This is the main theme of *Moral Man and Immoral Society* (1932). Niebuhr returns to the theme in other major works, *An Interpretation of Christian Ethics* (1935), esp. ch. 5, *The Nature and Destiny of Man* esp. vol. I (1941), ch. 8, and *The Children of Light and the Children of Darkness* (1944), esp. ch. 2.

28. The President's committee altered its report greatly before publication, largely to appease southern critics who disagreed with Myrdal's approach, or were offended by his failure to honor them in his report. But the committee remained Myrdalian in its basic thrust. On the President's committee and Humphrey, Southern, *Gunnar Myrdal and Black-White Relations*, 118–124.

29. Jackson also documents "an air of unreality, a lack of comprehension" among liberals of black America's political dynamism from roughly 1954 to 1960, noting that civil rights was "rarely a central concern of prominent white intellectuals outside the South" for the decade before that period. He suggests that "the gulf that opened in the mid-1960s between white and black advocates of civil rights" can be understood by examination of the content of white liberal thought in the period before the movement. See Jackson, "White Liberal Intellectuals and Civil Rights, 1954–1960," in Brian Ward and Tony Badger, eds., *The Making of Martin Luther King and the Civil Rights Movement* (New York: New York University Press, 1996), 96–114.

30. Richard King, *Civil Rights and the Idea of Freedom* (New York: Oxford University Press, 1992), 6, 38.

31. In his doctrine of man, King inclined at first towards liberalism, that is to say towards optimism, but even in his divinity school papers at Crozer (1948–51) he shows

an openness to pessimism, even before he apparently read Niebuhr. King himself is guilty of mislabeling Niebuhr "neo-orthodox": Answers to qualifying exam in History of Doctrine (1953). Yet even there, he notes that not only Niebuhr but "all of the outstanding Neo-orthodox theologians accept the latest results of Biblical and historical criticism, and yet hold to the most orthodox and traditional theological view." *PMLK* II, 213. In more thorough considerations of neo-orthodox thinkers, he leaves Niebuhr out of the discussion: "Contemporary Continental Theology" (1952) *PMLK* II, 128–38, and in qualifying exam answers in Systematic Theology, *PMLK* II, 228–31. He also notes that "Niebuhr differs from Barthianism" in that Niebuhr rejects Barth's radical (Augustinian) separation of God from man and combines "this-worldly and other-worldly hopes." "The Theology of Reinhold Niebuhr," paper read to the Dialectical Society (1954), *PMLK* II, 270.

32. "Rebel Prophet" was the term of T.C. Gordon, one of King's sources. In this essay, King warned that modern religionists needed to be especially wary of the status quo: "the worst disservice that we as individuals or churches can to do Christianity is to become sponsors of the status quo. How often has religion gone down, chained to a status quo it allied itself with. Durkheim and other sociologists rejoice to find in each religion simply the reflection of the State's opinion of itself foisted upon the divine, and along this they agree that no advancement can be looked for in spiritual affairs." Men like Jeremiah were therefore valuable *to religion*. But what was society's "reaction to such men?" King asked. "It has reacted, and always will re-act, in the only way open to it. It destroys such men." King, "The Significant Contributions of Jeremiah to Religious Thought," Crozer Theol. Sem., Nov. 1948, *PMLK* I, 181–95. The interest in Jeremiah comes up again in a subsequent essay on interpretive method; ibid., 255. The emphasis on the importance of "a higher standard," of "a prophet" who pushes values that are not "socially recognized," returns in an essay on W.K. Wright, *A Student's Philosophy of Religion* (1935), in *PMLK* I, 384–9. The emphasis on decline, or "breakdown in moral standards," also returns in his essay, "An Appraisal of the Great Awakening," *PMLK* I, 335–53.

33. Though August Meier brushes aside the intellectual content of King's speeches and writings as a "superficial" and "eclectic" amalgam of undigested and irreconcilable elements, he comes closer, I think, than anybody in capturing the essence of King's position in American culture in a single phrase, calling him "The Conservative Militant," in C. Eric Lincoln, ed., *Martin Luther King, Jr.: A Profile* (1970), 144–56. Robert Franklin and Lewis Baldwin capture a similar tension in describing King's thought as "prophetic radicalism." See Franklin, "Religious Belief and Political Activism in Black America: an Essay," *Journal of Religious Thought* 43 (Fall-Winter, 1986–87): 63–72, and Baldwin, *To Make the Wounded Whole: The Cultural Legacy of Martin Luther King, Jr.* (Minneapolis: Fortress Press, 1992), and *There is a Balm in Gilead: The Cultural Roots of Martin Luther King, Jr.* (Minneapolis: Fortress Press, 1991).

34. The most thorough articulation of this "prophetic" rejection of *both* liberalism and neo-orthodoxy is in Niebuhr's *Interpretation of Christian Ethics* (1935), but it is evident in all his works, even those that, like *Moral Man and Immoral Society* (1932), see liberalism as more prevalent and therefore more in need of criticism than neo-orthodoxy. Even the most careless reader could not come away from *Interpretation of Christian Ethics* with any thought that Niebuhr was trying to revive orthodoxy. Niebuhr's brother, H. Richard Niebuhr, gave "prophetic religion" a pointedly antinomian definition in his *The Kingdom of God in America* (1937), 10–11, and Andrew Delbanco has echoed this recently in his *Puritan Ordeal.* King developed his own prophetic streak in his essay, "Jacques Maritain" (1951), *PMLK* I, 436–9. Even if all he was doing here was cribbing from Walter Marshall Horton's *Contemporary Continental Theology* (1938), can he have failed to notice the echo of Jeremiah when he said Maritain thought Communism "originated chiefly through the fault of a Christian world unfaithful to its own principles"? Or when he observed that Maritain believed that the Christian-inspired system of democracy "has failed to remain true to its virtues. To[o] often has the democratic principle attempted to subsist without the Christian principle"? Why else emphasize those points in an 850-word essay?

Though Niebuhr spent much of his time denouncing the Social Gospel, the emphasis on, and much of the specific content of, his "prophetic" alternative originated with the leading theologian of the Social Gospel, Walter Rauschenbusch. Like most great thinkers, Rauschenbusch often transcended the limitations and oversimplifications of the school he headed, a point Niebuhr never acknowledged. His brother, as often, was more careful: "Washington Gladden and Walter Rauschenbusch. . . . distinguished themselves from their liberal contemporaries by keeping relatively close to evangelical notions of the sovereignty of God, of the reign of Christ and of the coming kingdom. In Rauschenbusch especially the revolutionary element remained pronounced; the reign of Christ required conversion and the coming kingdom was crisis, judgment as well as promise. Though his theory of the relations of God and man often seemed liberal he continued to speak the language of the prophets and St. Paul." *Kingdom of God in America* (1937), 194.

Rauschenbush stressed that prophetic tradition as his great source. See *Christianity and the Social Crisis* (NY: Macmillan, 1907), which begins with the Hebrew Prophets, pp. 1–44, and *A Theology for the Social Gospel* (1917; reprint, Nashville: Abingdon, 1945), esp. the core chapter, ch. XIII, "The Kingdom of God," which is a Jeremiad on how the community of Christians has fallen away from the original idea of the Kingdom of God.

35. In his notecards on Jeremiah, King noted, "Jeremiah was opposed to any form of humanism in the modern sense. It might well be that those of us who are opposed to humanism in the modern world would speak out against it as did Jeremiah and set out to give a rational defense of theism. [paragr.] It seems to me that one of the great services of neo-orthodoxy, notwithstanding its e[xt]remes[,] is its revolt against all forms of humanistic perfectionism. [Neo-orthodox theologians] call us back to a deeper faith in God. Is not this the need of the hour?. . . . Has not modern man placed to[o] much faith in himself and to[o] little faith in God?" In his notecard on the 72nd Psalm, he said, "Christianity was born among the poor and died among the rich. Whenever Christianity has remained true to its prophetic mission, it has taken a deep interest in social justice. Whenever it has fallen short at this point, it has brought about disastrous consequences. We must never forget that the success of communism in the world today is due to the failure of Christians to live to the highest ethical ten[et]s inherent in its system." See also similar remarks in the notecards on Amos. *PMLK* II, 165–7.

At the end of his essay on Karl Barth, King, like Niebuhr, criticized orthodoxy but felt it necessary to appropriate elements of Barth as correctives to liberalism. Barth's "cry," King said, "does call attention to the desperateness of the human situation. He does insist that religion begins with God and that man cannot have faith apart from him. He does proclaim that apart from God our human efforts turn to ashes and our sunrises into darkest night. . . . [etc.] Much of this is good, and may it not be that it will serve as a necessary corrective for a liberalism that at times becomes all to[o] shallow?" (Much of this, King's editors note, was lifted from an article by his old Crozer professor George Davis.) *PMLK* II, 106.

King explains how the Hebrew Prophets arrived at their "ethical monotheism" through "national and international disaster. The prophets had predicted that because of disobedience the nation would fall. Finally this day came when both the northern and southern kingdoms fell. . . . Unlike the Greek who came to monism through intellectualizing on the unity of the world, the Hebrew came to monotheism through the realistic experiences of history." Final exam answers, Old Testament, January 1953, *PMLK* II, 169–70.

36. King's "desire to be optimistic about human nature," he says, was tempered by experience and by his reading of what he calls neo-orthodox theologians. In "this transitional stage"—King does not indicate how long it has been going on—he is trying "to synthesize the best in liberal theology with the best in neo-orthodox theology and come to some understanding of man." How Modern Christians Should Think of Man," essay for Geo. Davis's Christian Theology for Today Course, Crozer Theol. Sem., winter quarter 1949–50, *PMLK* I, 273–9. The editors of King's papers say that in this essay, "King begins to depart" from liberalism. But he does not depart here—or later—from the aspects of

liberalism that he valued earlier, i.e., the Biblical criticism. (See: "Light on the Old Testament from the Ancient Near East," fall quarter 1948, *PMLK* I, 162–80, "The Ethics of Late Judaism as Evidenced in the Testaments of the Twelve Patriarchs," fall quarter 1949, *PMLK* I, 195–209, and "The Sources of Fundamentalism and Liberalism Considered Historically and Psychologically," fall quarter 1949, *PMLK* I, 236–42.) When King speaks favorably of liberalism, as he says in the "Sources" essay, "liberalism is a method not a creed." (p. 238) What King questions about liberalism is its doctrine of man, but that is not new in "How Modern Christians Should Think": King's earlier writings never showed any sympathy for a liberal doctrine of man. Moreover, his illiberal views on the doctrine of man in "How Christians Should Think" are similar to his earlier views on man (see esp. the Fall 1948 essay on Jeremiah, *PMLK* I, 181–95).

In "How Modern Christians Should Think," King's views are balanced—exactly as Niebuhr's are—between a rejection of optimism and a rejection of pessimism. His view of man does not change significantly later; the view in this essay is essentially the same as the one he later articulates in his "Autobiography of Religious Development," *PMLK* I, 359–63, and the "Pilgrimage to Nonviolence" he published in *Stride Toward Freedom* in 1958, which said among other things that he had come close to hating all white people. Throughout his life, his emphasis on the good of *liberalism* refers to its *Biblical criticism*, its rejection of fundamentalist literalism in a "Copernican universe." He later claims he was once inclined toward an optimistic view of man, but whenever the subject comes up in his divinity school and later essays, he is always at least ambivalent about liberalism's doctrine of man. On all other matters, the notes and annotations of the King Papers editors are insightful and meticulously researched, indeed indispensable for the kind of analysis being attempted here.

King himself emphasized the doctrine of man as the major shortcoming of liberalism—the only thing about it that he ever rejects—in his critique of his former professor, George Davis, in *PMLK* II, 94, 94–5n.

37. In a later essay at BU, King discusses Barth's doctrine of man, showing some sympathy for it, and notes the influence of existentialism on Barth and other "crisis theologians." "It seems the Kierkegaard has risen from the grave. For these men Biblicism takes the place of even the most exalted type of ordinary reason and experience. Philosophers and theologians are mere playboys sporting with the fad of reason." "Maybe man is more of a sinner than liberals are willing to admit. I realize that the sinfulness of man is often over-emphasized by some continental theologians, but at least we must admit that many of the ills of the world are due to plain sin. The tendency on the part of some liberal theologians to see sin as a mere 'lay of nature' which will be progressively eliminated as man climbs the evolutionary ladder seems to me quite perilous. I will readily agree that many of man's shortcomings are due to natural necessities, but ignorance and finiteness and hampering circumstances, and the pressure of animal impulse, are all insufficient to account for many of man's shortcomings . . . Only the one who sits on the peak of his intellectual ivory tower looking unrealistically with his rosey colored glasses on the scene of life can fail to see this fact. The word sin must come back into our vocabulary." "Again the continental theologians call us back to the dimension of depth in the Bible. This {is} not to say that the critical approach to the study of Scripture must be disregarded. But it does mean that Biblical criticism must remain a means, not an end. . . . The Bible is more than a piece of historical literature, as many liberals would reduce it to; it is a personal word from a living God." "Contemporary Continental Theology," (Jan. 1952) *PMLK* II, 133, 137–8.

King develops the Augustinian insistence that sin comes from rebellion against God, and identifies that insistence as a main theme in Niebuhr's thought, something he has in common with Barth and Brunner, against the insistence of Schleiermacher and other liberals, in his Qualifying exam on the History of Doctrine (November 1953), *PMLK* II, 213.

King's essay on Christian Hope in the New Testament sides with Paul Minear's *The Eyes of Faith* (1946) (against Rudolf Bultmann), affirming that the Kingdom of God is a present reality for Christians as well as a future event. But he is compelled to add, "there is no warrant in the N.T. for looking upon the kingdom as an 'idealized social order' but we must say that whenever there are advances in that direction there is an expression of he power of the kingdom." *PMLK* II, 206–7.

38. In addition to being more original, King's work on Niebuhr is far less tainted by the flattery that seems to taint his references to the only other contemporary theologians who have been identified as influences on King, the Boston Personalists. (Some scholars suggest that the leading Personalist, Edgar Sheffield Brightman, is the culmination and synthesis of King's intellectual influences, the closest thing to a single intellectual model.) King has no practical reason to flatter Niebuhr.

39. The personalist emphasis is in Warren Steinkraus, "Martin Luther King's Personalism and Nonviolence," *Journal of the History of Ideas* 34 (Jan.-Mar. 1973): 97–110, and in Kenneth L. Smith and Ira G. Zepp, *Search for the Beloved Community: The Thinking of Martin Luther King, Jr.* (Lanham, Maryland: University Press of America, 1986). While Smith and Zepp exaggerate the influence of personalists at the expense of Niebuhr, their book remains extremely useful and thorough as an introduction to King's thought. The other major attempt at an intellectual biography of King, John Ansbro, *Martin Luther King, Jr.: The Making of a Mind* (Maryknoll, NY: Orbis, 1982), also seems to me to overplay the personalism, but it too is sober, intelligent and thorough. These books remain the best introduction to King's thought other than King's own works.

King's most influential professor at Crozer, George W. Davis, was also drawn to Niebuhr's blend of certain liberal or modernist tendencies with a neo-orthodox-inspired doctrine of man. King came closest to putting a label on his own theological synthesis near the end of his time in Boston, when he wrote to Davis from Boston in December 1953, saying he recalled Davis's classroom as "saturated with a warm evangelical liberalism." He said he found something similar in DeWolf's classroom at Boston. He noted that DeWolf (whose 1953 book, *A Theology of the Living Church*, Davis had just reviewed in the *Journal of Bible and Religion*) "refers to himself as an evangelical liberal and as I remember, this is about the same position that you would hold." King summed up his own theological thinking: "I find myself still holding to the liberal position." But he seemed to mean by this a rejection of fundamentalism more than anything else. More and more King was seeing "there are certain enduring qualities in liberalism which all the vociferous noises of fundamentalism and neo-orthodoxy can never destroy." When he came to issues of doctrine, as opposed to method, particularly the doctrine of man that Davis had emphasized in his article, "Liberalism and a Theology of Depth," he found fault with liberalism. "I must admit that in the last two years, I have become much more sympathetic towards the neo-orthodox position than I was in previous years. By this I do not mean that I accept neo-orthodoxy as a set of doctrines, but I do find in it a necessary corrective for a liberalism that became all too shallow and too easily capitulated to modern culture. . . . Neo-orthodoxy certainly has the merit of calling us back to the depths of the Christian faith." King to Davis, 1 December 1953, *PMLK* II, 223–4. He does not specify Niebuhr as the model for the synthesis, but it is nearly identical with Niebuhr's.

40. I do not mean to countenance the racial charge in any form. But there may be some of the perhaps unconscious flattery that often appears in grad students in King's references to Brightman, and after Brightman dies in 1953, the flattery may linger as an uncritical reverence for the dead, and/or a living appeal to Brightman's protégé, Harold DeWolf, King's professor and dissertation reader. It should be noted, however, that Brightman, at least, encouraged King to criticize his ideas, and that King did criticize personalism in general and Brightman in particular—in a very Niebuhrian tone. See the note below on King's essay on the problem of evil.

41. Garrow, *Bearing the Cross* (New York: Morrow, 1984), 649. See also, Stephen Oates, "Intellectual Odyssey of Martin Luther King," *Mass. Review* XXII (Summer 1981): 301–ff.

42. Rustin, "The Negro and Nonviolence," *Fellowship*, October 1942, repr. in *Down the Line: The Collected Writings of Bayard Rustin* (Chicago: 1971), 8–12.

Notes to pages 17–24   181

43. [Rustin,] Martin Luther King Jr., "Our Struggle," *Liberation* I (April 1956), 3–6. Rustin published his own views on Montgomery in "Montgomery Diary," in the same issue of *Liberation*, repr. in *Down the Line*, 55–61.
44. Simkins speech notecards, n.d. [ca. 1948], Simkins Papers, University of South Carolina, Modern Political Collections, Columbia, box 5.
45. Simkins speech typed on back of campaign flyer [ca. 1960s?] of W.C. Mahaffey, Simkins papers, box 5.
46. Lawson, "From a Lunch Counter Stool," speech to SNCC conference, Raleigh, N.C., April 1960, in Francis Broderick and August Meier, eds., *Negro Protest Thought in the 20th Century* (Indianapolis: Bobbs-Merrill, 1965), 274.
47. Interview with John Lewis, *Dialogue Magazine*, Spring 1964, reprinted in Broderick and Meier, *Black Protest Thought*, 313–21.
48. Lewis called on all his listeners to join the "revolution," and said "we are not interested in becoming Madison Avenue types." On the background of the speech, see the interview printed in William Beardslee, *The Way out Must Lead in* (1977; reprint, Westport, Conn.: Lawrence, Hill, 1983), 1–35. A copy of the sanitized speech appears in *Student Voice* 4 (October 1963), 1, 3.

Notes to THE CIVIL RIGHTS MOVEMENT AS THEOLOGICAL DRAMA
by Charles Marsh

1. Martin Luther King, Jr., "A Christmas Sermon on Peace," in *A Testament of Hope: The Essential Writings and Speeches of Martin Luther King, Jr.*, edited by James Melvin Washington (San Francisco: Harper, 1986), p. 255.
2. W. E. B. DuBois cited in Richard Lischer, *The Preacher King: Martin Luther King, Jr., and the Word that Moved America* (New York: Oxford University Press), p. 21.
3. Andrew Young, *A Way Out of No Way: The Spiritual Memoirs of Andrew Young* (Nashville: Thomas Nelson Publishers, 1994), p. 57.
4. John Lewis, Interview with the author.
5. In his book, *The Culture of Disbelief*, the Yale Law professor Stephen Carter observes the same indifference or disregard toward belief and its practices that we find in academic life. "[When] pundits discuss the work of Reverend Martin Luther King, Jr.," says Carter, "the only member of the clergy whose life we celebrate with a national holiday, the fact of his religious calling is usually treated as a relatively unimportant aspect of his career, if, indeed, it is mentioned at all." *The Culture of Disbelief: How American Law and Politics Trivialize Religious Devotion* (New York: Basic Books, 1993).
6. King cited in Lischer, *The Preacher King*, p. 225.
7. Martin Luther King, Jr., "The Significant Contributions of Jeremiah to Religious Thought," *The Papers of Martin Luther King, Jr.*, Volume I, edited by Ralph E. Luker and Penny Russell (Berkeley: University of California Press, 1992), p. 191.
8. Lischer, *The Preacher King*, p. 198.
9. "The Student Nonviolent Coordinating Committee (as revised in conference, April 29, 1962)," The Charles Sherrod Papers, file 24, State Historical Society of Wisconsin.
10. John Lewis, interview with the author.
11. "The Student Nonviolent Coordinating Committee," April 29, 1962. Charles Sherrod Papers, File 24. State Historical Society of Wisconsin.
12. See Jürgen Moltmann, *The Spirit of Life: A Universal Affirmation*, translated by Margaret Kohl (Minneapolis: Fortress Press, 1994), p. 10ff.
13. King, *The Papers of Martin Luther King, Jr.* edited by Clayborne Carson (Berkeley and Los Angeles: University of California Press, 1997), volume III, p. 344.
14. Richard King, *Civil Rights and the Idea of Freedom* (New York: Oxford University Press, 1992), p. 99. For an interesting discussion of the term's philosophical antecedents, see John E. Smith, "Royce: The Absolute and the Beloved Community Revisited," in

Leroy Rouner, *Meaning, Truth and God* (Boston: Boston University Press, 1982), pp. 135–153.

15. "Letter to the National City Lines, Inc.," in *The Papers of Martin Luther King, Jr.*, volume III.

16. King, "Non-Aggression Procedures in Interracial Harmony," in *The Papers of Martin Luther King, Jr.*, p. 327.

17. See Richard Lischer, *The Preacher King*, and Ralph Luker's fine essay, "Kingdom of God and Beloved Community in the Thought of Martin Luther King, Jr.", in this volume.

18. Josiah Royce, *The Christian Doctrine of Life*, p. 196.

19. Georg Wilhelm Friedrich Hegel, *Lectures on the Philosophy of Religion*, volume III, edited by Peter C. Hodgson, translated by R. F. Brown, P. C. Hodgson and J. M. Stewart (Berkeley: University of California Press, 1985), p. 372.

20. Hegel, *Lectures on the Philosophy of Religion*, volume III, p. 347.

21. Josiah Royce, *The Christian Doctrine of Life*, p. 196.

22. Josiah Royce, *The Christian Doctrine of Life*, p. 201.

23. Another example of Royce's reconceptualization is the doctrine of Grace, which he describes in terms of the virtue of loyalty. Loyalty to community pulls individuals out of their isolation into social relation. Royce explains, "And the community to which, when grace saves him, the convert is thenceforth to be loyal, we may here venture to call by a name which we have not hitherto used. Let this name be 'The Beloved Community.' This is another name for what we before called the Universal Community. Only now the universal community will appear to us in a new light, in view of its relations to the doctrine of grace. And the realm of this Beloved Community, whose relations Christianity conceives, for the most part, in supernatural terms, will constitute what, in our discussion, shall be meant by the term 'The Realm of Grace.' " (125) from *The Christian Doctrine of Life*.

24. Josiah Royce, *The Real World and the Christian Ideas*.

25. Casey Nelson Blake, *Beloved Community: The Cultural Criticism of Randolph Bourne, Van Wyck Brooks, Waldo Frank, and Lewis Mumford* (Chapel Hill: University of North Carolina Press, 1990), p. 2.

26. Blake, *The Beloved Community*, p. 118.

27. Blake, *The Beloved Community*, p. 121.

28. Blake, *The Beloved Community*, p. 121.

29. Richard Lischer, *The Preacher King*, p. 124.

30. Dietrich Bonhoeffer, *Letters and Papers from Prison*, p. 310.

31. Dietrich Bonhoeffer, *Ethics*, translated by Neville Horton Smith (New York: Macmillan, 1978), pp. 197–200.

32. Cited in Richard Lischer, *The Preacher King*, p. 123. Or as Bonhoeffer wrote from Tegel concentration camp in one of his final letters before his execution: "It is certain that we may always live close to God and in the light of his presence, and that such living is an entirely new life for us; that nothing is then impossible for us, because all things are possible with God; that no earthly power can touch us without his will, and that danger and distress can only drive us closer to him. . . . In Jesus God has said Yes and Amen to it all, and that Yes and Amen is the firm ground on which we stand." Dietrich Bonhoeffer, *Letters and Papers from Prison*, p. 391.

33. Richard Lischer, *The Preacher King*, p. 20.

34. Eugene McCarraher, *Christian Critics: Religion and the Impasse in Modern American Social Thought* (Ithaca, New York: Cornel University Press, 2000), p. 15.

35. King, *The Papers*, volume III, p. 306.

36. King, *The Papers*, volume III, p. 306.

37. King, *The Papers*, volume III, p. 306.

38. King, *The Papers*, volume III, p. 328.

39. King, *The Papers*, volume III, p. 328 (my emphasis).

40. King, *The Papers*, volume III, p. 417.

41. King, *The Papers*, volume III, p. 462.

42. King, *The Papers*, volume III, p. 418.

43. King, *The Papers*, volume III, p. 328.

44. King, *The Papers*, volume III, p. 462; King, *The Papers*, volume III, p. 17.

45. King, *A Testament of Hope: The Essential Writings and Speeches of Martin Luther King, Jr.* (San Francisco: Harper, 1986), p. 17.

46. King, *A Testament of Hope*, p. 24.

47. King, *The Papers*, volume I, p. 249.

48. King, *The Papers*, volume I, p. 249.

49. King, *A Testament of Hope*, p. 17.

50. Karl Barth, *Church Dogmatics*, IV/3, translated by G. W. Bromiley (Edinburgh: T & T Clark, 1961), p. 116.

51. Karl Barth, *Church Dogmatics*, IV/3, p. 116.

52. Karl Barth, *Church Dogmatics*, IV/3, p. 117.

53. Karl Barth, *Church Dogmatics*, Volume IV/3/1, p. 114.

54. Cited in McCarraher, *Christian Critics*, pp. 14–16.

55. King, "Paul's Letter to American Christians: Sermon Delivered at Dexter Avenue Baptist Church," *The Papers*, volume III, p. 416.

56. King, *The Papers*, volume III, p. 420.

57. See my book, *Reclaiming Dietrich Bonhoeffer: The Promise of His Theology* (New York: Oxford University Press, 1994), pp. 3–33.

58. Barth cited in Jurgen Moltmann, *The Coming of God: Christian Eschatology*, translated by Margaret Kohl (Minneapolis: Fortress Press, 1996), p. 18.

59. Karl Barth, *The Humanity of God* (Atlanta: John Knox Publishers, 1978), pp. 39.

60. Paul Deats, "Introduction to Boston Personalism," *The Boston Personalist Tradition*, edited by Paul Deats and Carol Robb (Macon, Georgia: Mercer University Press, 1986), p. 3.

61. John H. Lavely, "Reflections on a Philosophical Heritage," *The Boston Personalist Tradition*, p. 272.

62. Lischer, *The Preacher King*, p. 53.

63. King, *The Papers*, volume II, p. 136.

64. Barth, *The Word of God and the Word of Man* (Gloucester, MA: Peter Smith, 1978), p. 4.

65. King, *The Papers*, volume II, p. 137.

66. King, *The Papers*, volume II, p. 137.

67. Lischer, *The Preacher King*, p. 234.

68. King, "I See the Promised Land," cited in *A Testament of Hope*, p. 279.

Notes for KINGDOM OF GOD AND BELOVED COMMUNITY IN THE THOUGHT OF MARTIN LUTHER KING, JR.
by Ralph E. Luker

1. Kenneth L. Smith and Ira G. Zepp, Jr., *Search for the Beloved Community: The Thinking of Martin Luther King, Jr.* (Valley Forge, PA: Judson Press, 1974), 119.

2. King, "Rediscovering Lost Values," 28 February 1954, in Clayborne Carson, Ralph E. Luker, et al., eds., *The Papers of Martin Luther King, Jr.* (Berkeley: University of California Press, 1991), II, 249; King, "Paul's Letter to American Christians," 4 November 1956, and King, "Facing the Challenge of a New Age,"3 December 1956, in Carson, Stewart Burns, et al., eds., *Papers of Martin Luther King*, III, 415, 456–7; King, "The American Dream," 6 June 1961, in James M. Washington, ed., *A Testament of Hope: The Essential Writings of Martin Luther King, Jr.* (New York: Harper and Row, 1986), 269; King, "The Man Who Was a Fool," in King, *Strength to Love* (New York: Harper and

Row, 1963), 54; King, "Letter from Birmingham Jail," in King, *Why We Can't Wait* (New York: Harper & Row, 1963, 1964), 77; King, *Where Do We Go From Here? Chaos or Community* (New York: Harper & Row, 1967), 171–2 and 181; King, "A Christmas Sermon on Peace," in King, *The Trumpet of Conscience* (New York: Harper & Row, 1967), 69–70; and King, "Remaining Awake Through a Great Revolution," 31 March 1968, in Washington, ed., *Testament of Hope*, 209.

3. King's abandon of references to the "beloved community" in the last years of his life is noted by Richard Lischer, *The Preacher King: Martin Luther King, Jr. and the Word That Moved America* (New York: Oxford University Press, 1995), 168–9.

4. Martin Luther King, Jr., "An Autobiography of Religious Development," 12 September-22 November 1950, in Carson, Luker, et al., *Papers of Martin Luther King*, I, 359–61. King's reference to a "friendly universe" uses language common among white liberal Protestant preachers such as John Sutherland Bonnell, Charles R. Brown, Harry Emerson Fosdick, John Haynes Holmes, Ernest Fremont Tittle, and Leslie D. Weatherhead in the years between World War I and World War II. As late as 1965, a King sermon would ask "Is the Universe Friendly?" See: Lischer, *The Preacher King*, 56, 76, 168, 282n, and 286n; and Keith D. Miller, *Voice of Deliverance: The Language of Martin Luther King, Jr., and Its Sources* (New York: The Free Press, 1992), 214 and 257n.

5. Roger L. Rice, "Residential Segregation by Law, 1910–1917," *Journal of Southern History*, 34 (May 1968): 179–99; John Dittmer, *Black Georgia in the Progressive Era, 1900–1920* (Urbana: University of Illinois Press, 1977), 13–15; Michael L. Porter, "Black Atlanta: An Interdisciplinary Study of Blacks on the East Side of Atlanta, 1890–1930" (unpublished doctoral dissertation, Emory University, 1974), 126–58; Blaine A. Brownell, "The Commercial-Civic Elite and City Planning in Atlanta, Memphis, and New Orleans in the 1920s," *Journal of Southern History*, 41 (August 1975): 339–68; and Ronald H. Bayor, *Race & the Shaping of Twentieth-Century Atlanta* (Chapel Hill: University of North Carolina Press, 1996), 53–8.

6. King, "Autobiography of Religious Development," 12 September-22 November 1950. Carson, Luker, et al., *Papers of Martin Luther King*, I, 362–3. A slightly different version of this story appears in: Martin Luther King, Jr., *Stride Toward Freedom: The Montgomery Story* (New York: Harper & Row, 1958), 18–19.

7. The best biographical treatments of King's youth are: David J. Garrow, *Bearing the Cross: Martin Luther King, Jr., and the Southern Christian Leadership Conference, A Personal Portrait* (New York: William Morrow, 1986), 32–44; Taylor Branch, *Parting the Waters: America in the King Years, 1954–63* (New York: Simon and Schuster, 1988), 27–90; and "Introduction," in Carson, Luker, et al., eds., *Papers of Martin Luther King*, I, 28–46.

8. On the fundamentalist/modernist controversy, see: Ernest R. Sandeen, *The Roots of Fundamentalism: British and American Millenarianism, 1800–1930* (Chicago: University of Chicago Press, 1970); George R. Marsden, *Fundamentalism and American Culture: The Shaping of Twentieth-Century Evangelicalism, 1870–1925* (New York: Oxford University Press, 1980); Kenneth Cauthen, *The Impact of American Religious Liberalism* (New York: Harper and Row, 1962); and William R. Hutchison, *The Modernist Impulse in American Protestantism* (Cambridge: Harvard University Press, 1976). There were fundamentalist and modernist spokesmen in white southern and in African American Protestantism, but a prevailing conservative evangelical orthodoxy largely sheltered them from the cataclysmic debates that divided northern white Protestants in the first half of the twentieth century. The 1916 and 1962 rifts in the National Baptist Convention resulted from power struggles rather than theological differences. The struggle in the Southern Baptist Convention was delayed into the second half of the twentieth century, when it was a division between moderate evangelicals and fundamentalists.

9. On the public intellectuals' debates about community in the 1920s, see: Christopher Lasch, *The True and Only Heaven: Progress and Its Critics* (New York: W. W. Norton & Co., 1991); Casey Nelson Blake, *Beloved Community: The Cultural Criticism of*

Randolph Bourne, Van Wyck Brooks, Waldo Frank, & Lewis Mumford (Chapel Hill: University of North Carolina Press, 1991); Eugene McCarraher, "Heal Me: 'Personality,' Religion, and the Therapeutic Ethic in Modern America," *Intellectual History Newsletter*, 21 (1999): 31–40; and Ian Nicholson, "From the Kingdom of God to the Beloved Community, 1920–1930: Psychology and the Social Gospel in the Work of Goodwin Watson & Carl Rogers," *Journal of Psychology and Theology*, 22 (Fall 1994): 196–206.

10. Josiah Royce coined the term, "beloved community," in his *The Problem of Christianity* (New York: The Macmillan Company, 1913). John Ansbro notes that King's graduate advisor, L. Harold DeWolf, included Royce on recommended reading lists at Boston University. King never referred to Royce as a significant influence on his thinking and professors who annually reproduce recommended reading lists have a sense of how far such recommendations reach. See: John J. Ansbro, *Martin Luther King, Jr.: The Making of a Mind* (Maryknoll, NY: Orbis Books, 1982), 319. After Royce, the term achieved a much broader currency in the influential essays of American social critic Randolph Bourne, in the works of such American liberal Protestants as George A. Buttrick, F. Ernest Johnson, Paul E. Johnson, Eugene William Lyman and Harry F. Ward, and its fullest explication by an Anglican clergyman, Roger Lloyd, the Canon of Winchester. It may also have occurred in works by King's personalist mentors at Boston University, so it is impossible to say that King never encountered the term prior to 1956.

11. King, "Six Talks in Outline," 13 September 1949–23 November 1950, in Carson, Luker, et al., eds., *Papers of Martin Luther King*, I, 250.

12. Smith and Zepp, *Search for the Beloved Community*, 129; Ansbro, *Martin Luther King, Jr.*, 187–97 and *passim*; and Kelly Miller Smith, *Social Crisis Preaching: The Lyman Beecher Lectures, 1983* (Macon, GA: Mercer University Press, 1984), 65–6. See also: Zepp, "The Intellectual Sources of the Ethical Thought of Martin Luther King, Jr., as Traced in His Writings with Special Reference to the Beloved Community" (unpublished doctoral dissertation, St. Mary's Seminary and University, 1971), 279–318. The problem with Smith and Zepp's thesis and Ansbro and Smith's assumption is that it treats King's mind as an ahistorical fixed abstraction. That both short-changes understanding how his mind changed by experience over the course of time and confuses discussion, for example, of his admittedly troubled attempt to interpret agape as a sure and sufficient basis for creating the beloved community.

13. Specifically, compare: Smith and Zepp, *Search for the Beloved Community*, 129; King, "The Christian Pertinence of Eschatological Hope," 29 November 1949–15 February 1950, and King, "Six Talks Based on *Beliefs That Matter* by William Adams Brown," 29 February 1949–15 February 1950, in Carson, Luker, et al., eds., *Papers of Martin Luther King*, I, 272–3 and 283–4; and William Adams Brown, *Beliefs That Matter: A Theology for Laymen* (New York: Scribner, 1928), 56–9.

14. Benjamin E. Mays, ed., *A Gospel for the Social Awakening: Selections from the Writings of Walter Rauschenbusch* (New York: Association Press, 1950); Carson, Luker, et al., eds., *Papers of Martin Luther King, Jr.*, I, 37n, 49, 55, 462; King, "Pilgrimage to Nonviolence," in King, *Stride Toward Freedom*, 91; and King, "Pilgrimage to Nonviolence," in King, *Strength to Love*, 137–8. See also: Carson, Stewart Burns, et al, eds., *Papers of Martin Luther King*, III, 381, 397–8.

15. See: Reinhold Niebuhr, "Walter Rauschenbusch in Historical Perspective," in Niebuhr, *Faith and Politics: A Commentary on Religious, Social and Political Thought in a Technological Age*. Edited by Ronald H. Stone (New York: George Braziller, 1968), 33–45; and Christopher Lasch, "Religious Contributions to Social Movements: Walter Rauschenbusch, the Social Gospel, and Its Critics," *Journal of Religious Ethics*, 18 (Spring 1990): 7–25.

16. Carson, Luker, et al., *Papers of Martin Luther King*, I, 55, 230–1, 231n and 433. See also: Smith and Zepp, *Search for Beloved Community*, 62–3.

17. King, "Reinhold Niebuhr," King, "Reinhold Niebuhr's Ethical Dualism," and King, "The Theology of Reinhold Niebuhr," in Carson, Luker, et al., eds., *Papers of Mar-*

tin *Luther King*, II, 139–41, 141–52 and 269–79; and Reinhold Niebuhr, *Moral Man and Immoral Society* (New York: Charles Scribner's Sons, 1932), 249–56.

18. King, "Pilgrimage to Nonviolence," in King, *Stride Toward Freedom*, 97–100. Bayard Rustin drafted at least a portion of this discussion of Niebuhr. See: Carson, et al., *Papers of Martin Luther King*, IV, 380n. In a revised, 1963 version of his "Pilgrimage to Nonviolence," however, King retained the discussion of Reinhold Niebuhr's influence on his thought, but he deleted all reference to Walter Rauschenbusch. Compare King, "Pilgrimage to Nonviolence," in King, *Stride Toward Freedom*, 90–107 and King, "Pilgrimage to Nonviolence," in King, *Strength to Love*, 135–42.

19. See, for example: "MIA Mass Meeting at Holt Street Baptist Church," 5 December 1955, King, "When Peace Becomes Obnoxious," 18/29 March 1956, Almena Lomax, "Mother's Day in Montgomery," 18 May 1956, King, "Walk for Freedom," May 1956, and King, "Annual Report, Dexter Avenue Baptist Church," 31 October 1956, in Carson, Burns, et al., eds., *Papers of Martin Luther King*, III, 72–4, 208, 266–7, 278 and 412. See also: King, *Stride Toward Freedom*, 84.

20. King, *Stride Toward Freedom*, 85–6.

21. King, "The Birth of a New Age," 11 August 1956, in Carson, Burns, et al., eds., *Papers of Martin Luther King*, III, 344.

22. King, "Facing the Challenge of a New Age," 3 December 1956, in Carson, Burns, et al., eds., *Papers of Martin Luther King*, III, 458.

23. King, "Address to MIA Mass Meeting at Holt Street Baptist Church," 14 November 1956, in Carson, Burns, et al., eds., *Papers of Martin Luther King*, III, 429.

24. King, "Paul's Letter to American Christians," 4 November 1956, in Carson, Burns, et al., eds., *Papers of Martin Luther King*, III, 417–18. For King's disappointment with and agenda for the church in the desegregation crisis, see: King, *Stride Toward Freedom*, 205–211; King, "Letter from the Birmingham Jail," in King, *Why We Can't Wait* (New York: Harper and Row, 1963, 1964), 89–93; "Playboy Interview: Martin Luther King, Jr.," January 1965, in Washington, ed., *Testament of Hope*, 345–6; and King, *Where Do We Go from Here: Chaos or Community* (New York: Harper and Row, 1967), 96–101.

25. See, for instance, King, "Facing the Challenge of a New Age," 1 January 1957, in Carson, et al., *Papers of Martin Luther King*, IV, 88.

26. King, "Nonviolence and Racial Justice," 6 February 1957, in Carson, et al., eds., *Papers of Martin Luther King*, IV, 120. With editorial variations, this article appeared in *Advance, Christian Century, The Churchman, Friends Journal, The Intercollegian, Jubilee, New South, Presbyterian Life*, and King, *Stride Toward Freedom*, 102–7. This passage appears in King, *Stride Toward Freedom*, 102. See also: "This Is SCLC" (Southern Christian Leadership Conference leaflet, revised edition, [1964?]), in Francis L. Broderick and August Meier, eds., *Negro Protest Thought in the Twentieth Century* (Indianapolis: The Bobbs-Merrill Company, Inc., 1965), 269–73.

27. See, for example: King, "Give Us the Ballot," 17 May 1957, and King, "Remarks in Acceptance of the NAACP Spingarn Medal," 28 June 1957, in Carson, et al., eds., *Papers of Martin Luther King*, IV, 213–14 and 232.

28. King, "The Birth of a New Nation," 7 April 1957, in Carson, et al., eds., *Papers of Martin Luther King*, IV, 162.

29. Clayborne Carson, ed., *The Autobiography of Martin Luther King, Jr.* (New York: Warner Books, 1998), 125. Interestingly, both references from his trips to newly emancipated nations observe amicable relations between newly empowered men of color and aristocratic white women.

30. King, "Paul's Letter to American Christians," 4 November 1956, in Carson, Burns, et al., *Papers of Martin Luther King*, III, 416; King, " 'A Look to the Future,' " 2 September 1957, in Carson, et al., eds., *Papers of Martin Luther King*, IV, 276; King, "The American Dream," 6 June 1961," in Washington, *Testament of Hope*, 215–16; King, "Transformed Nonconformist" and King, "A Knock at Midnight," in King, *Strength to Love* (New York: Harper & Row, 1963), 8–15, 43; King, "Letter from the Birmingham

Jail," in King, *Why We Can't Wait*, 91–2; and "Playboy Interview, Martin Luther King, Jr.," January 1965, in Washington, ed., *Testament of Hope*, 345–6. King's assertions of the importance of Christian maladjustment or nonconformity repeat arguments made by Harry Emerson Fosdick and other preachers of his era. Ultimately, as King noted, they reach back to Ralph Waldo Emerson's 1841 essay, "Self-Reliance": "Whoso would be a man must be a nonconformist." See: King, "Transformed Nonconformist,"in King, *Strength to Love*, 12; and Miller, *Voice of Deliverance*, 105–111, 164–5 and 213–14.

31. King, *Stride Toward Freedom*, 40. King quotes Matthew 10:34.

32. King, "How Should a Christian View Communism?" in King, *Strength to Love*, 99. This sentence also appears in: King, *Stride Toward Freedom*, 95.

33. King, *Stride Toward Freedom*, 105–6. The last sentence, at least, was ghostwritten by Bayard Rustin. The paragraph is part of a fuller interpretation of agape, in which King appears to paraphrase and plagiarize from Anders Nygren, *Agape and Eros* (Philadelphia: Westminster Press, [1953]) and Paul Ramsey, *Basic Christian Ethics* (New York: Scribner, 1950). Yet, his argument also seems to vary from each of theirs by degrees that are a function of his personalist theological orientation. See: Zepp, "Intellectual Sources of the Ethical Thought of Martin Luther King," 143–6; Smith and Zepp, *Search for the Beloved Community*, 62–7; Ansbro, *Martin Luther King, Jr.*, 8–36 and passim; and Carson, et al., *Papers of Martin Luther King*, IV, 380n–1n. The issue of King's use of sources in his interpretation of agape here and elsewhere needs re-examination. Unfortunately, it appears unlikely that the Martin Luther King Papers Project will produce a critical edition of *Stride Toward Freedom*, which would have been crucial to that re-examination. See also: King, *Stride Toward Freedom*, 219–20, King, "The Rising Tide of Racial Consciousness," December 1960, King, "An Address Before the National Press Club," 19 July 1962, and King, "The Case Against Tokenism," 5 August 1962, in Washington, ed., *Testament of Hope*, 148–9, 103, 110.

34. King, *Stride Toward Freedom*, 214.

35. King to Friends and Co-Workers of the MIA, 6 October 1958, in Carson, et al., eds., *Papers of Martin Luther King*, IV, 505.

36. King, "The Ethical Demands for Integration," 27 December 1962, in Washington, ed., *Testament of Hope*, 118, 122.

37. King, "Loving Your Enemies," in King, *Strength to Love*, 40.

38. Samuel Williams, conversation with the author, summer, 1962.

39. King, "The Death of Evil upon the Seashore," in King, *Strength to Love*, 64. King quotes Luke 17:21.

40. King, "Pilgrimage to Nonviolence," in King, *Strength to Love*, 142.

41. Compare: King, "Paul's Letter to American Christians," in King, *Strength to Love*, 127–134 and King, "Letter from Birmingham Jail," in King, *Why We Can't Wait*, 76–95. For a fine textual and contextual study of the composition of King's Birmingham "Letter," see: S. Jonathan Bass, *Blessed Are the Peacemakers: Martin Luther King Jr., Eight White Religious Leaders, and the "Letter from Birmingham Jail"* (Baton Rouge: Louisiana State University Press, 2001).

42. The phrase is from James F. Findlay, Jr., *Church People in the Struggle: The National Council of Churches and the Black Freedom Movement, 1950–1970* (New York: Oxford University Press, 1993).

43. King, "Letter from Birmingham Jail," in King, *Why We Can't Wait*, 92.

44. King, "Letter from Birmingham Jail," in King, *Why We Can't Wait*, 80.

45. Compare: Reinhold Niebuhr, *Beyond Tragedy* (New York: Charles Scribner's Sons, 1937), 85 with King, "The American Dream" and King, "I Have a Dream," in Washington, ed., *Testament of Hope*, 208–216 and 217–20.

46. Lyndon B. Johnson, "Remarks at the Lighting of the Nation's Christmas Tree, December 22, 1963," in *Public Papers of . . . . Lyndon B. Johnson, 1963–64* (Washington, DC: United States Government Printing Office, 1965), I, 81. Elizabeth Knowles, ed., *Oxford Dictionary of Quotations*. Fifth edition (New York: Oxford University Press, 1999),

408, correctly cites Johnson's speech as a source of this statement, but plays on "brotherhood" and "neighborhood" appear often in King's published work and likely occur in the sermons of his liberal Protestant mentors as well.

47. Johnson, "Remarks in Chicago at a Fundraising Dinner of the Democratic Club of Cook County, April 23, 1964," and Johnson, "Remarks at the University of Michigan, May 22, 1964," in *Public Papers of . . . . Lyndon B. Johnson*, 1963–64, I, 529–30 and 704. Richard Goodwin probably borrowed "Great Society" from Walter Lippmann's use of it in his *A Preface to Morals* (New York: The Macmillan Company, 1929), 232–313. Lippmann had borrowed the term from the English Fabian, Graham Wallas, who was his teacher in a seminar at Harvard in 1910. See: Wallas, *The Great Society: A Psychological Analysis* (New York: The Macmillan Company, 1914). In turn, Wallas could look back to the words of William Wordsworth, written in 1850:
There is
One great society alone on earth,
The noble Living, and the noble Dead.
Wordsworth, "The Prelude," II, 1, 393.

48. John Dittmer, *Local People: The Struggle for Civil Rights in Mississippi* (Urbana: University of Illinois Press, 1994), 272–316; Findlay, *Church People in the Struggle*, 99; Charles Marsh, *God's Long Summer: Stories of Faith and Civil Rights* (Princeton, NJ: Princeton University Press, 1997), *passim*; and Charles M. Payne, *I've Got the Light of Freedom: The Organizing Tradition and the Mississippi Freedom Struggle* (Berkeley: University of California Press, 1999), 340–1 and *passim*.

49. King, "Our God is Marching On!" 25 March 1965, in Washington, ed., *Testament of Hope*, 227–30.

50. King, *Where Do We Go from Here?*, 8–9.

51. King, "Nonviolence: The Only Road to Freedom," October 1966, in Washington, ed., *Testament of Hope*, 57–8.

52. Lischer, *The Preacher King*, 168–9; and Vincent Harding, "Introduction" to King, "Unfulfilled Dreams," in Clayborne Carson and Peter Holloran, eds., *A Knock at Midnight: Inspiration from the Great Sermons of Reverend Martin Luther King, Jr.* (New York: Warner Books, 1998), 188. Smith and Zepp, *Search for the Beloved Community*, 135, saw a change in King's thinking in the last three years of his life, but did not see that he no longer referred to "beloved community." See also Lischer's explication of "the Ebenezer Gospel" in Lischer, *The Preacher King*, 221–242.

53. King, *Where Do We Go from Here?*, 18–19 and 81–8.

54. King, *Where Do We Go from Here?*, 61, 128.

55. King, *Where Do We Go from Here?*, 83–4.

56. Vincent Harding, "The Religion of Black Power," 1968. Harding's article appears as "The Crisis of Powerless Morality," in C. Eric Lincoln, *Martin Luther King, Jr.: A Profile* (New York: Hill and Wang, 1984), 185–6.

57. King, "A Christmas Sermon on Peace," in King, *The Trumpet of Conscience* (New York: Harper & Row, 1967), 68. See also: King, "The Man Who Was a Fool," in King, *Strength to Love*, 54; and King, *Where Do We Go from Here?*, 171.

58. King, "A Testament of Hope," January 1969, in Washington, ed., *Testament of Hope*, 326.

59. King, "Nonviolence and Social Change," in King, *Trumpet of Conscience*, 60.

60. King, "A Christmas Sermon on Peace," in King, *Trumpet of Conscience*, 72. King expands upon Galatians 3:28.

61. See, for instance: King, "Three Dimensions of a Complete Life," in King, *Strength to Love*, 67–77. See also: Lischer, *The Preacher King*, pp. 96–7.

62. King, "Remaining Awake Through a Great Revolution," 31 March 1968, in Washington, ed., *Testament of Hope*, 277–8. King quotes Revelations 21: 5a, 4c. Compare this conclusion with King, "Three Dimensions of a Complete Life," in King, *Strength to Love*, 77.

63. King, "I See the Promised Land," 3 April 1968, in Washington, ed., *Testament of Hope*, 282. King refers to many passages in Exodus, Leviticus, Numbers, Deuteronomy, Joshua, Jeremiah and Ezekiel which are commonly translated as "a land flowing with milk and honey."

Notes to BEACON LIGHT AND PENUMBRA: AFRICAN AMERICAN GOSPEL LYRICS AND MARTIN LUTHER KING, JR.'S "I HAVE A DREAM" by Keith D. Miller

1. Interview with James Farmer, 1 June 1985, Columbus, Ohio.

2. George Lakoff and Mark Johnson, *Metaphors We Live By* (Chicago: University of Chicago Press, 1980).

3. George Lakoff and Mark Turner, *More Than Cool Reason: A Field Guide to Poetic Metaphor* (Chicago: University of Chicago Press, 1989), 9–10.

4. Lakoff and Turner, *More Than Cool Reason*, 14–15.

5. Lakoff and Turner, *More Than Cool Reason*, 67.

6. Lyricists complicate these metaphors even further than this list indicates. For example, lyricists frequently elaborate DEATH IS ARRIVAL AND FULFILLMENT IN HEAVEN with HEAVEN IS A CITY OF GREAT WEALTH (filled, for example, with golden streets).

7. Lucie Campbell, "Heavenly Sunshine," in *We'll Understand It Better By and By: Pioneering African American Gospel Composers*, ed. Bernice Johnson Reagon (Washington, D. C.: Smithsonian Institution Press, 1992), 86–7.

8. Thomas Dorsey, "Precious Lord," in Michael W. Harris, *The Rise of Gospel Blues: The Music of Thomas Andrew Dorsey in the Urban Church* (New York: Oxford University Press, 1992), 234–5.

9. William Herbert Brewster, "I'm Climbing Higher and Higher," in *We'll Understand It Better By and By*, ed. Reagon, 207–8. Brewster titled one of his songs "Our God Is Able," which later served as the title of a King sermon. See William Herbert Brewster, "Our God Is Able," in *We'll Understand It Better By and By*, ed. Reagon, 200; Martin Luther King, Jr., *Strength to Love* (New York: Harper & Row, 1963).

10. Martin Luther King, Jr., *In Search of Freedom*, Mercury Records, SR 1170, undated.

11. Martin Luther King, Jr., "Dimensions of a Complete Life," 31 May 1959, King Center Archives, Dillard University, New Orleans, LA.

12. King, "Dimensions."

13. Martin Luther King, Jr., "Address to Southern Christian Ministers' Conference in Mississippi," 23 September 1959, King Center Archives.

14. King, "Address."

15. Martin Luther King, Jr., "MIA Mass Meeting at Holt Street Baptist Church," Montgomery, AL, 5 December 1955, in *Birth of a New Age: The Papers of Martin Luther King, Jr.*: Volume III, ed. Clayborne Carson, et al (Berkeley, CA: University of California Press, 1997), 71–9; Martin Luther King, Jr., "I Have a Dream," Washington D. C., 28 August 1963, in *A Testament of Hope: The Essential Writings of Martin Luther King, Jr.*, ed. James Washington (San Francisco: Harper & Row, 1986), 217–220. All further references to "I Have a Dream" are made to this version of the text.

16. These lines recall lyrics from Brewster's song, "Faith That Moves Mountains," in which the narrator recognizes "towering mountains" that "do obstruct your way" but promises that "God . . . can blast the rocks." See William Herbert Brewster, "Faith That Moves Mountains," in *We'll Understand It Better By and By*, ed. Reagon, 221–3.

17. Archibald Carey, "Address to the Republican National Convention," in *Rhetoric of Racial Revolt*, ed. Roy Hill (Denver: 1964), 149–154. For the relation between Carey's oration and "I Have a Dream," see Keith D. Miller, *Voice of Deliverance: The Language*

of Martin Luther King, Jr., and Its Sources (Athens: University of Georgia Press, 1998), 142–158.

18. For an analysis of "I Have a Dream" as an African American political jeremiad, see Elizabeth Vander Lei and Keith D. Miller, "Martin Luther King, Jr.'s 'I Have a Dream' in Context: Ceremonial Protest and African American Jeremiad," *College English* 62 (September 1999), 83–99.

19. For her encouragement and help on this essay, I thank Elizabeth Vander Lei.

Notes to FANNIE LOU HAMER: NEW IDEAS FOR THE CIVIL RIGHTS MOVEMENT AND AMERICAN DEMOCRACY
by Linda Reed

1. Mrs. Fanny [sic] Lou Hamer, *To Praise Our Bridges: An Autobiography*, ed. by Julius Lester and Mary Varela (Jackson, Mississippi: KIPCO, 1967), 11. Hamer spoke of her mother and her mother's death in almost all of her interviews.

Fannie Lou Hamer's mother is a contemporary, interestingly enough, of Mary McLeod Bethune, Ida B. Wells-Barnett, and W. E. B. DuBois, all of whom were born close to the 1871 date. Separated by education and class differences, their lives were similar only in the oppression encountered by the fact of their racial identity.

2. On cotton production: see Ulrich B. Phillips, *American Negro Slavery: A Survey of the Supply, Employment and Control of Negro Labor as Determined by the Plantation Regime* (New York, 1918; paperback reprint, Baton Rouge, LA, 1966).

3. See Paula Giddings, *When and Where I Enter: The Impact of Black Women on Race and Sex in America* (New York: Bantam Books), 293; Quotation taken from the Proceedings of the Democratic National Convention 1964: Credentials Committee, Atlantic City, New Jersey, Aug. 22, 1964, p. 32–45, folder 549, box 11, Ed King Papers (Coleman Library, Tougaloo College, Jackson, Mississippi).

4. All quotations from "Life in Mississippi: An Interview with Fannie Lou Hamer," in *Afro-American History: Primary Sources*, ed. by Thomas R. Frazier (Chicago, 1988 [reprint from *Freedomways*, 5 (No. 2, 1965). The paraphrasing is evident that Fannie Lou Hamer had paid attention to various national figures, at least John F. Kennedy who had said in his 1961 inaugural address, "Ask not what your country can do for you, ask what you can do for your country."

5. Aldon D. Morris, *The Origins of the Civil Rights Movement: Black Communities Organizing for Change* (New York: Free Press, 1984), esp. 1–16 where Morris sees the church as a central positive force within the movement. Charles M. Payne has a more tempered view on the role of the church in the civil rights movement. See Payne, *I've Got the Light of Freedom: The Organizing Tradition and the Mississippi Struggle* (Berkeley: University of California Press, 1995).

6. Letter, John Dittmer to Linda Reed, July 22, 1987, in author's possession. Fannie Lou Hamer is mentioned in scholarly works such as Clayborne Carson, *In Struggle: SNCC and the Black Awakening of the 1960s* (Cambridge: Harvard University Press, 1981), the most comprehensive academic study on SNCC, and Darlene Clark Hine, "Lifting the Veil, Shattering the Silence: Black Women's History in Slavery and Freedom," in *The State of Afro-American History: Past, Present, and Future* ed. by Darlene Clark Hine (Baton Rouge: LSU Press, 1986), 244–5. Recent publications about Fannie Lou Hamer include: Chana Kai Lee, *For Freedom's Sake: The Life of Fannie Lou Hamer* (Urbana: University of Illinois Press, 1999); Kay Mills, *This Little Light of Mine: The Life of Fannie Lou Hamer* (New York: Dutton, 1993).

7. "Autobiography of Fannie Lou Hamer [but written in third person], microfilm roll 1, folder 1, box 3, Fannie Lou Hamer Papers (Amistad Research Center, New Orleans); pamphlet: "We Want Ours Now!" folder 4, ibid. According to Donna Langston, "The Women of Highlander," in *Women in the Civil Rights Movement: Trailblazers and Torch-*

bearers, 1941–1965 ed. by Vicki L. Crawford, Jacqueline Anne Rouse, and Barbara Woods (Brooklyn, N. Y.: Carlson Publishing, Inc., 1990), 157, Fannie Lou Hamer attended citizenship schools at the Highlander School in Tennessee. A date would help to determine who Fannie Lou Hamer got to know there. *Women in the Civil Rights Movement* is volume 16 of a comprehensive collection of secondary material on *Black Women in United States History* with Darlene Clark Hine as general editor.

    8. Jerry DeMuth, "Tired of Being Sick and Tired," *Nation*, 198 (June 1, 1964), 548–51; Phyl Garland, "Builders of a New South," *Ebony*, 21 (Aug. 1966), 27–30; P. Marshall, "Hunger Has No Color Line," *Vogue*, 155 (June 1970), 126–7; Joyce A. Ladner, "Fannie Lou Hamer: In Memoriam," *Black Enterprise*, 7 (May 1977), 56; Eleanor Holmes Norton, "Woman Who Changed the South: Memory of Fannie Lou Hamer," *MS*, 5 (July 1977), 51; Alexis De Veaux, "Going South: Back to Where the Heart of the Civil Rights Movement Still Beats," *Essence*, 16 (May 1985), 54, 56, 224; Marita Golden, "The Sixties Live On: The Era of Black Consciousness Is Preserved as a State of Mind, ibid., 70–1; "Claiming Our Power," ibid., 101–3; Jean Carey Bond, "From the Bottom Up: Black Women a Source for Liberation of Both Race and the Gender," ibid., 105–8, 205–7. See Martin Luther King, Jr., *Stride Toward Freedom: The Montgomery Story* (New York: Harper & Row, 1958), 40–5.

    9. See Darlene Clark Hine, *Black Victory: The Rise and Fall of the White Primary in Texas* (Millwood, N.Y.: KTO Press, 1979) for details on disfranchisement and *Smith v. Allwright.* See also Ronald W. Walters, *Black Presidential Politics in America: A Strategic Approach* (Albany: SUNY Press, 1988), esp. 29–33; Paul Kleppner, *Continuity and Change in Electoral Politics, 1893–1928* (Westport, Conn.: Greenwood Press, 1987), esp. 154; Linda Reed, *Simple Decency and Common Sense: The Southern Conference Movement, 1938–1963* (Bloomington: Indiana University Press, 1991). It is important to note that Alfred E. Smith's Catholicism had much to do with southern support for the Republican Party in 1928.

    10. Donald S. Strong, *Issue Voting and Party Realignment* (University: University of Alabama Press, 1977), 47–8; Harvard Sitkoff, *A New Deal for Blacks: The Emergence of Civil Rights as a National Issue, Vol. I: The Depression Decade* (New York: Oxford University Press, 1978), viii–ix, 58–9, 317–23; Linda Reed, *Simple Decency and Common Sense.*

    11. Aaron Henry interviewed by William M. Simpson, December 5, 1973, p. 13 (Transcript in National Series/Subseries Democratic Party, Aaron Henry Papers, Special Collections, Tougaloo College, Mississippi); Steven F. Lawson, *Running for Freedom: Civil Rights and Black Politics in America since 1941* (New York: McGraw-Hill, 1991), 94–101, 106–15.

    12. Steven F. Lawson, *In Pursuit of Power: Southern Blacks and Electoral Politics, 1965–1982* (New York: Columbia University Press, 1985), 4, 12; Meeting of the Commission on Party Structure and Delegate Selection of the Democratic Party for Alabama and Mississippi, May 22, 1969, Heidelberg Hotel, Jackson, Mississippi, Aaron Henry Papers (Hamer quotation p. 93). The 210-page document contains many descriptions of voting rights violations and the MFDP's and the National Democratic Party's efforts to curb them.

    13. Meeting of the Commission on Party Structure and Delegate Selection of the Democratic Party for Alabama and Mississippi, May 22, 1969, Heidelberg Hotel, Jackson, Mississippi, Aaron Henry Papers (Hamer quotation p. 96).

    14. Julian Bond, "The Impact of Student Activism on Black Politics, 1965–1968," paper delivered at Southern Historical Association Meeting, New Orleans, Nov. 1990, p.17; Bond believed that by 1965 SNCC fielded the largest number of workers than any civil rights organization, which kept it closer to grass roots community. This, in turn, made SNCC's outreach to people like Fannie Lou Hamer more likely and possible. Bond also believed that MFDP served as a model for "black power" in 1965. In 1969, the Supreme Court case of *Allen v. State Board of Education* is seen as a result of MFDP. Finally, he emphasized that the larger voter participation between 1965 and 1968 made it possible for the number of elected black officials to go over 300.

Harry A. Ploski and James Williams, comps. and eds., *The Negro Almanac: A Reference Work on the Afro-American* (New York: John Wiley & Sons, 1983), 354; Alex Poinset, "How to Get More Blacks into Congress: Enforcement of the Voting Rights Act Is Regarded as the Most Important Step," *Ebony* (May 1986), 124–31.

15. Meeting of the Commission on Party Structure and Delegate Selection of the Democratic Party for Alabama and Mississippi, May 22, 1969, Henry Papers; see also, Poinsett, "How to Get More Blacks into Congress."

16. Richard J. Hughes (New Jersey Governor & Chair, Special Equal Rights Committee of the Democratic National Committee) to "Chairman [for Mississippi this was Aaron Henry], July 26, 1976, folder 9, box 2182, Mississippi AFL-CIO Records, Special Collections (Georgia State University, Atlanta); memo, Aaron Henry to Coahoma County Convention of the Democratic Party, May 21, 1968, ibid.; Henry and Hodding Carter to "Loyal Democrat [Democrats who abided by rules of the National Democratic Committee], June 21, 1968, ibid.; Claude Ramsay (President, Mississippi AFL-CIO) to Henry, June 24, 1968, ibid.; Henry to "Supporters," ibid.; Henry to Steering Committee of Loyal Democrats of Mississippi, July 8, 1968, ibid.; "Coalition Is Formed for Demo Seats," *Clarion-Ledger*, July 23, 1968, p. 9; "Negro Alternate Bucks Delegation," *Memphis Commercial Appeal*, July 24, 1968.

17. Henry interviewed by Simpson, p. 11. In 1976 South Carolina had its first Republican governor when James Edwards won the election. See Grace Jordan McFadden, "Septima P. Clark and the Struggle for Human Rights," in *Women in the Civil Rights Movement*, 89.

18. A recent example is Herbert Denmark, Jr., "F. L. Hamer Convention Develops Platform, Economic Bill of Rights," in Local, Church and Inter-Scholastic News Section of *The Atlanta Voice*, July 30–Aug. 5, 1988, pp. 1, 3. This is with the National Democratic Party Convention in 1988.

19. See Fannie Lou Hamer interviewed by Neil McMillen in 1973 (Mississippi Oral History Program of the University of Southern Mississippi, Vol. 31, 1977) esp. part I, p. 2.

Notes to "CLOSET MODERATES": WHY WHITE LIBERALS FAILED, 1940–1970 by Tony Badger

1. Terry Sanford interview with Jack Bass and Walter DeVries, Southern Oral History Program, Southern Historical Collection, Chapel Hill, NC. Margaret Birdsong Price interview with the author, 20 May 1970. Raleigh *News and Observer* 23 January 2000.

2. John William Coon, "Kerr Scott, the 'Go Forward' Governor: His Origins, his program and the North Carolina General Assembly," (University of North Carolina: MA thesis, 1968) 32–65. For the Trigg appointment see Box 10, especially J. S. Davis to W. Kerr Scott, 28 April 1949, Scott to Davis, 19 May 1949, Papers of Governor W. Kerr Scott, North Carolina Division of Archives and History, Raleigh, NC.

3. Coon, "Kerr Scott," 33–9. Timothy J Minchin, *What Do We Need a Union For? The TWUA in the South, 1945–1955* (Chapel Hill: University of North Carolina Press, 1997), 81–2, 91.

4. Campaign Speech, 1936, Papers of W. Kerr Scott, North Carolina Division of Archives and History, Raleigh. Rob Christiansen, "The Scotts of Haw River," Raleigh *News and Observer* 17 Jan. 1999.

5. Julian M. Pleasants and Augustus M. Burns III, *Frank Porter Graham and the 1950 Senate Race in North Carolina* (Chapel Hill: University of North Carolina Press, 1990), 5–17, 156–9.

6. Jesse Helms to W. Kerr Scott, 16 September 1949, Governor W. Kerr Scott Papers, Southern Historical Collection.

7. Steve Niven, " 'The Slow Burn rebellion of Forgotten Americans': White Backlash in North Carolina, 1964–68." I am extremely grateful to Steve Niven for a copy of this

paper. David Cecelski, *Along Freedom Road: Hyde County, North Carolina and the Fate of Black Schools in the South* (Chapel Hill: University of North Carolina Press, 1994), 155–8. Robert W. Scott, Oral History Interview 1986, Southern Oral History Program, Southern Historical Collection, Chapel Hill.

8. Tony Badger to Iris and Kenneth Badger 23 February 1970 (in the author's possession). Thad Stem to Jonathan Daniels, 5 October 1970, Papers of Jonathan Daniels, Southern Historical Collection, Chapel Hill.

9. John Egerton, *Speak Now Against the Day: The Generation Before the Civil Rights Movement in the South* (New York: Alfred A. Knopf, 1995), 10–11.

10. Patricia Sullivan, *Days of Hope: Race and Democracy in the New Deal Era* (Chapel Hill: University of North Carolina Press, 1996), 69, 84–92, 141–9, 169–247, 273, 275. Patricia Sullivan, "Southern Reformers, the New Deal and the Movement's Foundation," in Armstead Robinson and Patricia Sullivan, eds., *New Directions in Civil Rights Studies* (Charlottesville: University of Virginia Press, 1991), 81–104. Adam Fairclough, *Race and Democracy: The Civil Rights Struggle in Louisiana, 1915–1972* (Athens: University of Georgia Press, 1995), xii, xiv. Robert Korstad and Nelson Lichtenstein, "Opportunities Found and Lost: Labor, Radicals and the Early Civil Rights Movement," *Journal of American History* 75 (1988) 786–811. Minchin, *What Do We Need a Union For?* 26–118.

11. Jennifer Brooks, "From Fighting Nazism to Fighting Bossism: Southern World War II Veterans and the Assault on Southern Political Tradition," (unpublished paper in the author's possession). Pamela Tyler, *Silk Stockings and Ballot Boxes: Women and Politics in New Orleans, 1920–1963* (Athens: University of Georgia Press, 1996), 78–168. Leslie Gale Parr, *A Will of Her Own: Sarah Towles Reed and the Pursuit of Democracy in Southern Public Education* (Athens: University of Georgia Press, 1998), 144–85.

12. Egerton, *Speak Now Against the Day*, 113. Tony Badger, "Whatever Happened to Roosevelt's New Generation of Southerners?" in Robert A. Garson and Stuart Kidd, eds., *The Roosevelt Years: New Essays on the United States, 1933–1945* (Edinburgh: Edinburgh University Press, 1999), 122–38; Ira Katznelson, Kim Geiger and Daniel Kryder, "Limiting Liberalism: The Southern Vote in Congress," *Political Science Quarterly* 108 (1993) 283–306.

13. Hugh Davis Graham and Numan Bartley, *Southern Politics and the Second Reconstruction* (College Park: Johns Hopkins University Press, 1975); Tony Badger, "Fatalism, not Gradualism: Race and the Crisis of Southern Liberalism, 1945–1965," in Brian Ward and Tony Badger, eds., *The Making of Martin Luther King and the Civil Rights Movement* (London: Macmillan, 1996).

14. Frank Smith, *Congressman from Mississippi* (New York: Pantheon Books, 1964) 69–74. Tony Badger, "Southerners Who Refused to Sign the Southern Manifesto," *The Historical Journal* 42, 2 (1999) 517–34. John Drescher, *Triumph of Goodwill: How Terry Sanford Beat a Champion of Segregation and Reshaped the South* (Jackson: University Press of Mississippi, 2000), 10–14. Nahfiza Ahmed, "Race, Class, and Citizenship: The Civil Rights Struggle in Mobile, Alabama, 1925–1985," (Ph.D. dissertation, Leicester University, 1999), 108–22.

15. Elaine M. Paull to Terry Sanford, 31 May 1954, W. Kerr Scott Papers. Badger, "Fatalism not Gradualism," 87–8.

16. Minchin, *What do we need a Union for?* 48–68, 199–209. Bryant Simon, *A Fabric of Defeat: The Politics of South Carolina Millhands, 1910–1948* (Chapel Hill: University of North Carolina Press, 1998), 221.

17. James C. Cobb, "World War II and the Mind of the Modern South," in Neil R. McMillen, ed., *Remaking Dixie: The Impact of World War II on the American South* (Jackson: University Press of Mississippi, 1997), 6–9. Brooks, "Fighting Nazism." Brian Lewis Crispell, *Testing the Limits: George Armistead Smathers and Cold War America* (Athens: University of Georgia Press, 1999), 8–74; Thad Stem to Jonathan Daniels, 24 September 1967, Jonathan Daniels Papers.

18. Bruce J. Schulman, *From Cotton Belt to Sunbelt: Federal Policy, Economic Devel-

opment, and the Transformation of the South, 1938–1980 (New York: Oxford University Press, 1991), 321. Carl Grafton and Anne Permaloff, Big Mules and Branchheads: James E Folsom and Political Power in Alabama (Athens: University of Georgia Press, 1985), 62. Badger, "Southerners Who refused to Sign the Southern Manifesto," 517–34.

19. Kari Frederickson, The Dixiecrat Revolt and the End of the Solid South (Chapel Hill: University of North Carolina Press, 2001), 101–73. Pete Daniel, Lost Revolutions: The South in the 1950s (Chapel Hill: University of North Carolina Press, 2000), 257, 281–2. Pleasants and Burns, Frank Porter Graham, 121.

20. Carl Elliott and Michael D'Orso, The Cost of Courage: The Journey of an American Congressman (New York: Doubleday, 1992), 181. Sullivan, Days of Hope, 221–75. Morton Sosna, In Search of the Silent South (New York: Columbia University Press, 1977), 165. Michael Klarman, "How Brown Changed Race Relations: The Backlash Thesis," Journal of American History 81 (1994) 81–118.

21. Sullivan, Days of Hope, 221–75. Korstad and Lichtenstein, "Opportunities Found and Lost," 786–811. Fairclough, Race and Democracy, xiii. Numan Bartley, The New South, 1945–1980 (Baton Rouge: Louisiana State University Press, 1995), 70, 73.

22. Numan Bartley, comment, 40th Anniversary of Little Rock Conference, University of Arkansas at Little Rock, 27 September, 1997. Klarman, "How Brown Changed Race Relations," 81–118; Korstad and Lichtenstein, "Opportunities Found and Lost," 786–811. Jim Sleeper, "Color Blind," New Republic, 2 March 1998.

23. Gary Huey, Rebel with a Cause: P. D. East, Southern Liberalism and the Civil Rights Movement, 1953–71 (Wilmington, Del.: Scholarly resources Inc., 1985), 106–8. Alan Brinkley, The End of Reform: New Deal Liberalism in Recession and War (New York: Knopf, 1995), 265–71.

24. Frank Smith, interview with the author, 7 November 1995. Maury Maverick, Jr. Interview, Texas Oral History Interview, Woodson Research Center, Rice University, Houston. Michael Heale, McCarthy's Americans: Red Scare Politics in State and Nation, 1935–1965 (Athens: University of Georgia Press, 1998), 214–17. William J. Billingsley, Communists on Campus: Race, Politics, and the Public University in Sixties North Carolina (Chapel Hill: University of North Carolina Press, 1999), 1–87.

25. Calvin Trillin, "Reflections: Remembrance of Moderates Past," New Yorker, 21 March 1977.

26. David Chappell, Inside Agitators: White Southerners in the Civil Rights Movement (Baltimore: Johns Hopkins University Press, 1994), 1–49. David Chappell, "The Divided Mind of Southern Segregationists," Georgia Historical Quarterly 82 no. 1 (1998) 45–72. David Chappell, "Religious Ideas of Segregationists," Journal of American Studies 32, no. 2 (1998) 237–62. J. Mills Thornton III, "Municipal Politics and the Course of the Movement," in Robinson and Sullivan, New Directions in Civil Rights Studies, 41–4. Badger, "Fatalism not Gradualism," 77–8, 85–86. Fairclough, Race and Democracy, 35.

27. Badger, "Fatalism not Gradualism," 85. Badger, "Southerners who did not sign the Southern Manifesto," 534.

28. Smith, Congressman from Mississippi, 77–92. Dennis J. Mitchell, "Frank E. Smith: Mississippi Liberal," Journal of Mississippi History 48 (1986) 91–3. Frank Smith to Hodding Carter, 26 August 1949, quoted in Dennis J. Mitchell, Mississippi Liberal: A Biography of Frank E. Smith (Jackson: University Press of Mississippi, 2001), 69. Badger, "Fatalism not Gradualism," 77–8.

29. Robert J. Norrell, Reaping the Whirlwind: The Civil Rights Movement in Tuskegee (New York: Knopf, 1985), 85.

30. Brooks Hays, Interview, Columbia Oral History program, Lawrence Brooks papers, Special Collections Division, University of Arkansas Libraries, Fayetteville, Arkansas; J. William Fulbright to Mrs Walter Bell, 31 August 1948, Papers of J. William Fulbright, Special Collections Division, University of Arkansas, Fayetteville, Arkansas. Randall B. Woods, Fulbright: a Biography (Cambridge: Cambridge University Press, 1995), 114–9, 52.

31. Sidney McMath Interview, by John Egerton, 8 September 1990, Southern Oral

History Program, Southern Historical Collection. Bartley and Graham, *Southern Politics and the Second Reconstruction*, 38–40, 76–8. Earl Black, *Southern Governors and Civil Rights* (Cambridge, Mass: Harvard University Press, 1976), 45.

32. Terry Sanford interview, 14 May 1976, Southern Oral History Program, Southern Historical Collection. Drescher, *Triumph of Goodwill*, 16–19.

33. 17 May 1954 Statement, Sanford statement [n.d], W. Kerr Scott Papers. Albert Gore to Mrs. Talley, 12 October 1954, Papers of Albert Gore, Gore Research Center, Middle Tennessee State University, Murfreesboro, TN. Estes Kefauver to P. L. Prattis, 19 May 1956, Kefauver to B. L. Fonville, 10 May 1956, Papers of Estes Kefauver, University of Tennessee, Knoxville. Robert Dallek, *Lone Star Rising: Lyndon Johnson and his Times, 1908–1960* (New York: Oxford University Press, 1991), 445.

34. Albert Gore Interview, 13 March 1976, Southern Oral History program, Southern Historical Collection. Richard Russell to Walter R. McDonald, 15 Feb. 1956, Papers of Richard Russell, Richard B. Russell Library, University of Georgia, Athens, GA.

35. Fulbright interview with Stewart Alsop, *Washington Post*, 8 April 1956 box 71, J. William Fulbright Papers, Special Collections Division, University of Arkansas Libraries, Fayetteville, AR. Sam Englehardt to John Sparkman, 15 March 1956, Papers of John Sparkman, W. S. Hoole Library, University of Alabama, Tuscaloosa, AL. Typed statement [n.d.] Fulbright Papers. Randall B. Woods, "Dixie's Dove: J. William Fulbright, the Vietnam War, and the American South," *Journal of Southern History* 9 (1994) 541. Memorandum, John Lang, 3 February 1956, Papers of Charles B. Deane, Southern Baptist Historical Collection, Wake Forest University, Winston-Salem, NC. William Cochrane interview with the author, September, 1988. Brooks Hays Interview 1970, 26–8, Columbia University Oral History Program, Hays Interview, 1971, 26, Lyndon Baines Johnson Library, Brooks Hays Papers.

36. Jack Bass, *Unlikely Heroes: The Dramatic Story of the Southern judges of the Fifth Circuit who Translated the Supreme Court's Brown Decision into a Revolution for Equality* (New York: Simon and Schuster, 1981), 68–74, 78–80. Virginia Van der Veer Hamilton, *Lister Hill: Statesman from the South* (Chapel Hill: University of North Carolina Press, 1987), 212–55. Virginia Durr to Hugo Black, November 1962, Virginia Foster Durr Papers, Arthur and Elizabeth Schlesinger Library, Cambridge, Mass. (I am very grateful to Pat Sullivan for this reference).

37. Tony Badger, *Race and War: Lyndon Johnson and William Fulbright* (Reading: The University of Reading, 2000), 11–12.

38. William Cochrane interview. "North Carolina's Man on the Hill," *Carolina Alumni Review* (Spring 1984), 13–14. Jonathan Houghton, "The Politics of Sly Resistance: North Carolina's Response to Brown," (Paper given at the Organization of American Historians' meeting, 11 April 1991). Sylvia Ellis, "The Road to Massive Resistance: North Carolina and the Brown Decision" (Graduate paper in the author's possession). Drescher, *Triumph of Goodwill*, 51–2.

39. Sidney McMath Interview, by John Egerton, 8 September 1990. Jim Lester, *A Man for Arkansas: Sid McMath and the Southern Reform Tradition* (Little Rock: Rose Publishing Co., 1976), 233–5.

40. Sims, *The Little Man's Big Friend*, 175–188.

41. Badger, "Southerners who did not sign the Southern Manifesto," 532–4. James C. Cobb, *The Selling of the South: the Southern Crusade for Industrial Development, 1936–1980* (Baton Rouge: Louisiana State University Press, 1982), 122–50.

42. Badger, "Southerners who did not sign the Southern Manifesto," 525–32. Tony Badger, "Albert Gore, Sr. and Civil Rights," paper given at the Gore Research Center, Middle Tennessee State University, Murfreesboro, TN, 8 November 1997 (copy in the author's possession). Charles L. Fontenoy, *Estes Kefauver: A Biography* (Knoxville: University of Tennessee Press, 1980), 236–43, 285–301.

43. Badger, *Race and War*, 7, 10–11.

44. Hamilton, *Lister Hill*, 170. John Horne to Lister Hill, 20 October 1955, Ed Dun-

nelly to Lister Hill, 25 Jan.1956, Tully A. Goodwin to Lister Hill, 22 Feb. 1956, Bart P
Chamberlain to Lister Hill, 22 February 1956, Papers of Lister Hill, University of Ala-
bama. John Sparkman Interview 31 Jan. 1974, Southern Oral History Program, Southern
Historical Collection.

45. Elliott, *The Cost of Courage*, 212–58.

46. Chappell, "The Divided Mind of Southern Segregationists," 45–72.

47. J. D. Messick to Terry Sanford, 16 April 1954; Sanford to Messick, 24 April 1954,
W. Kerr Scott to Clark Brown, 15 June 1954, W. Kerr Scott Papers. Sims, *The Little
Man's Big Friend*, 167–8. Sidney McMath Interview, by John Egerton, 8 September 1990.
Terry Sanford interview, 14 May 1976, Drescher, *Triumph of Goodwill*, 162–3. Dante
Fascell interview with the author, 27 Feb. 1997.

48. Jack Bass and Marilyn W Thompson, *Ol' Strom: An Unauthorized Biography of
Strom Thurmond*, 123, 131. Edwin E. Dunaway interview with John A. Kirk, 26 September 1992 (I am very grateful to John Kirk for permission to quote from this interview).

49. Bartley, *The New South*, 174; Woods, *Fulbright*, 211.

50. J. Mills Thornton, "Challenge and Response in the Montgomery Bus Boycott,"
Alabama Review 33 (1980) 163–235. Nahfiza Ahmed, "Race, Class and Citizenship,"
chapters 4, 5.

51. Hollinger F. Barnard ed., *Outside the Magic Circle: The Autobiography of Virginia
Foster Durr* (University, AL: University of Alabama Press, 1985), 32. John A. Salmond,
The Conscience of a Lawyer: Clifford J. Durr and American Civil Liberties, 1899–1975
(Tuscaloosa: University of Alabama Press, 1990) 208. John A. Salmond, *A Southern Rebel:
The Life and Times of Aubrey Willis Williams, 1890–1965* (Chapel Hill: University of
North Carolina Press, 1983). Drescher, *Triumph of Good Will*, xv.

52. Bartley and Graham, *Southern Politics and the Second Reconstruction*, 71.

53. Bartley and Graham, *Southern Politics and the Second Reconstruction*, 56–7, 67–8,
111–34.

54. Cobb, *The Selling of the South*, 149. Davison M. Douglas, *Reading, Writing and
Race: The Desegregation of the Charlotte Schools* (Chapel Hill: University of North Carolina Press, 1995), 88, 103. Glenn T. Eskew, *But for Birmingham: the Local and National
Movements in the Civil Rights Struggle* (Chapel Hill: University of North Carolina Press,
1997), 111–2, 189–90, 235–6, 269–97. Grafton and Permaloff, *Big Mules and Branchheads*, 165–66, 189–90. Robert Gaines Corley, "The Quest for Racial Harmony: Race
Relations in Birmingham, Alabama, 1947–63," (Ph. D. dissertation, University of Virginia,
1979), 180–6.

55. Bartley and Graham, *Southern Politics and the Second Reconstruction*, 138–41,
162–3. Woods, *Fulbright*, 663.

56. Linda Flowers, *Throwed Away: Failures of Progress in Eastern North Carolina*
(Knoxville: University of Tennessee Press, 1990), 52.

57. Cecelski, *Along Freedom Road*, 39. Frank A. Rouse, interview, Southern Oral History Program, Southern Historical Collection.

58. Tony Badger, "The Rise and Fall of Bi-Racial Politics in the South," in Jan Nordby
Gretlund, ed., *The Souths of the 1990s* (Columbia: University of South Carolina Press,
1999), 30–45.

59. Bartley, *The New South*, 466.

Notes to THE STRUGGLE AGAINST EQUALITY: CONSERVATIVE
INTELLECTUALS IN THE CIVIL RIGHTS ERA, 1954–1975
by Richard H. King

1. Numan V. Bartley, *The New South, 1945–1980* (Baton Rouge, LA: LSU Press,
1995), chapter two makes this point about post-war liberalism quite strongly. At an international level, the basic tenets of post-war universalism were articulated in the UN Char-

ter, the articulation and implementation of the Nuremberg Principles in international law, the Convention against Genocide, The UN Declaration of Human Rights, and the UNESCO Statement on Race.

2. Still basic and most comprehensive is George H. Nash, *The Conservative Intellectual Movement in American since 1945* (New York: Basic Books, 1979). Also useful are Patrick Allitt, *Catholic Intellectuals and Conservative Politics in America, 1950–1985* (Ithaca and London: Cornell University Press, 1995) and Eugene D. Genovese, *The Southern Tradition* (Cambridge, MA: Harvard University Press, 1994). William F. Buckley, *Up from Liberalism* (New York: Ivan Obolensky, 1959) was crucial in establishing the framework of post-1945 American conservatism, while John B. Judis, *William F. Buckley, Jr.: Patron Saint of Conservatives* (New York: Simon and Schuster, 1988) is a good place to start in understanding what made Buckley tick. Finally, Alan Brinkley, "The Problem of American Conservatism," *American Historical Review*, 99 (April 1994): 409–29 is an indispensable, but mainstream liberal guide to the problems of the historiography of American conservatism.

3. See Peter Novick, *The Holocaust in American Life* (New York: Houghton Mifflin and Co., 1999), p. 313 (footnotes 14–19). Novick does note a strange incident where Buckley had to admit that American Nazi Leader George Lincoln Rockwell had been commissioned to help promote *National Review*. For a brief discussion of liberal scepticism about Israel (before 1967), see D. D. Guttenplan, "The Holocaust on Trial," *The Atlantic Monthly* (February 2000), p. 3 (Internet WebSite <theatlantic.com/issues/2000/02/002quttenplan.htm>

4. Nash, *The Conservative Intellectual Movement*, p. 217. More recently, Jacob Heilbrunn, "Apologists Without Remorse," *American Prospect* 36(January-February 1998) has asserted that "Just as conservatives were on the side of repression in the American civil rights battle, so they joined ranks with the tyrants in South Africa"(p. 29). I hope to show in what follows that things are a bit more complicated than that—but not a whole lot. In retrospect, even white southern liberals had not transcended inherited attitudes on race. In the 1940s, for instance, Hugo Black privately voiced views on race which later would sound more appropriate coming from the lips of confirmed segregationists. See Greg Robinson and Peter Eisenstadt, "Two Dilemmas: Ralph Bunche and Hugo Black in 1940," *Prospects* 22, 453–78. On the other hand, UNC sociologists Howard Odum and Guy Johnson publicly rejected biological racism before 1954, but were privately opposed to the *Brown* decision as too drastic a first step. See Richard Kluger, *Simple Justice* (New York: Alfred Knopf, 1976) for a thorough discussion of the attempts of both sides in the school segregation cases to obtain public support from social scientists. There were few profiles in courage to be drawn in these matters.

5. Brinkley, "The Problems of American Conservatism," p. 415.

6. Quoted in Daniel Bell, "The Cultural Wars: American Intellectual Life, 1965–1972," *The Wilson Quarterly* XVI, 3 (Summer 1992), p. 83.

7. On these matters, see Leo Strauss, *Natural Right and History* (Chicago: University of Chicago Press, 1953), chapters I and II.

8. See Daryl Scott, *Contempt and Pity: Social Policy and the Image of the Damaged Black Psyche, 1880–1996* (Chapel Hill, N.C.: UNC Press, 1997), pp. 126–8 for this point about the absence of conservative social scientists. I.A. Newby, *Challenge to the Court: Social Scientists and the Defense of Segregation*, rev. ed with commentaries (Baton Rouge, LA.: LSU Press, 1969) is also extremely informative on this issue, though not uncontroversial with the academics and intellectuals it analyzed.

9. Newby, *Challenge to the Court*, p. 171. See also Michael Lind, *Up from Conservatism* (New York: The Free Press, 1996), chapter eight for the observation that the 1990s have seen the re-emergence of explicit racism on the conservative end of the political spectrum.

10. M. E. Bradford, "Introduction," *From Eden to Babylon: The Social and Political Essays of Andrew Nelson Lytle* (Washington, D.C.: Regnery Gateway, 1990), xviii.

11. See Richard Weaver, *Ideas Have Consequences* (Chicago, IL: University of Chi-

cago Press, 1948); Eric Voegelin, *The New Science of Politics* (Chicago: University of Chicago Press, 1952), p. 49; and Friedrich A. Hayek, *The Road to Serfdom* (Chicago, IL.: University of Chicago Press, 1944).

12. Bradford, "Some Southern Thoughts at Dartmouth," *Remembering Who We Are: Observations of a Southern Conservative* (Athens, GA.: University of Georgia Press, 1985), p. 69.

13. Michael Oakeshott, *Rationalism in Politics* (London: Methuen, 1981), p.21; Voegelin, *The New Science of Politics*, pp. 188–9.

14. Voegelin, p. 175.

15. Andrew Nelson Lytle, "The Quality of the South," *National Review* V, 10 (March 8, 1958), 236.

16. Daniel Bell, *The End of Ideology* (Glencoe, IL: The Free Press, 1960), p. 370.

17. Bradford, "The Heresy of Equality: A Reply to Harry Jaffa," *A Better Guide than Reason: Studies in the American Revolution* (LaSalle, IL: Sherwood Sugden and Co., 1979), p. 34.

18. Wilmoore Kendall, *The Conservative Affirmation* (Chicago, IL: Henry Regnery, 1963), ix; Garry Wills, *Confessions of a Conservative* (Harmondsworth, U.K.: Penguin, 1980), chapter 5.

19. Wills, *Confessions*, 17.

20. Kendall, "Equality and the American Political Tradition," in *Keeping the Tablets: Modern American Conservative Thought*. Ed with Introductions by William F. Buckley and Charles Kesler (New York: Harper and Row Publishers, 1988), p. 75.

21. Ibid. p. 76.

22. Ibid. p. 83.

23. Kendall, "The Civil Rights Movement and the Coming Constitutional Crisis (1964)," *Wilmoore Kendall Contra Mundum* ed. by Nellie D. Kendall (New Rochelle, N.Y.: Arlington House, 1971), p. 366; p. 374.

24. Ibid., p. 383.

25. Kendall, "Who Killed the Civil Rights Movement?" in *Contra Mundum*, p. 461; p. 464; p. 468.

26. Harry Jaffa, *Crisis of the House Divided: An Interpretation of the Issues in the Lincoln-Douglas Debate* (Garden City, N. Y.: Doubleday and Co., Inc., 1959), p. 374; p. 229; p. 238.

27. Jaffa, "Equality as a Conservative Principle" (1978), in Buckley and Kesler (eds.), p. 94. Garry Wills' *Lincoln at Gettysburg: Words that Remade America* (New York: Touchstone Books, 1992) offers a reprise of Kendall's (and Bradford's) position. Though Wills seems to accept the validity of Kendall's position as such, he also recognizes that Lincoln "won" the argument historically and thus his interpretation of the Declaration has carried the day.

28. Bradford, "The Heresy of Equality," p. 34.

29. Ibid., p. 42; p.215; p.56. It is not hard to see why Bradford's nomination to be head of the National Endowment for the Humanities in 1980–1981 was opposed, and eventually defeated, by northern (neo-) conservatives such as George Will and Irving Kristol.

30. Editorial, *National Review*, 1, 15 (February 29 1956), pp. 5–6. Later on the tenth anniversary of the *Brown* decision, Buckley, ever the irreconcilable, contended that the 1954 decision had "been an abysmal failure strictly on its own terms," as though conservatives like Buckley had not done everything they could do to thwart its implementation, even on "its own terms." See *National Review*, XVI, 22 (June 2, 1964), p. 434.

31. Editorial, *National Review* IV, 9 (August 24, 1957), pp. 148–9. See Buckley's *Up From Liberalism* for substantially the same discussion.

32. Brent Bozell, *National Review* IV, 9 (September 7, 1957), p. 209; Buckley, *Up From Liberalism*, p. 148; p. 146. Significantly, Buckley did not call for the disfranchisement of black Americans in the North where they could vote.

33. Buckley, *Up From Liberalism*, p. 144; Judis, p. 185. See also Heilbrunn, pp. 23–39.

Judis notes in his biography of Buckley that Buckley traveled to several African countries under the sponsorship of their colonial regimes (Judis, p. 207). Two caveats here: first, Buckley in 1969 seemed to offer support for some sort of compensatory aid for black Americans; second, in the late 1980s, Buckley, when asked if he would join the ANC if he were a black South African, answered in the affirmative.

34. Editorial, *National Review* XXI, 39 (October 7 1969), pp. 996–7. Except for libertarians, few, if any, conservatives were, or are, champions of the First Amendment, despite their strong anti-statist views.

35. Ernest van den Haag, "Intelligence or Prejudice," *National Review* XVI, 48 (December 1 1964), p. 1061.

36. In particular, see van den Haag, "Social Science Testimony in the Desegregation Cases—A Reply to Professor Kenneth Clark," *Villanova Law Review* 6(Fall 1960), pp. 69–79. Van den Haag's original critique of Clark appeared in his *The Fabric of Society* (New York: Harcourt, Brace, and Co., 1957), pp. 161–6. For discussions of this controversy, see Newby, *Challenge to the* Court, 180–3 and also Daryl Scott, *Contempt and Pity*, chapter seven.

37. Bruno Bettelheim, "Discrimination and Science," review of Kenneth Clark, *Prejudice and Your Child* in *Commentary* 21 (April 1956), pp. 384–6. Bettelheim's overall point here was not the same as van den Haag's. It was rather that "social and political equality are issues of justice and morality, not of psychological utilitarianism."

38. Van den Haag, "Negroes and Whites: Claims, Rights, and Prospects," *Modern Age* 9 (1964–1965), p. 359

39. Ibid., p. 359. I have no evidence that van den Haag and Arendt had any connections, though both had links with the New School for Social Research. See Richard H. King, "American Dilemmas and European Experiences," *Arkansas Historical Quarterly* LVI, 3(Autumn 1997), pp. 314–33 for an analysis of Arendt's (largely) mistaken position.

40. Ibid., pp. 361–2.

41. See Kenneth C. Blanchard, Jr., "Ethnicity and the Problems of Equality, "*Interpretation* 20, 3(Spring 1993), pp. 309–24 for a clear discussion of the relationship between talents and rights, abilities and moral status, from a natural law point of view.

42. Jaffa, *Crisis of the House Divided*, pp. 339–40. One immediate objection to Jaffa's position on Western cultural superiority might take the following form: did other cultures than the West have a notion of biologically inferior races? If not, that would suggest Western inferiority on the issue. The larger point is that there is no one single criterion for determining cultural superiority or inferiority.

43. This is Kenneth Blanchard's point in his above cited article.

44. See Judis, p. 192.

45. *National Review* XX, 12 (March 26 1968), for instance, included two lengthy articles by Frank Meyer and Ernest van den Haag analyzing—and largely rejecting—the conclusions of the Kerner Commission.

46. It also helped that neo-conservatives had the means to make themselves heard. Increasingly in the late 1960s and early 1970s, Norman Podhoretz's *Commentary* moved rightward. Even more important for airing political and social disillusionment with conventional liberal policies was *The Public Interest* (1965), a quarterly originally edited by Bell and Irving Kristol.

47. See Garry Wills, *Confessions*, p. 56 for a brief discussion of this tradition which is highly skeptical of the universally beneficent effects of the free market.

48. Daniel Patrick Moynihan, "The Schism in Black America," *The Public Interest* 27 (Spring 1972), p. 8.

49. Moynihan, "The President and the Negro: The Moment Lost," *Commentary* 43, 2 (February 1967), p. 45.

50. Edward Banfield, *The Unheavenly City: The Nature and Future of Our Urban Crisis* (Boston: Little, Brown and Co., 1970), p. 83.

51. Daniel Bell, *The Cultural Contradictions of Capitalism* (New York: Basic Books, 1976). See also Irving Howe, "The New York Intellectuals," *Commentary* (1967).

200 Notes to pages 131–37

52. Philip Rieff, *Fellow Teachers* (New York: Harper and Row, 1973), p. 94; p. 91. As an example of considerable overkill, Rieff was scathing on the claims for a black culture as such. He read it as "a negative transference to whites, a slogan of political and psychological warfare;" and he went on to assert that "Without their inherited spirituality, American blacks are exactly like the rest of us Americans, spiritually disinherited, rancorous, deeply worried at the sign of any inferiority" (p. 91).

53. In his well-known essay, "Meritocracy and Equality," in *The Public Interest* 29 (Fall 1972), pp. 29–68, which was reprinted in *The Coming of Post-Industrial Society* (New York: Basic Books, 1973) as "Meritocracy and Equality," Bell described this redefinition as "socialist" in nature, a strange comment since Bell always described himself as a socialist in economics. If so, then Bell should have supported the shift in basic principle. Crucially, equality of results went beyond advocating the removal of impediments to the pursuit of individuals' plans and projects and recommended preferential treatment for certain groups. Bell linked this sea-change in the idea of equality to the work of his Harvard colleague, John Rawl's *A Theory of Justice* (1972). This was quite unfair, since it was not at all clear that Rawls's principles of justice would allow for group preferential treatment over equal access to positions. Nor was his justification for inequalities—that they had to work for the benefit of the "least well off"—linked specifically to the position of African Americans. The respect in which Rawls's work might have been open to Bell's reading lay in Rawls's rejection of merit as a sufficient justification for social advantage.

54. Bradford, "The Heresy of Equality," p. 30.

55. Richard M. Weaver, *The Southern Tradition at Bay: A History of Postbellum Thought*, ed. by George Core and M. E. Bradford (Washington, D.C.: Regnery Gateway, 1989), p. 379. For a fuller discussion of these matters, see Richard H. King, "Anti-Modernists All!," *The Mississippi Quarterly* XLIV, 2 (Spring 1991), p. 193–201. See also, Fred D. Young, *Richard M. Weaver, 1910–1963: A Life of the Mind* (Columbia, Mo.: University of Missouri Press, 1995) and Michael Kreyling, "Richard Weaver and the Outline of Southern History," *Inventing Southern Literature* (Jackson, MS.: University Press of Mississippi, 1998), pp.19–32.

56. Weaver, *Southern Tradition*, p. 244; p. 247.

57. Ibid., pp. 251–2; p. 246.

58. Weaver, *Ideas Have Consequences*, p. 85; p. 87. On the left, Theodor Adorno also had a notorious blind spot concerning jazz. It is of course difficult now to recapture the time when jazz was seen either as a force for revitalization in, or uniquely sinister for, the future of the West.

59. Richard Weaver, "The Regime of the South," *National Review*, VI, 21(March 14, 1959), p. 387.

60. Ibid., p. 387.

61. Ibid., p. 588. In a later article "The Importance of Cultural Freedom," *Modern Age*, 6 (Winter 1960–61), Weaver noted that "A culture is like an organic creation in that its constitution cannot tolerate more than a certain amount of what is foreign or extraneous." (p. 23).

62. M. E. Bradford, "A Fire Bell in the Night: The Southern Conservative View," *Modern Age* 17 (Winter 1972–73), p. 10.

63. Garry Wills, "What Color is God?" *National Review*, XIV, 20 (May 21 1963), 408–17. Wills's piece should be contrasted with M. E. Bradford's "Faulkner, James Baldwin, and the South," *Georgia Review*, 20 (Winter 1966), pp. 431–43.

Notes to JIM JOHNSON OF ARKANSAS: SEGREGATIONIST PROTOTYPE
by Elizabeth Jacoway

1. Elizabeth Jacoway interview with Jim Johnson, August 6, 1999.
2. Elizabeth Jacoway interview with Jim Johnson, May 22, 1999.

Notes to pages 137–43

3. Pete Daniel and Elizabeth Jacoway interview with Jim Johnson, January 27, 1997.
4. Harry Ashmore, *Civil Rights and Wrongs: A Memoir of Race and Politics, 1944–1994* (New York: Random House, 1994), p. 124; Herbert Mitgang, *Saturday Review*, as quoted on the dust jacket of Numan V. Bartley, *The Rise of Massive Resistance: Race and Politics in the South During the 1950's* (Baton Rouge: Louisiana State University Press, 1969); Neil McMillen, *The Citizens' Councils: A History of Organized Southern White Resistance to the Second Reconstruction, 1954–1964* (Urbana: University of Illinois Press, 1971), pp. 95, 114.
5. George Fisher, *The Best of Fisher: 28 years of Editorial Cartoons from Faubus to Clinton* (Fayetteville: University of Arkansas Press, 1993); a taped copy of the Gridiron roast can be found in the Jim Johnson Papers, Arkansas History Commission, Little Rock (hereinafter cited as JJP).
6. Extensive examples of Johnson's handwritten style can be found in JJP.
7. Jacoway interview with Johnson, May 22, 1999.
8. Jacoway interview with Johnson, August 6, 1999.
9. Ibid.
10. Elizabeth Jacoway interview with Jim Johnson, August 26, 1999.
11. Jacoway interviews with Johnson, May 22 and August 6, 1999.
12. Jim Johnson to Elizabeth Jacoway, October 6, 1995.
13. Richard Kluger, *Simple Justice: The History of Brown V. Board of Education and Black America's Struggle for Equality* (New York: Random House: 1975), pp. 710–11.
14. Elizabeth Jacoway interview with Orval Faubus, October 23, 1976.
15. Roy Reed, *Faubus: The Life and Times of an American Prodigal* (Fayetteville: University of Arkansas Press, 1997), pp. 121–4.
16. Jacoway interview with Johnson, August 6, 1999.
17. Reed, p. 170.
18. An incomplete collection of *Arkansas Faith* can be found in JJP.
19. Reed, p. 174; Johnson still maintains this position, Jacoway interview with Johnson, August 6, 1999.
20. Numan Bartley quoted the following figures on attendance at these rallies drawn from Citizens' Council information included in *Arkansas Faith*, November, 1955 and March, 1956: Dewitt, 500; Lake Village, 500; Hoxie-Walnut Ridge, 1,500; Dermott, 800; England, 350; Sheridan, 400; Forrest City, 1,000; Hamburg, 2,500; England, 2,000, from Bartley, *The Rise of Massive Resistance*, p. 100.
21. Reed, p. 170.
22. Jacoway interview with Johnson, August 6,1999; the recordings can be found in JJP.
23. *Life Magazine*, " 'A Morally Right Decision,' " xxxix (July 25, 1955). pp. 29–31.
24. Neil R. McMillen, "White Citizens' Council and Resistance to School Desegregation in Arkansas," *Arkansas Historical Quarterly*, XXX (Summer, 1971), pp. 97–8; see also Reed, Faubus, pp. 172–3; for early coverage of the Hoxie affair, see "Hoxie Schools Desegregate in Arkansas without Incident," *Southern School News* (hereinafter cited as SSN), August, 1955, p. 15; "Protests Lead to Closing of Schools 2 Weeks Early at Hoxie, Arkansas," *SSN*, September, 1955, p. 10; and Cabell Phillips, "Integration: Battle of Hoxie, Arkansas," *The New York Times Magazine*, September 25, 1955, pp. 12, 68–76.
25. Reed, *Faubus*, p. 173.
26. "Special Judge Is Chosen to Hear Hoxie Case in Arkansas," *SSN*, December, 1955, p. 9.
27. This recording and others are included in JJP. Neil McMillen claims that these recordings were a fraud; he writes: "Somewhat later this spurious document was exposed when a country editor from Georgia revealed that 'Professor Williams' was known to neither Howard nor the NAACP . . .", McMillen, "White Citizens' Council and Resistance to School Desegregation in Arkansas," p. 99; McMillen also writes: "According to a Council newspaper [*Arkansas Faith*], the tape proved that 'the NAACP and their insolent agitators

are little concerned with an education for the "ignorant nigger"; but rather, are "demand-ing" integration in the white bedroom.' " My hearing of the three recorded NAACP speakers—Roy Wilkins and Clarence Mitchell as well as Williams, is quite different; the only reference to bedrooms is when "Roy Wilkins" claims: "We're neither for intermar-riage or against intermarriage; we want protection for the Negro woman!" The tape sounds credible to me, and the Williams tape discloses promises that Orval Faubus was said to have made, through his head of the Arkansas Industrial Development Commission Winthrop Rockefeller, to Arkansas blacks if they would support him in the statehouse. Faubus always carried large numbers of black precincts.

28. "Arkansas' Segregation Laws Again Are Ruled Unconstitutional," *SSN*, February, 1956, p. 11.

29. Neil McMillen, "The Citizens' Councils: A History of Organized Southern White Resistance to the Second Reconstruction," unpublished Ph.D. dissertation, Vanderbilt University, 1969, p. 144.

30. Bartley, *The Rise of Massive Resistance*, p. 121.

31. Ibid.

32. Ibid., p. 123.

33. JJP.

34. Bartley, *The Rise of Massive Resistance*, p. 119.

35. "Arkansas' Segregation Laws Again Are Ruled Unconstitutional," *SSN*, February, 1956, p. 11.

36. Reed, Faubus, p. 178.

37. Ibid.

38. Bartley, *The Rise of Massive Resistance*, p. 132.

39. Reed, *Faubus*, p. 175.

40. Ibid., p. 174.

41. Ibid., p. 179.

42. Jacoway interview with Johnson, May 22, 1999.

43. Jacoway interview with Johnson, August 6, 1999.

44. Reed, *Faubus*, pp. 175–6.

45. Ibid., p. 177.

46. "Three Court Cases Dominate School Scene in Arkansas; U. S. Intervenes," *SSN*, March, 1956, p. 4.

47. Bartley, *The Rise of Massive Resistance*, p. 142.

48. Reed, *Faubus*, p. 178.

49. Ibid., p. 179.

50. Bartley, *The Rise of Massive Resistance*, p. 142.

51. Ibid., p. 260.

52. Jacoway interview with Johnson, May 22, 1999.

53. Reed, *Faubus*, pp. 365–7.

54. Elizabeth Jacoway interview with Jim Johnson, January 19, 2000; Johnson admits that no political solution would have removed his personal abhorrence of miscegenation, Ibid.

55. Roy Reed interview with Jim Johnson, March 24, 1994, Archives and Special Col-lections, University of Arkansas Libraries, Fayetteville, Arkansas; the fullest elaboration of the events remembered as the Little Rock crisis is to be found in Elizabeth Jacoway and C. Fred Williams, eds., *Understanding the Little Rock Crisis: An Exercise in Remem-brance and Reconciliation* (Fayetteville: University of Arkansas Press, 1999).

56. JJP.

57. Ibid.; Reed interview with Johnson, March 24, 1994; Johnson claims that the most critical letter he has ever received came when he was on the Supreme Court from a young lawyer in Pine Bluff, Jay Dickey (now a member of the Arkansas Congressional delega-tion) lambasting him for finding in favor of the black defendant against Dickey's white client, Jacoway interview with Johnson, January 19, 2000.

58. Reed interview with Johnson, March 24, 1994.
59. Jacoway interview with Johnson, August 26, 1999.
60. Ibid.
61. Ibid.
62. Ibid.
63. Ibid.
64. Jacoway interview with Johnson, May 22, 1999.
65. Sheldon Hackney, "Southern Violence," *American Historical Review*, volume lxxiv, number iii, February, 1969, pp. 906–25.
66. Dan T. Carter, *The Politics of Rage: George Wallace, The Origins of the New Conservatism, and the Transformation of American Politics* (New York: Simon and Schuster, 1995).
67. George M. Fredrickson, *The Black Image in the White Mind: The Debate on Afro-American Character and Destiny, 1817–1914* (New York: Harper and Row, 1971), p. 321.
68. McMillen, *The Citizens' Councils*, pp. 159–88.
69. Fred Hobson, *But Now I See: The White Southern Racial Conversion Narrative* (Baton Rouge: Louisiana State University Press, 1998).
70. Kluger, *Simple Justice*, see especially chapter 23.
71. Ibid. p. 742.
72. *Arkansas Democrat-Gazette*, May 16, 1999.
73. *Arkansas Democrat-Gazette*, June 3, 1999.

Notes to DOUBTLESS SINCERE: NEW CHARACTERS IN THE CIVIL RIGHTS CAST
by Lauren F. Winner

1. David L. Chappell, *Inside Agitators: White Southerners in the Civil Rights Movement* (Baltimore: The Johns Hopkins University Press, 1994). S. Jonathan Bass, *Blessed Are the Peacemakers: Martin Luther King, Jr., Eight White Religious Leaders, and the "Letter from Birmingham Jail"* (Baton Rouge: LSU Press, 2001). Diane McWhorter, *Carry Me Home: Birmingham, Alabama, The Climactic Battle of the Civil Rights Revolution* (New York: Simon and Schuster, 2001). Matthew D. Lassiter and Andrew B. Lewis, *The Moderates' Dilemma: Massive Resistance to School Desegregation in Virginia* (Charlottesville: University Press of Virginia, 1998); Charles Marsh, *God's Long Summer: Stories of Faith and Civil Rights* (Princeton: Princeton University Press, 1997).
2. Glenda Gilmore, *Gender and Jim Crow: Women and the Politics of White Supremacy in North Carolina, 1896–1920* (Chapel Hill: University of North Carolina Press, 1996), xviii, passim. Adam Fairclough, *Teaching Equality: Black Schools in the Age of Jim Crow* (Athens: The University of Georgia Press, 2001), 12.
3. Carter G. Woodson, "Negroes Not United for Democracy," *The Negro History Bulletin*, Vol. VI, No 8 (May 1943), 170.
4. Anne Moody, *Coming of Age in Mississippi* (New York: Dell, 1968), 261. Pat Watters and Reese Cleghorn, *Climbing Jacob's Ladder: The Arrival of Negroes in Southern Politics* (New York: Harcourt, Brace, and World, 1967), 128–40. Everett Carll Ladd, *Negro Political Leadership in the South* (New York: Atheneum, 1969 ed.), 154.
5. Donald R. Matthews and James W. Protho, *Negroes and the New Southern Politics* (New York: Harcourt, Brace, and World, 1966), 340.
6. Ibid., 340.
7. "Affairs of the State" by Charles M. Hills, *The Clarion Ledger*, September 16, 1961.
8. Zora Neale Hurston, "A Negro Deplores the Segregation Decision," *Asheville Times*, August 30, 1955 (reprinted from the *Orlando Sentinel*).
9. Her biographers have suggested that Hurston opposed integration because she was most familiar with Eatonville, Florida, a place where African Americans led relatively

autonomous lives, far freer from the menace of Jim Crow than, say, African Americans in the Mississippi black belt. They also point to Hurston's commitments to folklore and celebrating African American culture. She believed there was great value in southern black culture, and thought integrationism implicitly devalued it, suggesting that all black people wanted to be with, and be like, white people. Robert Hemenway has suggested that Hurston was unable to see that one could simultaneously celebrate black culture and criticize the oppressive social system that gave rise to it. In Hemenway's view, Hurston, who was violently ant-Communist, simply "group[ed] them all together, party members and NACCP conservatives, and interpret[ed] their criticism [of Jim Crow] as resulting from a philosophical belief in a pathology of black life. She was an instinctive black nationalist—or at least a cultural nationalist—without quite realizing the implications of her position." Ultimately, Hemenway suggests, Hurston's politics were simply incoherent. Larry Neal shares the assessment: "at one moment she could sound highly nationalistic. Then at other times she might mouth statements which in terms of the on-going struggle for black liberation were ill-conceived and even reactionary." Robert E. Hemenway, *Zora Neale Hurston: A Literary Biography* (Urbana: University of Illinois Press, 1977), 328–9. Zora Neale Hurston, "I Saw Negro Votes Peddled." *American Legion Magazine* 49 (Nov., 1950), 12–13, 54–7, 59–60.

10. Zack J. Van Landingham to Director, State Sovereignty Commission, August 11, 1959, Coleman Papers, 55, Box 21, Folder 37, Department of Archives, University of Southern Mississippi, Hattiesburg, MS. The fullest discussion of white segregationists' search for black allies is in David Chappell, *A Stone of Hope* (Chapel Hill: The University of North Carolina Press, forthcoming).

11. Roy Wilkins, "The Negro Wants Full Equality," in Rayford W. Logan, ed., *What Does the Negro Want?* (Chapel Hill: The University of North Carolina Press, 1944), 127. (I am citing the 1969, Agathon Press reprint ed., NY). J. L. Chesnut with Julia Cass, *Black in Selma: The Uncommon Life* of J.L. Chestnut, Jr. (New York: FSG, 1990), 48.

12. Watters and Cleghorn, *Climbing Jacob's Ladder*, 101. King quoted in Ralph David Abernathy, *And the Walls Came Tumbling Down* (New York: Harper and Row, 1989), 255. Peter Maass, "The Secrets of Mississippi: Post-Authoritarian Shock in the South," *The New Republic* December 21, 1998. Myrlie Evers, *For Us, The Living* (Jackson: The University Press of Mississippi, 1996), 145–8. Julius E. Thompson, *Percy Greene and the Jackson Advocate: The Life and Times of a Radical Conservative Black Newspaperman, 1897–1977* (Jefferson, NC: McFarland and Company, 1994), 119–121. Harry Holloway, *The Politics of the Southern Negro: From Exclusion to Big City Organization* (New York: Random House, 1969), 128–30.

13. Chesnut, *Black in Selma*, 48–9. Charles Evers, *Have No Fear: The Charles Evers Story* (New York: John Wiley and Sons, 1997), 194. Paul Lewinson, *Race, Class, and Party, A History of Negro Suffrage and White Politics in the South* (New York: Grosset and Dunlap, 1932), 120, 154, 199. Abernathy, *And the Walls*, 114. Daniel C. Thompson, *The Negro Leadership Class* (Englewood Cliffs: Prentice-Hall, 1963), 62–3. James Q. Wilson, *Negro Politics: The Search for Leadership* (New York: The Free Press, 1960), 118–19. Roi Ottley, *"New World A-Comin": Inside Black America* (Boston: Houghton Mifflin, 1943), 238–9.

14. Mays quoted in David R. Goldfield, *Black, White and Southern: Race Relations and Southern Culture 1940 to the Present* (Baton Rouge: LSU Press, 1990), 90. Gunnar Myrdal, *The American Dilemma: The Negro Problem and Modern Democracy* (New York: Harper and Brothers, 1944), 940.

15. Reed Sarratt, *The Ordeal of Desegregation: The First Decade* (New York: Harper & Row, 1966), 283. Harry Tipper, "Sermon on Marriage," circa summer 1955, copy in author's possession. "New Negro Association Draws NAACP Criticism," *Southern School News* 6 (February 3, 1955), 6. W. R. Farley, "From A Southern Negro," 3–4, Luther Hodges Papers, Box 118, "Segregation" folder, North Carolina Division of Archives and History, Raleigh, NC.

16. As Adolph Reed has recently noted, contemporary bourgeois African Americans have created a cottage industry of nostalgic memoir, filled with a longing for "the organic community black Americans supposedly lost with the success of the civil rights movement." Reed numbers Henry Louis Gates, Harold Cruse, Clifton Taulbert, and William Julius Wilson among those black writers who have "romanced" their Jim Crow childhoods, "yearning for a prelapsarian black communal order, churning out "inspirational memoir. . . . Once Upon a Time . . . We Were Segregated and Happy." As Reed makes clear, these memoirists' visions of the good old days are, at best, rose colored: they mistake "the apparent simplicity of childhood for the simplicity of a social order." Adolph Reed, *Class Notes: Posing as Politics and Other Thoughts on the American Scene* (New York: The New Press, 2000), 14–24. Goldfield, *Black, White, and Southern*, 90.

17. Henry Lewis Suggs, ed., *The Black Press in the South, 1865–1979* (Westport, 1983), 303. Sarratt, *Ordeal of* Desegregation, 250. (White social scientists did echo Lee's claim that segregation had propped up the middle class, but they came to different conclusions: as Duke sociologist Edgar T. Thompson put it, "No matter how much modern Negro leaders may inveigh against these segregated areas, it is reasonable to suppose that in them were incubated and protected the occupations and institutions that trained large number [sic] of Negroes in middle-class skills and values." But the Negro middle class would only become stronger, said Thompson, as more black southerners "refuse[d] to play the role assigned to [them] by the traditional status system." Edgar T. Thompson, "The South and the Second Emancipation," in Allan P. Snider, ed., *Change in the Contemporary South* (Durham: Duke University Press, 1963), 114–15.)

18. Davis Lee, "The Viewpoint of a Negro,"*The Roanoke Times*, August 2, 1948. Farley, "From a Southern Negro," 3.

19. Farley, "From a Southern Negro," 4. Watters and Cleghorn, *Climbing Jacob's Ladder*, 97–8. Woodson, "Negroes Not United," 177.

20. Grace Halsell, *Soul Sister* (New York: World Pub., 1969), 175–6. Myrlie Evers, *For Us, The Living*, 146.

21. Jeffrey J. Crow, Paul D. Escott, and Flora Hatley, *A History of African Americans in North Carolina* (Raleigh: Division of Archives and History, North Carolina Department of Cultural Resources, 1992), 167. "Talk Made at a Meeting of the Fairfax Kiwanis Club by Professor Freeman Burns, Negro Superintendent of the Rehobeth School District, Fairfax, Alabama," Box 731, Segregation-Integration Folder 3, Dwight D. Eisenhower Papers, Central Files, Official Files D, Dwight Eisenhower Library, Abilene, Kansas. Thanks to Daryl M. Scott for calling this document to my attention.

22. Matthews and Protho, *Negroes and the New Southern Politics*, 340. Myrlie Evers, *For Us, The Living*, 146–51.

23. Mary Simmons, interview with author, Mocksville, North Carolina, December 7, 1998.

24. Ted Ownby, *American Dreams in Mississippi: Consumers, Poverty, and Culture, 1830–1999* (Chapel Hill: University of North Carolina Press, 1999). Robert Weems, *Desegregating the Dollar: African American Consumerism in the Twentieth Century* (New York: New York University Press, 1998).

25. Charles Evers, 89. Myrlie Evers, *For Us, The Living*, 84, 193–5. Sara Peters, interview with author, Chapel Hill, North Carolina, December 5, 1998.

Contributors

TONY BADGER is Paul Mellon Professor of History at Cambridge University and Vice-Master of Sidney Sussex College. He is author of *Prosperity Road: The New Deal, Tobacco, and North Carolina* and *The New Deal: The Depression Years, 1933–1940*; coeditor of *The Making of Martin Luther King and the Civil Rights Movement* and *Contesting Democracy: Substance and Structure in American Political History, 1775–2000*; and is writing a biography of Albert Gore, Sr.

DAVID L. CHAPPELL is associate professor of history at the University of Arkansas. He is the author of *Inside Agitators: White Southerners in the Civil Rights Movement* and the forthcoming *A Stone of Hope: Religion, Culture, and the Triumph of Civil Rights*.

ELIZABETH JACOWAY is the author of *Yankee Missionaries in the South: The Penn School Experiment* and coeditor of *Understanding the Little Rock Crisis: An Exercise in Remembrance and Reconciliation*, *Southern Businessmen and Desegregation*, and *The Adaptable South: Essays in Honor of George Brown Tindall*.

RICHARD H. KING is professor at Nottingham University and has been a fellow at the Robert Penn Warren Center for the Humanities and Vanderbilt University. He is the author of *Civil Rights and the Idea of Freedom*, *A Southern Renaissance: The Cultural Awakening of the American South*, and *The Party of Eros: Radical Social Thought in the Realm of Freedom*.

RALPH E. LUKER is author of the *Historical Dictionary of the Civil Rights Movement*, *The Social Gospel in Black and White: American Racial Reform, 1885–1912*, and *A Southern Tradition in Theology and Social Criticism, 1830–1930*. He edited Mary Ovington's *Black & White Sat Down Together: The Reminiscences of an NAACP Founder*, was an editor on two volumes of *The Paper of Martin Luther King, Jr.*, and is editing a book on the work of Vernon Johns.

CHARLES MARSH is associate professor of religious studies and director of the Project on Lived Theology at the University of Virginia. He is the author of *God's Long Summer: Stories of Faith and Civil Rights*, *Reclaiming Dietrich Bonhoeffer: The Promise of His Theology*, and the autobiographical *The Last Days: A Son's Story of Sin and Segregation at the Dawn of a New South*.

KEITH D. MILLER is associate professor of English at Arizona State University. He is the author of *Voice of Deliverance: The Language of Martin Luther King, Jr. and Its Sources* and coeditor of *New Bones: Contemporary Black Writers in America*.

TED OWNBY is professor of history and southern studies at the University of Mississippi. He is author of *Subduing Satan: Recreation, Religion, and Manhood in the Rural South, 1865–1920* and *American Dreams in Mississippi: Consumers, Poverty, and Culture, 1830–1998* and editor of *Black and White: Cultural Interaction in the Antebellum South*.

LINDA REED is professor of history and African American studies at the University of Houston. She is the author of *Simple Decency and Common Sense: The Southern Conference Movement, 1938–1963*, coauthor of *America: Pathways to the Present*, and coeditor of *"We Specialize in the Wholly Impossible"*: *A Reader in Black Women's History*. She is coauthor of a forthcoming volume entitled *Black Women in America, 1619–2001* and is writing a study of the life of Fannie Lou Hamer.

LAUREN F. WINNER is a doctoral candidate at Columbia University. She is coauthor, with Randall Balmer, of a book about contemporary American Protestantism.

Index